THE GROUNDS OF
MORAL JUDGEMENT

THE GROUNDS OF MORAL JUDGEMENT

BY

GEOFFREY RUSSELL GRICE

Lecturer in Philosophy in the University of East Anglia

CAMBRIDGE

AT THE UNIVERSITY PRESS

1967

Published by the Syndics of the Cambridge University Press
Bentley House, 200 Euston Road, London, N.W. 1
American Branch: 32 East 57th Street, New York, N.Y. 10022

© Cambridge University Press 1967

Library of Congress Catalogue Card Number: 67-17008

Printed in Great Britain
at the University Printing House, Cambridge
(Brooke Crutchley, University Printer)

To

FRANK McEACHRAN

who made me aware of philosophy

CONTENTS

Acknowledgements   *page* xi

Introduction   1

1 Moral Grounds   2

2 Prichard's Mistake   5

3 Three Impediments   6

CHAPTER 1. MOTIVE, REASON AND OBLIGATION   8

1 Reason for Acting and Reason for Judging   9

2 Reason for Acting and Desire   10

3 Motive   13

4 Desire and Interest   15

5 Reason for Acting   17

6 Better Reason Than   21

7 Obligation and its Modes   24

8 The Reason-for-Acting/Obligation Schema   26

9 Independent Interest   29

10 Abstract and Actual Obligation   31

11 Residual Uses of 'Ought'   33

CHAPTER 2. RIGHTS AND CONTRACT   36

1 The Concept of a Right   37

2 Basic Obligation and Rights   40

3 Abstract Obligation   42

4 The Promising Function   45

5 The Assertion Theory   47

6 Apparent Counter-Examples   52

7 Utilitarianism: the Particular Case   57

8 Obligation, Promising and Other Moral Concepts *page* 63
 Rights   63
 Blameworthiness   69
 Moral Good   70
 Trustworthiness   70
 Reason for Acting   71

9 Utilitarianism: the General Rule   74

10 The Reason for Keeping a Promise   77

11 Promises extracted by Threats   79

12 Criminal Promises   84

CHAPTER 3. THE GROUND OF BASIC OBLIGATIONS   87

1 The Programme   87

2 Edicts and Obligation Principles   90

3 The Contract Argument   93
 First Deductive Chain (A)   94
 The Contract Ground   95
 Second Deductive Chain (B)   95
 Conclusion   97
 Complementary Proof   97
 An Objection   98

4 Contractually Harmonized Interests   99

5 Entrenched Legal Institutions   102

6 The Tyrant   104

7 Societies and Basic Obligation   106

8 Material Objections   109

9 The Time of Contract and Complementary Classes   111

10 Punishment   115

11 The Law Giver and the Genesis of Morality   117

12 Specific Obligation Principles and Actual Obligations   120
 Conflict of Obligations   121
 Interpretation   126

13 Reason for Acting and Basic Obligation   *page* 131

14 The Master Criminal   135

15 Promising Again   140

16 Morality, Justice and Law   143

17 Natural Rights   147

18 Nations and Other Societies   150

CHAPTER 4. THE GROUND OF ULTRA OBLIGATIONS   155

1 Ultra Obligation and Rights   155

2 Christianity, Ultra Obligation and Rights   159

3 Fulfilment   164

4 Reason for Adopting a Mode of Life   166

5 Ultra Obligation and Altruistic Motives   169

6 The Ground of Ultra Obligations   172

7 Ultra Obligation and Reason for Acting   174

CHAPTER 5. GOOD   177

1 Morally Better Than   177

   Motives   178

   Actions   179

   Men   180

2 Morally Good   180

3 Moral Good and Ultra and Basic Obligation   181

4 A Man's Good   183

5 Good and its Modes   187

6 Utilitarianism and Contract Theory   190

   Moore   193

   Sidgwick   195

7 Rule Utilitarianism   197

Epilogue   201

Index   205

ACKNOWLEDGEMENTS

This book is based upon a doctoral dissertation approved by the University of Cambridge in 1965.

I have several debts which it is a pleasure to acknowledge: to the Master and Fellows of Churchill College who, by electing me to the College Research Studentship in 1963, enabled me to stay in Cambridge and complete my work; to Dr A. C. Ewing whose support made possible my return to philosophy after several years in less congenial fields, and with whom I have discussed, always with profit to myself, most of the points in the book; to Professor R. B. Braithwaite who has kindly discussed several questions with me and saved me from at least one howler; to Mrs Philippa Foot whose criticism of my argument at crucial places has helped me, I hope, to improve it; and to Mr Alan Dutton whose philosophical companionship has been invaluable over a number of years.

My debt to my wife is of a different kind: it is quite certain that without her sustaining influence I should have had no opportunity to acknowledge any debts.

University Plain   G. R. G.
Norwich.
10 April 1967

INTRODUCTION

When we make moral judgements and are challenged upon their correctness, the more articulate of us are usually able to support them. If, for example, one of us were to say, in a particular situation, that a dying man had the right to be told that he was dying; that a man who knowingly allows another to be punished for his crime is evil; that discrimination against coloured people is unjust or that abortion, with proper safeguards, ought to be legalized; and if we were challenged upon the correctness of our judgement, we should usually be able to say something in defence of it. And if in turn this defence were challenged, we should normally think it proper to take part in a discussion, an argument, whose purpose was to determine the correctness or otherwise of the original judgement. In doing so, we should be considering reasons for and against it.

Let us, in the first instance, leave judgements about rights, justice, good and evil on one side and confine our attention to judgements of obligation. If we survey the reasons brought forward in support of such judgements, we shall find, apparently, a wide variety of propositions fulfilling this role. As reasons, some of them will no doubt be good and others bad. But when the bad ones are eliminated, a wide diversity is still to be found among those which remain. The point, I believe, does not need labouring. It is enough to think of half a dozen arguments about what ought to be done in a concrete situation to be impressed with the variety in the reasons adduced. There does not appear to be any proposition of which we could say: This is *the* reason for judgements of moral obligation.

It would be naïve to suppose that a distinguished line of moral philosophers have been ignorant of the diversity which a cursory examination reveals. Yet philosophers of a very distinguished line have believed that there is some proposition of which we can say that it is, in a perfectly good sense, *the* reason for such judgements. And a large part of the history of moral philosophy, though by no means the whole of it, has been an attempt to find this proposition. Utilitarianism, in one or other of its forms, is a good example of the outcome of this quest. In its purest form, Utilitarianism is the thesis that *the* reason for any moral judgement of obligation is that the action enjoined produces more good than any other action open to the agent at the time. Most Utilitarians, it is true, qualify their claim in an attempt to avoid well known difficulties about justice to which it gives rise. But in its purest form, as expounded, for example by G. E. Moore,[1] Utilitarianism is the view that *the* reason for any moral ought judgement is that the action enjoined produces more good than any alternative. A Utilitarian is free to admit that the reasons which appear, in all their variety, in day to day moral argument are reasons in a perfectly good sense of the word. He may say that they are reasons just because they support the proposition which he claims is *the* reason; and that the measure of how strongly they support it is the measure of how good they are as reasons.

Utilitarianism, I shall argue, is a false answer to the question it attempts to answer. But the question, I believe, is a proper one: there is significance in the question, 'What is *the* reason for moral judgements of obligation?' even though, in defending particular judgements of that kind, the diversity in the reasons advanced will be most conspicuous. The question is widened, and expressed in a superior way, by asking, 'What are the grounds of the different kinds of moral judgement: judgements of obligation, rights, justice and good and evil?' It is the central purpose of this work to set out these grounds as elements in a coherent structure which shall be explanatory of the moral demand and of moral appraisal.

I. MORAL GROUNDS

Justice, and good and evil, present little difficulty once the ground of judgements of obligation is established, and it is to this task that the major part of this work is devoted. The ground of judgements of obligation is a proposition, making an assertion about doing an action x, which implies, whatever action x may be, that x ought to be done. The word 'implies' will be used throughout in such a way that p implies q if and only if (1) it is logically im-

---

[1] *Principia Ethica* (Cambridge).

possible that p is true and q is false, and (2) the impossibility is not a consequence of either the impossibility of p or the necessity of q. But as thus defined, p may imply q without being a ground of q. For example, the proposition that I know that r implies that r, but it is not a ground of r. If I were to say, 'The editor of the Times caused the last war' and were asked for my ground, I should not be answering if I were to say, 'I know that the editor of the Times caused the last war'. Even though what I now say implies that I have a ground, I have not, in so answering, given a ground.

It would be idle to pretend that I can give a complete and satisfactory analysis of the notion of a ground. But I hope to be able to say enough to enable us to proceed in moral philosophy. The proposition, making an assertion about doing an action x, which is, as I shall argue, the ground of judgements of obligation, has a characteristic in addition to that of implying that x ought to be done; it also explains why x ought to be done. I work with a largely unanalysed notion of explanation, but I think it will be agreed, as we go along, that the thesis presented does have explanatory power in a high degree. Some propositions which imply ought judgements lack explanatory power. For example, 'x is an act of murder' implies, as will readily be conceded, 'x ought not to be done'. But it does not explain why x ought not to be done. A man is not unintelligible, it seems to me, who says, 'You have shown me that x is an act of murder, and I am persuaded that it follows logically that I ought not to do x, but you still have not explained to me why I ought not to do it. Suppose I enjoyed doing murders as, apparently, some people do. If you were to say that I ought not to act in this way, despite the enjoyment it gives me, I think I should be justified in asking you to explain why I ought not to. And you simply have not provided an explanation in showing me that x is an act of murder and pointing out that "x is an act of murder" implies "x ought not to be done".' Because I sympathise with a man who argues in this way, I do not wish to say that the antecedent of this implication is a ground of its consequent. The ground is a proposition of much greater generality which implies the consequent and which also explains the obligatoriness of the action to which both refer.

It may be conceded by one who argues in this way that 'x ought not to be done' implies that there are reasons for not doing x, and he may express his objection by saying that although we have established that there *are* reasons for not doing murder, we have not told him *what* they are. The point he makes is correct and is seen to be correct provided a certain confusion is avoided. If a man is aiming at avoiding acts of murder, and we are able to show him that an action which he thought was, say, justifiable homicide was in fact an act of murder, then we have given him a reason for not doing that act. Given his aims, there is no great problem in understanding what has to be done to provide him with a reason. But the man we have been considering has, we may suppose, no such aims: he enjoys doing murders. And the problem of giving him a reason for not murdering is a very different and a much more difficult one. Now I shall argue in the appropriate place that the proposition which I propose as the ground of judgements of obligation does, if it is true when asserted of doing x, constitute a reason for doing x. Consequently the objection cannot be lodged, as it can in the murder case, that in showing that the ground implies the ought judgement, we have not *given* a reason for doing x. We *have* given a reason: the truth of the ground *is* a reason for acting in that way. If the ground is true as asserted of x, then it is a reason for doing x; and if it is true as asserted of not doing x, then it is a reason for not doing x. Part, but not the whole, of the explanatory force of the ground proposed lies in its constituting a reason for acting. For the remainder, I find I am unable to do more than allow it to emerge as we go along.

In the pages which follow, I hope to show that we may properly speak of *the* reason, or the ground, of judgements of obligation, and of moral judgements of other kinds. It is not possible to make a simple general statement about the relations between the ground and the reasons given for moral judgements in day to day discussion because of the diversity in kind of these reasons. But once the ground is established, we shall be able to see how any individual reason is related to it. And the relations will be seen to explain our discrimination between some reasons as good and others as not so good. Establishing the ground of judgements of obligation is explanatory not only in the way described in the previous paragraph, but in this way also.

2. PRICHARD'S MISTAKE

It has been the aim of many, though not all, the greatest moral philosophers to establish the ground of judgements of obligation. No proposal so far made has won general acceptance, and it is inevitable that after more than two thousand years of unsuccessful investigation, the question should arise whether there is or could be any proposition of the kind moral philosophers have been seeking. It fell to the lot of H. A. Prichard to argue that there could not: that the whole subject, as so conceived, asks an improper question and rests therefore upon a mistake.[1] Prichard held that once we ask for the ground of moral judgements of obligation, only three answers are, 'from the necessities of the case', possible:[2]

(1) Action in the way enjoined is, when all things are considered, seen to be for the agent's own good, or, as he prefers to put it, for the agent's own advantage or, better again, his own happiness.

(2) That something realised *by* acting in the way enjoined is good, i.e., that such action produces something other than an action, e.g., a state of affairs, which is good. This thesis he calls 'Utilitarianism in the generic sense in which what is good is not limited to pleasure'.

(3) That something realized *in* acting in the way enjoined is good, i.e., that such an action is good in itself or intrinsically good.

Having stated that these answers 'from the necessities of the case' exhaust the possibilities, he examines each in turn and rejects them all to make way for his own thesis that the truth of moral ought judgements 'can only be apprehended directly in an act of moral thinking'.[3] His view is that there is no possibility of speaking of the ground of moral ought judgements in the way outlined in the previous section; that there could be no proposition of which we could say, 'This proposition is the ground of such judgements'.

It is difficult to believe that any contemporary philosopher who examines Prichard's arguments will think them successful in demolishing the claims made on behalf of the answers he considers.

---

[1] 'Does Moral Philosophy rest upon a Mistake?' *Mind* (1912), reprinted in *Moral Obligation* (Oxford).

[2] *Moral Obligation*, p. 2.   [3] *Op. cit.*, p. 16.

But however that may be, it makes no matter, for as I hope to show at length the answers he considers do not exhaust the possibilities. His claim that they do is undefended in his pages and it is false. Argument by the elimination of possibilities breaks down disastrously if the philosopher who uses it fails to envisage all the possibilities. The mistake to which Prichard's paper draws attention is not a mistake made by moral philosophers at large. It is a mistake made by Prichard.

It is now time to introduce an overall qualification to the claim I have been making. In the previous sections, I have spoken of the ground, in the singular, of judgements of obligation. I shall argue in fact that judgements of moral obligation divide into two distinct kinds each of which has its own ground. I shall speak here of judgements of basic obligation and judgements of ultra obligation; and the programme includes setting out the ground of judgements of each of these kinds. The grounds of the two kinds of obligation judgement are quite different; but neither of them is any of the three possibilities envisaged by Prichard.

3. THREE IMPEDIMENTS

The search for the grounds of judgements of obligation has been impeded, it seems to me, by two major mistakes and one serious lack of clarity. The first of these mistakes is the failure to notice the distinction between judgements of basic obligation and judgements of ultra obligation. It is a distinction which will occupy us at length, and no more will be said about it at this point. The second mistake is the almost universal assumption that the ground of moral ought judgements must be some quite simple proposition to the effect that something is good. Prichard has already revealed himself as guilty of this assumption in saying that 'from the necessities of the case' the ground of moral ought judgements can only be a proposition asserting of the action enjoined either (*a*) that it is for the agent's own good, or (*b*) that it leads to a state of affairs which is good, or (*c*) that it is intrinsically good. The assumption led Prichard to say that moral ought judgements can have no ground; it has led others to defend either one or another of the apparent possibilities and to look no further. By contrast, Kant wrote:

The concept of good and evil must not be determined before the moral law (of which it seems as if it must be the foundation), but only after it and by means of it.[1]

In speaking of good and evil, Kant is speaking of moral good and evil, and he is saying that the ground of a judgement that something is morally good or evil must include a judgement of obligation and not vice versa. He is denying that a judgement of obligation must be grounded in a proposition asserting something to be morally good. I believe that on this point Kant is most profoundly right: that if we make Prichard's contrary assumption, we shall not only fail to find the ground of moral ought judgements; we shall fail also to obtain any grasp of the concepts of good and evil. These remarks should not be understood as threatening a deontological theory. The theory for which I shall argue is teleological.

The third impediment is a lack of clarity first on the distinction between a motive and a reason for acting, and secondly on the distinction between a reason for acting and a reason for a judgement. I want to devote a chapter to these distinctions before broaching the main task of setting out the grounds of judgements of obligation. Principally, a clear understanding of the notion of reason for acting makes, I think, for a clear understanding of the notion of obligation, including Sir David Ross's important conception of *prima facie* obligation. But secondly, if the distinctions are not clear, my thesis about ultra obligations may seem to be egoistic, which I believe it is not. Accordingly, we turn first to the distinctions between a motive, a reason for acting and a reason for a judgement, and to the connections between the concepts of reason for acting and obligation.

---

[1] *Critique of Practical Reason*, ed. Abbott, 1907, p. 154.

CHAPTER I

MOTIVE, REASON AND OBLIGATION

Philosophers have only recently become much interested in the concept of reason for acting. Until some fifteen years ago, they were content to use 'motive' (and, of course, 'cause') when speaking of the antecedents of action, and to reserve 'reason' for the grounds of propositions. Indeed, it was generally thought proper to do so and incorrect to do otherwise. The change appears to have begun with the publication of Dr Stephen Toulmin's *The Place of Reason in Ethics* in 1950. In his Critical Notice of this work, Professor C. D. Broad represented the earlier position when he wrote,

. . . there is no doubt a perfectly good sense of 'reason' in which one can ask, 'What was X's reason for giving that order?' or 'What reason is there why Y should obey that order of X's?' But 'reason' here means *motive* for or against acting in a certain way . . .[1]

Does it? Have recent philosophers, in using the term 'reason for acting' introduced an expression which is otiose and whose work is done adequately by 'motive'? Or does the classical position miss a distinction of importance in identifying 'reason for acting' with 'motive'?

Broad would have been right in saying that his predecessors, with a few exceptions, drew no distinction; he would have been right in predicting that some of his successors would use 'reason' when they meant motive; he would have been right again had he said that some later philosophers would use 'reason for acting' when they meant a reason for a judgement. But he was wrong in thinking there was no distinction to be drawn between a reason for acting and a motive. I shall argue that there are three distinct concepts to be isolated in this region: the concepts of motive, reason for acting and reason for judging a proposition true or false. 'Reason for judging' will be used as an abbreviation for the latter.

[1] *Mind* (Jan. 1952), p. 96.

I. REASON FOR ACTING AND REASON FOR JUDGING

If there is no distinction between reasons for judging and reasons for acting, the use of the expression 'reason for acting' can only be misleading; for what are so described are nothing but reasons for judging. If there is no such distinction, the classical position is right: there are motives and reasons for judging; and 'reason for acting', if it does not mean one of these, means nothing.

It will be argued here that reason for acting and reason for judging are distinct concepts, but that the distinction between them is often concealed by the misapplication of the term 'reason for acting'. Philosophers often apply it to propositions which are not themselves reasons for acting but which provide inductive support for other propositions which are. They apply it, that is, to reasons for judging propositions true. 'The ice is thin', 'It is a beautiful day' and 'There is a restaurant nearby' are typical examples of reasons for acting cited by philosophers. They may be cited as reasons for avoiding the ice, taking a picnic on the river and pulling the car off the main road respectively. At first sight it seems that such reasons are reasons only for a man who wants to do something or wants something. That the ice is thin is a reason for avoiding it for a man who wants to keep dry; for another who wants to see what it is like to fall through it is a reason for going onto it. That there is a restaurant nearby is a reason for pulling off the main road only for someone who wants food, or for someone who wants his companion to have food, and so on. This is the position which first suggests itself and has suggested itself to many philosophers. For example, Professor A. I. Melden writes, '... "there is a restaurant nearby" would be no reason for stopping the car unless there was something wanted and to be gotten by performing that action ...'[1] Professor P. H. Nowell-Smith[2] holds a view which is similar but not identical; that a man cannot have a reason for acting unless he has a pro-attitude towards the action or towards some state of affairs to be attained by the action. Wanting, for Nowell-Smith is one of many pro-attitudes, and although it is not quite fair to say without qualification that he holds the view in question, it is fair to say that his use of the term 'pro-attitude'

[1] *Free Action* (Routledge), p. 146.
[2] *Ethics* (Penguin Books), ch. 8.

conceals distinctions of importance and makes it difficult to say decisively whether he holds it or not.

This position confuses reasons for acting with reasons for judging, and it also confuses reasons for acting with motives. To take the first point first, the propositions considered are not reasons for acting at all: they are part of the inductive support for propositions which are and are thus reasons for judging. For example, 'It is a beautiful day', has been considered as a reason for taking a picnic on the river. But it is properly understood not as a reason for acting but as part of the reason for judging that the agent would enjoy taking a picnic on the river. It is the latter which is a reason for acting. That a man would enjoy taking a picnic on the river is a reason for doing so; that it is a beautiful day is part of the inductive support for this proposition or part of the reason for judging it to be true. Similarly, 'There is a good restaurant nearby', is part of the reason for judging that by pulling the car off the main road, the agent would be able either to enjoy a good lunch or relieve his hunger; and either of the latter is a reason for pulling the car off the main road.

If there is to be any hope of isolating the concept of reason for acting, it is essential to keep clear the distinction between propositions which are reasons for acting and other propositions which provide inductive support for them. The latter are reasons for judging, and to call them 'reasons for acting' can lead to nothing but confusion. The present discussion of the distinction is far from complete, but it cannot be taken further at this stage. Reason for acting is an elusive concept which can be pinned down only by a series of discussions some of which cannot be completed at the stage at which they have to be introduced. I turn now to the second confusion in the position advocated by Nowell-Smith and Melden.

2. REASON FOR ACTING AND DESIRE

It is wrong to hold that a proposition can be a reason for acting only for a man who wants something to be attained by the action. Reasons for acting are logically independent of desires. Suppose James is home from school for the summer holidays. It is a beautiful day and the river is at its best. One of James's delights is punting. His friends, home from other schools, are all going on the river, taking a picnic with them. There are girls in the party too, and James likes girls. But alas! he is in one of those dreadful moods of ennui. He is consumed with lethargy and as miserable as sin. He is in the kind of mood which we all know and which most of us sometimes suffer. He does not want to go on the river. All he wants to do is slouch around at home. Despite his lack of desire, we can suppose that he would enjoy it on the river if he would make the effort to conquer his present mood. We can suppose that he would enjoy it more than anything else he could do and certainly much more than a day spent moping. If this is so, there is good reason for his going on the river even though he does not want to. In staying at home, he is being stupid, foolish and unreasonable. He is wasting his time. The case shows that there being good reason for a man's doing so-and-so is logically independent of his wanting to do it or wanting to achieve anything to be attained by doing it.

The conclusion of the previous paragraph may be reached by a more direct route. Suppose a man would enjoy a certain activity more than any other he could do at the time. If this is so, there is a reason for his doing it. It follows immediately that there can be a reason for a man's doing something even though he does not want to do it, for it may not have crossed his mind to do it. And if it has not crossed his mind, he cannot want to do it. Whether there is a reason or not is logically independent of his desires. It may seem that this argument applies only if 'want' is used episodically, and that the fact adduced is no reason for acting unless he has a disposition to want to do the kind of action in question. But the truth is that a disposition to want is no more necessary that his wanting episodically. It may be possible to establish that a man would most enjoy playing golf one afternoon even though he has never in his life thought of playing golf and never wanted to do so: it may be an afternoon on which the alternatives are not exciting; it may be possible to infer from his known skills that he would be good at golf, and known that he enjoys activities which he does well. This is enough to establish that there is good reason for his playing golf. Yet, ex hypothesi, he has no disposition to want to: the thought of playing golf has *never* crossed his mind.

As a final illustration, suppose a certain action would win a man promotion. If it has not occurred to him to do it, he cannot want (episodically) to do it. But it may seem that there is a reason for his doing it only if he (dispositionally) wants promotion. This again is false. Whether there is a reason for his doing the action or not depends not upon whether he *wants* promotion but upon whether it is in his *interest* to have it. He may be perfectly contented in his rut and have no desire to emerge. But it remains possible that he would be happier if promoted, and to establish that he would is to establish that there is a reason for his doing the action whatever his desires may be.

I have spoken throughout this section of *there being* a reason for a man's acting in a certain way and not of *his having* a reason. At a later stage, I shall draw a distinction between *A's having* a reason for doing *x* and *there being* a reason for *A*'s doing *x*, where '*A*' represents, as throughout, any agent and '*x*' any action. But for the moment I want to consider the objection that the point about the independence of reasons and desires holds only for the latter and not for the former, i.e., that a man cannot *have* a reason for doing *x* unless he wants something to be attained by the action, although it is conceded that there can *be* a reason for his doing it even if he does not want any such thing. This objection arises only because reasons are confused with motives. It may be seen to be unfounded by considering again the case of the boy suffering from ennui. Suppose he knows all the facts of the case as set out. It is conceded that there is a reason for his going on the river. It follows that, if he knows all the facts, he knows that there is. It cannot now be said that he does not have a reason for going on the river: there is a reason, and he knows it. Any inclination to object to this is the result, as will be seen, of confusing the proposition that he does not have a *reason* with the proposition that he does not have a *motive*. He does not have a motive because he does not *want* to go on the river: all he wants to do is mope. When this confusion of reason with motive is avoided the temptation to say that he has no reason for going on the river if he does not want to is overcome. He does not have a motive, but he does have a reason. The formula *No reason without a desire* is false. But the formula *No motive without a desire* is true. This is the first important point of distinction between a reason for acting and a motive.

3. MOTIVE

Philosophical discussion of motives has been bedevilled by the assumption that 'vanity', 'considerateness', 'avarice', 'patriotism', 'indolence' and such like are the names of motives. The list is Professor Gilbert Ryle's.[1] The only reason for thinking these terms are the names of motives is that we often answer the question, 'Why did he do so-and-so?' by saying 'Vanity' or 'Out of patriotism' or 'Because he is considerate'; and these answers are in some sense motive explanations. But it by no means follows that the motive is explicitly named in them. The alternative remains that such answers explain why a certain motive, which is not explicitly named, was a motive for a particular man: Such-and-such was a motive for this man because he is vain, but not for that man because he is not vain; such-and-such is a motive for this man because he is considerate, but not for that man because he is not.

Bentham held that avarice, indolence, benevolence and such like are motives only in a figurative sense of the term.[2] A motive in the unfigurative sense is the expectation of an 'individual lot of pleasure or pain'. If we abandon Bentham's view about the omnipotence of pleasure and pain, and substitute 'belief' for 'expectation', his position takes the form that to have a motive for an action is to believe that some end will be furthered by doing it. This is a necessary condition of having a motive, but it is not sufficient. It is also necessary to *want* to further that end. *A* and *B* may both believe that the action would lead to their children's happiness, but *A* can have a motive for doing it while *B* has not: *A* may want his children to be happy while *B* does not. Again, *A* and *B* may both believe a certain action would lead to riches. But if *A* wants riches and *B* does not, *A* has a motive for the action while *B* does not. The formula *No motive without a desire* is true.

In both these cases, the question whether *A* and *B* have motives is independent of whether there is a reason for their acting in certain ways. In the latter case, it may be possible to show that *B* would be happier if he were possessed of riches, and if this is so, there is a reason for his doing the action whatever he may think and whatever he may want. This is a prudential case in which it is

---

[1] *The Concept of Mind* (Hutchinson), p. 85.
[2] *Principles of Morals and Legislation*, 1879, p. 99.

easy to see what the reason might be. The former case is moral, and the kind of reason appropriate cannot be given yet. But it is clear that it may be possible, as it is in the prudential case, to give a reason for *B*'s acting so as to make his children happy even though he does not wish to make them happy and has no motive for doing so. Whether, in showing him that there was such a reason, we should supply him with a motive is another question again. The answer to it depends upon how his desires are affected when he is shown that there are reasons for acting in certain ways. It is indeed true that the intellect alone cannot move the will to action; but it is also true that the intellect alone supplies us with reasons for action.

Suppose a man has acted so to ease his neighbour's burden and that his action is explained as done from considerateness. The suggestion that the motive is explicitly named has been rejected, and it remains to show how the explanation functions. It functions in a two-fold way. First, it explains why the belief that a certain action would ease his neighbour's burden was a motive for this man whereas there are many others for whom it would not be a motive. It does this by pointing out that the former man is considerate whereas some others are not; by pointing out that it is characteristic of him to be moved by such a belief. But secondly it explains by revealing the kind of belief which provided the motive for the action. In being told that it was done out of considerateness, we are being told that he was moved by the belief that the action would help his neighbour and not by the belief that he would be judged a benevolent man, nor that his neighbour would return the kindness to him. Had one of the latter pair been the case, the explanation would have been not 'Out of considerateness' but perhaps, 'Out of vanity' or 'Out of prudence' respectively. Similarly, when an action is explained in terms of lust, greed, curiosity, sympathy or benevolence the explanation singles out the kind of belief involved in the motive. The second of these two elements has more explanatory force than the first, and together they do just about as much to explain a man's actions as we think is done by answers of this kind.

I have been arguing for the truth of the formula *No motive without a desire* and the falsity of the formula *No reason without a desire*. To establish that the second formula is false is to establish that the question whether a man can be given reasons for acting in certain ways is independent of any question about his desires. This is not to say that it is independent of his interests, considered either independently of the interests of other people or in conjunction with them. Reasons for acting and peoples' interests are intimately connected in ways to be seen. But reasons are independent of desires, and this is one of the ways in which the concepts of reason for acting and motive differ.

It may be objected to this thesis that 'I want to do x' is itself a reason for doing x. But the truth is that it is not. It appears to be only because it is usually a fair assumption that it is in a man's interest to do what he wants to do. If it is to be established that there is a (prudential) reason for a man's doing x, it has to be established that it is in his interest to do x. Given that he wants to do x, it has to be established that, in the case in question, it is in his interest to do what he wants to do. That he wants to do it is not a reason. To say, 'I want to do x' is not to contribute to a discussion of whether it is rational for me to do x. It is to exhibit truculence—unless it is brought forward because, in the particular case, it is understood that it is in my interest to have what I want.

4. DESIRE AND INTEREST

In the previous sections, I have drawn a distinction between a man's desires and his interests. And I have argued that although his having a reason for doing x, and there being a reason for his doing x, are independent of his desires, they are not independent of his interests and the interests of other people; while, on the other hand, his having a motive for doing x is not independent of his desires, but is independent of his interests. To have a motive for doing x, it is not, of course, necessary that he should want to do that action. For example, we often have motives for doing morally right actions without wanting to do those actions. But it is necessary that something is wanted: to see oneself as a moral person, for example, or to enjoy the good opinion of one's neighbours.

Now plainly it may be in a man's interest to do an action even though he does not want to do it: it may be in his interest to invest his inheritance even though he wants to exhaust it in purchasing an expensive car. Certainly there may be a reason for a man's acting in a certain way even though he does not want to do that *action*. But so tame a truth is a far cry from the claim that his having a reason, or there being a reason, for his doing the action is totally independent of his desires. And it may seem that the only way of establishing that it is in his interest to invest his inheritance, that there is a reason for his doing so, is by drawing attention to other things which he desires, e.g., the improvement in his standard of living which an additional income would make possible. Thus, it may appear that the distinction between interests and desires cannot be driven home, and that the distinction between reasons and motives, so far as it rests upon it, breaks down. A man may have a motive for doing x or he may have a reason for doing x: in neither case is it necessary that he should want to do x; but in both cases it is necessary that something should be wanted which will be attained by doing x.

The reply to this objection is that the premiss on which it rests is false. It is not true that when a man does not want to do something we can show that it is in his interest to do it only by appealing to other desires which he has. Suppose a man of no talent and no financial resources is embarked upon a wretched career as an actor. He lives in poverty. He has no chance of success. He is thoroughly discontented and unhappy. It may be that despite his discontent and unhappiness, despite his poverty and the certainty of failure, he wants, and wants more than anything else, to persist in the life he has chosen. But it may also be that, despite his desires, and in addition to the facts cited, there are all sorts of hints to be found in his life that it is in his interest to tear himself away from the stage and sink himself in some other career. It would need a novelist, not a philosopher, to do justice to the description of such hints, but they need not be any facts about what he wants in his present condition: if, of any consequence of the alternative career, we were to ask, 'And don't you want that?' he may reply correctly, 'No, not if it is incompatible with my being an actor'. I am not saying that we can establish that it is in his interest to abandon the stage without also establishing that, if he would make the break, he would *come to want* the alternative career rather than his acting career. But the fact remains that, whatever his desires may *be*, it may be possible to establish that it is in his interest to make the break; and thus there may be a reason for his acting in a certain way even though he wants nothing to be attained by acting in that way. On the other hand, he cannot have a motive for an action unless he does, there and then, desire something to be attained by the action. The distinction between the notions of reason and motive does not break down in the way alleged.

5. REASON FOR ACTING

So far the only examples given of reasons for acting have been that A would enjoy doing x, and that it is in A's interest to have the promotion to which x would lead. Consider now the very general reason that it is in A's interest to do x, and let this proposition be represented by 'P'. The truth of P is a reason for A's doing x, but it is not the only reason in terms of P. The truth of the proposition that A has good reason for judging that P is also a reason. To deny this leads to paradox. Suppose A decides to catch the 3.05 train to London. It may be true that the train is going to crash with the death of all passengers and therefore false that it is in his interest to catch it. But if he has no good reason for thinking it will crash, and good reason to think that by catching it he will reach London in time for an appointment, then he has good reason for judging that it is in his interest to catch it. And if this is so, it cannot be denied that he has a reason, and good reason, for catching that train. The use which is required of 'A has good reason for judging that P' allows for the individuality of A's situation—that it is different, for example, from the situation of those about to engineer the destruction of the train. At the same time, it is necessary that certain canons of judgement are satisfied. These canons are such that, if they are satisfied, we can say that the judgements A made on this occasion were beyond criticism. I shall say that if P is true, *there is* a reason for A's doing x; and that if A has good reason for judging that P is true, A *has* (given the individuality of his situation) a reason for doing x.

Thus the truth of P and the truth of the proposition that A has good reason for judging that P are both reasons for A's acting. It will save verbiage if I speak of the proposition as a reason for acting, and this device will be adopted frequently. Whenever I speak in this way, it is a shorthand for referring to either the truth of the proposition or the truth of the proposition that A has good reason for judging it true. With this understanding, it is false to say that *any* proposition can be a reason for acting. It is false, for example, of the propositions that it is a beautiful day, that the specific heat of copper is 0·1, that the ice is thin and that Bentleys are expensive. It may seem that circumstances can be imagined in which any of these propositions is a reason for acting, but the fact is that circumstances can be imagined in which any of them may provide inductive support for a proposition which is a reason for acting. At this point the discussion under the heading *Reason for Acting and Reason for Judging* is taken a stage further. I said in that earlier discussion that philosophers often apply the term 'reason for acting' to propositions which are not reasons for acting but which provide inductive support for propositions which are; and that this was a confusion which must be avoided if the concept of reason for acting is to be isolated. I must now try to make clear my view upon what kinds of proposition can be reasons for acting.

In the section *Reason for Acting and Desire* we saw that the question of whether or not there is a reason for A's doing x is independent of his desires. But there was no suggestion that it was independent of his interests. Quite the reverse: in each case discussed the question depended upon whether A would enjoy doing x, or, more generally, whether it was in his interest to do x. The only propositions which are properly understood as reasons for acting—as reasons for A's doing x—are propositions which state either that x is *in some way* in accordance with A's interests or that x conduces to A's aims. One such proposition is that it is in A's interest to do x, but the action is not always related to the agent's aims or interests in this simple way. In the case of moral reasons a more complex relation holds between the interests of A, the interests of other people, and the action; but it still asserts that x is *in some way* in A's interests. The truth of a proposition of one of these kinds is a reason for acting; and so is A's having good reason for judging it true. The truth of any other kind of proposition is not; nor is A's having good reason for judging it true. Many other kinds of proposition may indeed, in various circumstances, provide inductive support for a proposition which is a reason for acting. But this is not to say that they are themselves reasons for acting.

This may seem like dogmatic assertion, or it may seem obvious once stated, or it may have seemed obvious before it was stated. But in any case I had better defend the position adopted. It can only be done at this stage by considering a prudential case in which no moral factors are involved. The claim will be argued independently for moral cases at a later stage. Suppose I establish to a man's satisfaction that it is going to be a beautiful day. It does not follow that I have established that there is a reason for his doing anything: he may be oblivious to the weather. Suppose I prove to him that the ice is thin. I have again not proved that there is a reason for his acting in any way: he may be in bed with a sprained ankle. Again, if I establish that there is a restaurant nearby, I have not established that there is a reason for his doing anything: he may be an ascetic who is not hungry. It is only when I have shown that it is in his interest to do something that I have shown that there is a reason for his doing it. I can establish any proposition I like which does not state that an action is in his interest and he can always intelligibly reply, 'You have not yet given me a reason for acting'. It is only when I have established that it is in his interest to act in a certain way that he cannot make this reply. 'It is in my interest to do x, but that is no reason for my doing x' is self-contradictory, while 'It is a beautiful day, but that is no reason for my doing x' is not.

The point is concealed in day to day discussions because so much is usually taken for granted. For example, when someone states that the ice is thin, other propositions are often taken for granted which, together with the one asserted, provide sufficient inductive support for the proposition that it is in the interest of all concerned to keep off. In such a case, it is established that there is a reason for doing so, though the argument is not explicitly set out. It thus seems that the proposition that the ice is thin is a reason for acting, because it is the only proposition asserted. But the fact is that it is part of the inductive support, the rest being implicit, for the proposition that it is in the interest of all concerned to keep off the ice. And this latter proposition is the reason for acting.

The most important point to be considered about reasons for acting is their assessment as good or bad. Two elements are involved in such an assessment. To avoid verbiage again, I shall let 'S' represent any proposition which asserts that x is *in some way* in accordance with A's interest or conduces to A's aims. Thus 'S' represents the kind of proposition which I have just been arguing can be a reason for acting. (Strictly speaking, as already explained, the truth of S and the truth of the proposition that A has good reason for judging that S are reasons for acting.) 'S' may represent any of a number of propositions for there are many ways, as we are to see, in which x can be in accordance with A's interest.

The first element involved in the assessment of a reason for acting as good or bad is as follows. It is a necessary and sufficient condition of *there being* a reason for A's doing x that some S is true. And it is a necessary and sufficient condition of A's *having* a reason for doing x that he should have good reason for judging some S true. These are necessary and sufficient for there being *a* reason and for A's having *a* reason respectively. They are necessary but not sufficient for there being *good* reason for A's doing x and for A's having *good* reason for doing x. It is a further necessary condition, that the S involved is of a certain kind. But before dealing with this point, which deserves a separate section, I must draw attention to the second way in which a reason for acting differs from a motive.

It has already been argued that having a motive implies having a desire but that neither having a reason nor there being a reason implies having a desire. Leaving there being a reason on one side— precisely parallel remarks apply to it—we now see that it is a necessary condition of A's having a reason for doing x that he has good reason for judging some S true. It is plain that this is not a necessary condition of his having a motive for doing x. It is sufficient for his having a motive that he should *believe* that some aim is furthered by his doing x and that he should want to further that aim. It is irrelevant whether he has good reason for his belief; his reasons may be abysmal, but it has no bearing upon whether or not he has a motive. It follows that one of the elements involved in the assessment of a reason for acting as good or bad, viz., that some S is true, or that he has good reason for judging some S true, is not available for the assessment of motives. Motives cannot be good or bad in the way that reasons for acting can. Motives can be assessed as morally good or bad, but that is a different matter.

6. BETTER REASON THAN

The second element in the assessment of reasons as good or bad is explained in this section. For simplicity of exposition, I shall leave on one side for the moment considerations about *A*'s having good reason for judging that some *S* is true and talk in terms of the truth of some *S*. The truth of some *S* is a necessary condition of there being good reason for *A*'s doing *x*, but it is not sufficient. It is not sufficient because the truth of some *S*'s is better reason for acting than the truth of some others. If an *S* is true of *x* it does not follow that there is good reason for *A*'s doing *x* because another *S* may be true of not-*x*, *and the truth of the second* S *may be a better reason for acting than the truth of the first.*

A distinction can be drawn between a man's present and his future interests. An action may be in his present interest because he would enjoy it, because it would give him immediate satisfaction, relieve an uneasy conscience, cure a pain or rid him of some other unpleasant sensation. It may be in his future interest because it will lead to an annual income of £5000 later, or to a happy retirement, or to his marrying the girl he wants, and so on. The distinction between present and future interests is not, of course, sharp. An action which is in his present interest may also be in his future interest and vice versa; but an action which is in his present interest may be against his future interest and an action which is in his future interest may be against his present interest. When such conflicts occur we need a way of referring to the action it is in his interest to do, and for this purpose I speak of his overall interest. The action which is in his overall interest is the action it is in his interest to do when his present and future interests conflict. It is not always in a man's overall interest to do the action which is in his future interest. 'One splendid indiscretion', Ernest de Selincourt said, 'Is worth a world of caution'. It can be in a man's overall interest to cater for either his present or future interests. There need be nothing momentous about deciding an action to be in one's overall interest. I may decide that it is in my overall interest to go for a walk one afternoon because I would enjoy it and doing so will have no effect upon my future life. Vast numbers of decisions which we take are like this. On the other hand, such decisions are sometimes immensely important.

The proposition that x is in A's present interest and that x is in A's future interest are both reasons for his doing x. But the proposition that it is in his overall interest to do x is a better reason than either, for they both leave open the possibility, which it does not, that it is against his overall interest to do x. The point is that the truth of one proposition relating A's interest to x is a better reason for acting than the truth of other propositions relating his interest to x. It will be clear that this is distinct from the claim that if A believes that x is in his overall interest he has a stronger motive; he very often does not, and life would be easier if he did.

The point about this superiority of reason, which has been made in terms of the action x, must be related to any action incompatible with x. Such an action will be referred to as not-x. The relation is stated in the following way: the truth of the proposition that it is in A's overall interest to do x is a reason for his doing x which is better than any *in terms of his present or future interests* for doing either x or not-x. There are linguistically simpler ways of expressing this, e.g., 'It is a good prudential reason'; but I am adopting the more cumbersome expression deliberately so that certain structural similarities will stand out later.

A technical case will provide a second illustration of the truth of one proposition being a better reason for acting than the truth of another. Suppose A is aiming at an end E, and that M is the most effective means to that end, N being a less effective means. The truth of the proposition that A is aiming at E and that M is the most effective means to E is a better reason than the truth of the proposition that A is aiming at E and that N is a less effective means to E: the former is a better reason for choosing M than the latter is for choosing N. This is so obvious that the point seems hardly worth making. It may however be expressed in a way parallel to that used in the previous case: the truth of the proposition that A is aiming at E and that M is the most effective means to E is a reason for doing M which is better than any reason in terms of means to E for doing either M or not-M.

The points of the previous two paragraphs may plainly be made in terms of A's having good reason for judging the proposition true as well as in terms of the propositions being true. The important point for this work is that although the truth of some S is a necessary condition of there being good reason for A's doing

x; and although A's having good reason for judging some S true is a necessary condition of his having good reason for doing x, these conditions are not sufficient. For the S which satisfies them may be a poorer reason than another S which also satisfies them. It is useful, I think, as we go along, to relate what is being said now to what will be said about moral argument later. The fact that the truth of some propositions constitutes better reason for acting than the truth of some others is important in dealing with moral cases. I hope to show in the chapters which follow that certain propositions connecting the interests of A, the interests of other people and actions which are morally right (i.e., actions which we have a basic or an ultra obligation to do) constitute better reason for A's doing these actions than any proposition which relates his interest alone to these actions or any alternatives. I should not like the strength of this claim to be underestimated.

There have been philosophers, wishing to maintain the rationality of moral discourse, who have been prepared to say that there is 'good reason' for doing x simply on the basis that x is an action which ought to be done. If the expression 'good reason' is used in this way, it is doing no work at all; and its introduction, far from showing moral discourse to be rational, is worthless. If, where x is a morally right action, it is claimed that some proposition in terms of A's interests, the interests of other people and the action x, is a better reason for A's doing x than any proposition in terms of A's interests alone, then it has to be shown that it *is* a better reason without employing the premiss that x is a morally right action. If this is not done, the introduction of 'better reason' is idle. It is also important, I believe, to be tough minded about the application of 'better reason'. It will never be claimed here that S_1 as a reason for a man's doing an action x is better than S_2 as a reason for his doing not-x unless I think that, whoever he may be, he would be convinced that it is; provided *only* that he understands what is being said to him. Good will is not presupposed.

The reasons which can or cannot be given for a man's acting in certain ways are, it will be remembered, logically independent of his desires. The claim made is that reasons can be given for acting morally not only to a man who wants to be moral but also to a man who does not care a brass farthing whether he is moral or not. And reasons can also be given for acting morally not only to a man who is aiming at being moral but also to a man who is aiming at no such thing. It will be clear that the claim made is distinct from the claim that such a man can always be provided with a motive. To provide him with a motive involves bringing him into a condition in which he wants certain things, and it may or may not be possible to accomplish this by reasoning. But a *reason* for a man's acting morally does not fail to be a reason for his acting just because he does not want to be moral or just because he is not aiming at being moral.

7. OBLIGATION AND ITS MODES

Philosophers have drawn distinctions between (1) subjective and objective obligation; (2) prudential and moral obligation; and (3) *prima facie* and actual obligation. Something must be said about the first distinction at this point. It has often been held that if a man has good reason for thinking a certain action right then he ought to do it. But it remains possible that it is wrong, and that he ought therefore not to do it. It seems then that he ought both to do it and not do it. This dilemma was resolved by Richard Price in his *Review of the Principal Questions of Morals*[1] by saying that two different senses of 'ought' are involved and that the contradiction is apparent, not real. In recent times Price has been followed in offering this solution by Dr A. C. Ewing.[2] The difficulty has been traditionally expressed in terms of 'sincerely thinking that he ought', but I have deliberately substituted for this 'having good reason for thinking that he ought'.

The distinction between prudential and moral obligation is also sometimes expressed by speaking of different senses of 'ought'; and Sir David Ross's distinction between *prima facie* and actual obligation might be expressed in the same way. Philosophers who speak about different senses seem to be committed to recognizing an embarrassingly large number, although it would be naïve to interpret them as holding that there are several senses of 'ought' in the sense in which 'chair', 'sincerity', 'woman' and 'goblin' have different senses. Even so, if this is not what they meant, I think it is fair to say that it has not been made clear what they did mean. In contrast to this threatened proliferation of senses, the

---

[1] *British Moralists*, ed. Selby-Bigge, vol. 2, pp. 175–6.
[2] *The Definition of Good* (Routledge), p. 120.

most favoured contemporary view seems to be that 'ought' has just one sense.

I do not take sides in this dispute because it does not seem to me to be a helpful way of discussing the problems involved. To say that 'ought' has only one sense is to obscure distinctions of importance. To say it has many senses, and leave it at that, is to suggest that the distinctions are more thorough-going than they are. There is certainly not more than one sense of 'ought' in the sense in which there is more than one sense of 'bank': and there is certainly not just one sense of 'ought' in the sense in which there is just one sense of 'centimetre'. The truth of the matter is best expressed by saying that obligation is a complex concept with several distinguishable modes. It is a central theme of this work that the common element which holds the modes together is that every ought proposition asserted of an action x implies a proposition in terms of the concept of *better reason for doing* x *than*, i.e., the proposition

A ought (   ) to do x
implies
... better reason for doing x than ...

The modes of the concept selected by different occupants of the brackets in the implicans are distinguished, some partly, some completely, by different completions of the implicandum.

Distinctions can be drawn between subjective and objective modes of the concept; between prudential and moral modes; and between *prima facie* and actual modes. The first distinction will be dealt with here and then left on one side. Apart from a paragraph in the next section, the objective mode will be employed throughout. The distinction between subjective and objective modes is required to deal with the dilemma which Richard Price resolved by postulating two senses of 'ought'. The distinction between these two modes lies in the completion of the first space in the implicandum, the second being completed in the same way. The proposition that A ought (objectively) to do x implies that *there is* a reason for A's doing x better than ...; the proposition that A ought (subjectively) to do x implies that A *has* a reason for doing x better than ... The distinction between *There is* ... and A *has* ... has been considered earlier: it is a necessary condition of the truth of the former that a proposition stating that x is in some way in accordance with A's interest is true; of the latter that A has good reason for judging such a proposition true. The dilemma is resolved by seeing that what has been expressed as 'He ought to do x and he ought not' is properly expressed by saying, 'He ought (subjectively) to do x but (objectively) he ought not to' with the implication that *he has* good reason (given the individuality of his situation) for doing x, but *there is* good reason for his not doing x. But it is an oversimplification to say that two senses of 'ought' are involved: the second space in the implicandum may be completed in the same way for both ought propositions; indeed, to give rise to this dilemma, it must be.

It may seem that my handling of this problem is no less arbitrary than the postulation of two senses. Were it offered as an isolated treatment of an isolated problem, I should not claim otherwise. But the fact is that it is just one part of the complex structure of relations between obligation and reason for acting. The remaining parts of this structure have yet to be set out.

8. THE REASON-FOR-ACTING/OBLIGATION SCHEMA

As explained in the Introduction, 'implies' is used in such a way that p implies q if and only if (1) it is logically impossible that p is true and q is false, and (2) the impossibility is not a consequence of the impossibility of p or the necessity of q.

The general form of the Reason-for-Acting/Obligation Schema is as follows, 'S' representing a proposition asserting some action, x, or some class of actions, to be in some way in A's interest or, in moral cases, in the interest, in some way, of a group of people:

S
implies
A ought (   ) to do x
implies
There is a reason for A's doing x which is better than . . .

The correct completion of the second implicandum depends upon the occupant of the brackets after 'ought'. If the occupant is 'prudentially', then the implicandum is completed in one way; if 'morally' in another. If the latter, the mode of the concept may be either *prima facie* or actual, and the implicandum is completed in different ways accordingly. Correspondingly, the proposition represented by '*s*', which is the ground of the ought judgement, differs from case to case.

The validity of the schema will be illustrated by considering its application to the prudential mode of the concept:

(*P*) It is in *A*'s overall interest to do *x* and *A* can do *x*
implies

(*Q*) *A* ought (prudentially) to do *x*
implies

(*R*) There is a reason for *A*'s doing *x* which is better than any *in terms of his present or future interest* for doing either *x* or not-*x*

i.e., *P* implies *Q* and *Q* implies *R*. The words italicised are important. The ought proposition does not imply that there is a reason for *A*'s doing *x* which is better, simpliciter, than any for doing either *x* or not-*x*. It does not imply it because *x* might be a morally wrong action, and in that case, as will be argued, there is a better reason for his doing not-*x*.

The validity of the schema may indeed be obvious as it is applied to the prudential mode. But if it is not we may argue for it by considering, in the first instance, a modified form of the schema in which the proposition *R* is replaced by

(*R'*) There is a conclusive prudential reason for *A*'s doing *x*.

In the previous sections, we have come a long way towards isolating, and obtaining an understanding of, the notion of reason for acting. The first step in coming to understand the notion of obligation is to realize that the function of an ought judgement is to say that there is a reason of a certain kind for doing the action enjoined by it. It is important that its function is not to say anything about motives; a point which has not always been clear to moral philosophers. The kind of reason depends upon the kind of ought judgement. The function of '*A* ought (prudentially) to do *x*', for example, is to say that there is a conclusive prudential reason for *A*'s doing *x*. In other words, we are saying that the propositions *Q* and *R'* imply each other.

It is now fairly easy to show that *P* implies *Q* by showing that *P* implies *R'*. The argument is that the proposition *P* *is* a conclusive prudential reason for *A*'s doing *x*, so that, in conjunction with the proposition asserting that it is, it implies that there is a conclusive prudential reason for A's doing x. Thus

> (P) It is in A's overall interest to do x and A can do x
> and
> (N) P is a conclusive prudential reason for A's doing x
> conjointly imply
> (R') There is a conclusive prudential reason for A's doing x;

and therefore, by virtue of the equivalence of Q and R', conjointly imply that A ought (prudentially) to do x. But N is a necessary proposition which may, uncontroversially, be dropped provided 'implies' is used in the way explained and P and Q and R' are contingent propositions. We thus have the conclusion that P implies Q, and the first implication of the schema for the prudential mode of the concept is established. The second implication, i.e., that Q implies R, is now easily shown to hold. For we have seen that Q and R' imply each other, and as it is obvious that R' implies R, it follows that Q implies R. I state the schema in terms of R rather than R' because I think it is better to avoid talking about prudential reasons. The argument of this section can be set out without doing so at the expense of greater complexity, but simplicity has seemed preferable.

It is understood that we have been speaking of an objective mode of the concept. The schema applies to the subjective mode also: in this case the proposition corresponding to P is that A has good reason for judging that it is in his overall interest to do x; and R begins with 'A has a reason better than . . .' instead of 'There is a reason better than . . .' And naturally, the proposition corresponding to Q speaks of a subjective mode instead of the objective mode understood in the exposition.

I am committed to establishing the Reason-for-Acting/Obligation schema for all modes of the concept of obligation to be discussed. I am committed to showing, that is, that whichever mode is selected by the term in brackets in the proposition corresponding to Q, the proposition implies a proposition corresponding to R, the words italicised being different for different modes of the concept; and to showing that for all modes of the concept, there is a proposition corresponding to P which implies, in the strong sense explained, the proposition corresponding to Q. This proposition is the ground of judgements of obligation. By showing, in each of the several cases, that it is a reason for acting of the kind specified in the proposition corresponding to R, we are able to explain the demand which the ought proposition makes upon us. To show that the schema applies to the moral modes of the concept of obligation is to show how morality can be practical, for it is to show that every proposition of the form, 'A ought to do x' implies that there is a reason for A's doing x which is better than. . . The problem of the practicality of morals is the main stimulus behind Prescriptive theories. One of my subsidiary aims is to show that this problem can be solved without abandoning the view that in moral discussion we are concerned with propositions. The Reason-for-Acting/Obligation schema, reveals, as it seems to me, the truth which Prescriptive theories seek to express, but which they fail to express with any clarity. The obscurity results, I believe, from the failure of their authors to make themselves clear about the concept of reason for acting.

9. INDEPENDENT INTEREST

In discussing the prudential case, the expression, 'a man's overall interest' was used. This has to be understood as his overall interest *assessed independently of the interests of other people*. And it has to be explained what this means. Sometimes none of the alternative actions between which a man is choosing has any foreseeable effect upon others. In such a case, in deciding what to do, he consults his own interest, in a straightforward sense, without considering the interests of others. This is certainly an assessment of his interest independently of the interests of other people. But the expression will be used here to cover also a different kind of case. The judgement that A ought to help B may be made on the ground that others are watching, that they will praise A if he offers help, and that A enjoys praise. The ground adduced may be said to involve an assessment of A's interest which is *not* independent of the interests of others, because it is in B's interest to receive help. Even so, as the expression will be used here, this counts as an independent assessment. B is being considered, to employ Kant's distinction, as a means and not as an end.[1] He is being considered

[1] *Groundwork of the Metaphysic of Morals*, ed. Paton, pp. 96–7.

as a means of bringing about a state of affairs which is in A's interest, viz., a state of affairs in which A experiences enjoyment. No premiss about B's interest is required to establish that it is in A's interest to act in the way in question. The only premisses needed are that A's acting in that way will occasion applause, and that it is in A's interest to be applauded. If A's interest is assessed in such a way that the interests of other people are considered *only* as a means to bringing about states of affairs which are in A's interest, then A's interest will be said to be assessed independently of the interests of others. It will be clear that the interests of groups can also be assessed independently of the interests of other groups and of individuals outside them. Interests, so assessed, will be referred to as *independent interests*.

On the other hand, it is sometimes in a man's interest to act in a certain way because it is in the interest of others that he should act in this way. A man of altruistic disposition characteristically acts in certain ways because it is in the interest of others that he should do so. His motive is the desire to help others and the belief that such actions are in the interests of others. But the point to be made is not about motives. The point is that there is a good sense in which it is in his interest to act in these ways; he is not, except occasionally, made more miserable by doing so. On the contrary, he is, on the whole, made happier. When we speak in this way of its being in his interest to act in the interests of other people, I wish to say that this is an assessment of his interest which is not independent of the interests of other people. To establish that it is in a man's independent interest to act in certain ways, no premiss asserting such actions to be in anyone else's interest is needed. But it cannot be established that it is in a man's non-independent interest to act in certain ways without employing a premiss that it is in the interest of other people that he should do so. The presence of this premiss in its ground distinguishes a proposition asserting a kind of action to be in a man's non-independent interest from a proposition asserting actions of the kind to be in his independent interest. It will be plain that the discussion here concerns the ground of propositions and that motives are not in question.

The distinction between the independent and non-independent assessment of interests explained in this section is important throughout and particularly important in chapter 4.

10. ABSTRACT AND ACTUAL OBLIGATION

Sir David Ross drew a distinction between *prima facie* and actual obligation which is of central importance.[1] The terminology is unfortunate as he himself recognized, and I shall speak of *abstract* and *actual* obligation instead of *prima facie* and *actual* obligation. The distinction has application only within the moral mode of the concept.

The distinction between the abstract and actual modes is simply drawn by employing the second part of the schema set out earlier. It has to be remembered that we are dealing with objective and moral modes:

A ought (abstractly) to do x
implies
There is a reason for A's doing x which is better than any in terms of his overall *independent* interest for doing either x or not-x

To speak of 'independent interest' is to speak of interest assessed independently of the interests of others as explained in the previous section. If A ought (abstractly) to do x, there may, of course, be reasons in terms of his independent interest for doing either x or not-x. But, however this may be, there is also a reason, and a better one, for his doing x which is not in terms of his independent interest. Thus from 'A ought (abstractly) to do x' it follows that there is a reason for his doing x however it may be with his independent interests; or, as we might say, in *abstraction* from his independent interests. Hence the choice of the name 'abstract obligation'.

'A ought (abstractly) to do x' does not imply that there is a reason for A's doing x which is better, simpliciter, than any for his doing x or not-x; only that it is better than any in terms of his overall independent interest. The proposition in terms of actual obligation has a stronger implication:

A ought (actually) to do x
implies
There is a reason for A's doing x which is better than any other reason of the same kind for doing either x or not-x.

[1] *The Right and the Good* (Oxford), p. 19.

The kind of reason referred to is the kind of which it is asserted, in the implicandum of '*A* ought (abstractly) to do *x*', that it is a reason better than any in terms of overall independent interest. In a particular situation, there may be more than one reason of this kind for *A*'s acting, and one may be a reason for doing *x* and the other a reason for doing not-*x*. This is the well known situation of a conflict of abstract (*prima facie*) obligations. If we judge that in such a situation *A* ought (actually) to do *x*, and that he ought (actually) not to do not-*x*, then we are committed to saying that the reason of the kind in question for doing *x* is better than the reason of this kind for doing not-*x*.

The distinctions so far drawn within the concept of obligation are familiar to philosophers. In the following chapter, I shall explain a distinction between two modes, basic and ultra obligation, which is not familiar. Both have an abstract and an actual mode, and the part of the schema just given applies to both. One of the differences between the basic and ultra modes is that the reasons referred to in the implicandum are of different kinds, although both are better than any reason in terms of independent interest. This difference is a consequence of the propositions which imply the ought propositions being different, i.e., the ground of propositions in terms of basic obligation is different from the ground of propositions in terms of ultra obligation.

In discussing the schema, it has become apparent that a proposition which is a reason for *A*'s acting, viz., that it is in *A*'s overall interest to do *x*, implies the proposition that *A* ought (prudentially) to do *x*. Thus some propositions which are reasons for acting imply ought propositions and are therefore also reasons for judging propositions true. This is not so of all propositions which are reasons for acting. For example, 'It is in *A*'s present interest to do *x*' does not imply an ought proposition. I only want to stress here that the point insisted upon earlier is not affected, viz., that some propositions are reasons for acting and others are not (1, 1; 1, 5);[1] and that although propositions which are not reasons for acting may provide inductive support for those which are, they are not thereby made reasons for acting themselves. This point is untouched by the truth which the schema makes evident,

[1] Cross-references are given in this way throughout. (1, 5), for example, represents chapter 1, section 5; (5, 4) represents chapter 5, section 4, and so on.

viz., that propositions which are reasons for acting can *also* be reasons for judging other propositions true. It is in any case evident, quite apart from the schema, that any proposition can be a reason for judging some other proposition true or false. But the fact remains that some propositions are reasons for acting and others are not.

II. RESIDUAL USES OF 'OUGHT'

There are uses of 'ought' additional to those in which it is employed to signify a prudential, basic or ultra obligation. Judgements in terms of such uses satisfy the second part of the schema:

> *A* ought to do *x*
> implies
> There is a reason for *A*'s doing *x* which is better than . . .

and by suitably sub-dividing them, i.e., marking off further distinguishable modes of the concept and specifying the completion of the implicandum above, they can be shown to satisfy the complete schema. Such judgements, however, do not have an integral part to play in the theory to be presented, and the distinctions will not be drawn. They will be grouped together as judgements in terms of residual uses of 'ought'. When 'ought' is used in such ways, it will be distinguished from other uses by writing, for want of a better way of doing it, the word 'rationally' immediately following it in brackets. And I shall say, without any attempt at further specificity, that the implication of such ought judgements is in terms of the notion of good reason. Thus

> *A* ought (rationally) to do *x*
> implies
> There is good reason for *A*'s doing *x*

The use of 'rationally' to mark off the residual uses is not entirely happy; but it will be understood that it does not carry any pejorative suggestions about other uses of 'ought'. The use to be given to 'good reason' does not exclude the possibility of there being better reason for doing something else, though in particular cases it may: it might mean 'good reason, other things being equal' or 'good reason, come what may'. We should be content to use 'good reason' in this way only because the uses of 'ought' in question are not of central importance in the work to be done. By drawing the distinctions of this chapter I have tried to show clearly what the claim that there is good reason for doing *x* comes to when *x* is the subject of ought judgements of the kinds which are of central importance: if the judgement is prudential the claim is that there is better reason for doing *x* than any in terms of present or future interests; if moral and abstract, that there is better reason than any in terms of overall independent interest, and so on.

A second point needs to be made about the uncritical use of 'good reason'. It is often said that the notion of implication is not needed in moral argument: 'We can give good reasons', it is said, 'What do we want with implications?' I hope to show that when it is made clear what is involved in a claim about 'good reason', the implications are transparent. Uses of 'good reason', without clarity about the implications of such uses, are, I believe, unfortunate in moral philosophy. It is not being said, of course, that the proposition which implies the ought proposition is itself implied by some other proposition or set of propositions; it is a proposition which makes a claim about human interests, and the appropriate ground for such a proposition is, in general, inductive.

Examples must now be given of the kinds of proposition I am grouping together in speaking of residual uses of 'ought'. G. H. Hardy describes a proof of a theorem which had:

... a very high degree of *unexpectedness*, combined with *inevitability* and *economy*. The arguments take so odd and surprising a form; the weapons used seem so childishly simple when compared with the far-reaching results; but there is no escape from the conclusions. There are no complications of detail—one line of attack is enough in each case.[1]

Hardy leaves the reader in no doubt that he thinks the proof, and the mathematician who made it, ought to be admired. This is a judgement made by employing a residual use of 'ought' and it implies that there is good reason for admiring such a proof.

A second example, which is an important one, concerns ends aimed at and the means to those ends. If *A* is aiming at an end *E* and *M* is the most effective means to it, then there is good reason for his choosing *M*. He ought (rationally) to choose *M*. This is not a prudential judgement, because the end at which he is aiming may be against his interest. But it remains true that,

[1] *A Mathematician's Apology* (Cambridge), p. 53.

given that he is aiming at E, he has good reason for doing M: given his aim, he ought (rationally) to do M. Kant distinguished this kind of case under the name 'imperative of skill':

Here there is absolutely no question about the rationality or goodness of the end, but only about what must be done to attain it.[1]

As a final example, consider a man who says that we ought to have a universal language. He commits himself to maintaining that there is good reason for doing so. It is true that this might be accommodated in the class of prudential judgements, and that he might be understood as saying that we ought (prudentially) to have a universal language. On the other hand, as this judgement is most naturally understood, its ground is that, in the long run, it is in everyone's interest to speak the same language; it is not that it is in the interest of the speaker assessed independently of the interests of others. It is not like the case in which a man thinks, of a poor product he wishes to sell, 'It's in my interest that people should buy it. Therefore I ought to advertise'. It is thus more appropriate to classify it under the residual uses of 'ought' than under the prudential uses.

The distinctions drawn in this chapter between different modes of the concept of obligation are neither so numerous nor so bewildering as may appear. I have drawn, or said I will draw, distinctions between

    prudential obligation
    basic moral obligation
    moral ultra obligation

All these modes may be subjective or objective, and the last two may be also either abstract or actual. I have also spoken of uses of 'ought' which fall outside this classification, and we shall take it that such uses imply that there is good reason for doing whatever is enjoined by judgements which employ them. To take it so is, I believe, superficial; but it is justified by the facts that such uses have no important part to play in what is to be said, and that complexity should be avoided when it is avoidable.

[1] *Groundwork of the Metaphysic of Morals*, ed. Paton, pp. 82–3.

CHAPTER 2

RIGHTS AND CONTRACT

In the philosophical study of moral thought two separate but related logical structures have to be recognized which are keyed in distinct modes of the concept of obligation: basic obligation and ultra obligation. The ground of basic obligations is different from the ground of ultra obligations; if the proposition corresponding to Q in the schema for prudential obligation (1, 8) is that A has a basic obligation to do x, the complex proposition corresponding to P is of one kind; but if it is that A has an ultra obligation to do x, the proposition corresponding to P is of a different kind.

The ground of propositions of basic obligation is in a sense, but not in any of the senses which first come to mind, contractual. For this reason the greater part of this chapter deals with the notion of contract, but reference will be made to ultra obligations from time to time. I must therefore say something on the subject however unsatisfactory, at this point. An ultra obligation is an obligation to do more for other people than a basic obligation requires, and it is an obligation to act from altruistic motives. The ground of a proposition of ultra obligation, is a proposition whose truth value depends upon the character of the man. Thus ultra obligations vary from man to man: whether or not A has an ultra obligation to do x depends upon the character of A. Ultra obligations are personal in a way that basic obligations are not. These points are set out briefly here so that I may occasionally speak of ultra obligations without mystifying the reader, before dealing with them more fully.

Propositions of ultra obligation comprise what is sometimes called the ethical part of morality while propositions of basic obligation comprise the legalistic part. The correspondences are approximate. At this point the second important difference between basic and ultra obligations can be stated: a basic obligation implies and is implied by a right, but not so an ultra obligation. More fully, the proposition that A has a basic obligation to B implies and is implied by the proposition that B has a right against A. No such connection holds between ultra obligation and rights. Before supporting these claims it is important to examine the concept of a right which has to bear a heavy burden in this chapter.

I. THE CONCEPT OF A RIGHT

One of the defects of classical Utilitarian theory is the scant attention paid to the concept of a right. Moore, for example, does not mention it throughout his writings, and Rashdall dismisses it in less than a page of less than compelling argument.[1] There is, as will be seen, a special reason for this shyness, but for the moment another possible explanation must be considered. It may be said that the concept of a right is not a moral concept at all; only a legal one. It is easily seen that this is an impossible position. Suppose a man has been taken ill, and the doctor urgently summoned. After the examination, he watches the doctor and his wife whispering. He fears the worst. He calls the doctor to him. 'I have the right to know', he says. He does not speak of a legal right, for there is no law which binds the doctor to tell him the truth. But he has not been speaking nonsense. It is not as if he had said he had the wealth to know or the power. He has made an intelligible claim about his rights where no legal right is in question. I find no alternative but to say he has claimed a moral right. Again, a man does not speak nonsense if he claims the right to his wife's fidelity, but there is no law in this country against adultery, and he cannot be claiming a legal right. Finally, suppose a man complains to his wife about a neighbour's failure to help him in a particular spot of trouble. His wife may reply that he has no right to expect help, and he may answer, 'I have indeed. Just think of all the help I have given him from time to time'. Again no law is involved: it is a moral right which is claimed. I want to point out here, for the sake of future argument, that the last case involves a perfectly proper use of the term 'a right'. We can properly speak of having a right to expect help from another.

Philosophers have sometimes written as if there are two or sometimes three different kinds of rights. Professor M. G. Singer is a recent example. He speaks of:

(a) *action rights*, which are rights to do certain things, to act in certain ways; (b) what may be called *receivatory* or *treatment rights*, which are

[1] *The Theory of Good and Evil* (Oxford), vol. i, p. 227.

rights to *receive* certain things, or to be *treated* in certain ways; and (*c*) *property rights*, which are rights *in* or *to* something.[1]

There is plainly some sort of distinction here: we speak of rights *to do*; of rights *to be treated* in certain ways; and of rights *in* (property) and rights *to* (our lives). But it is not a distinction that is important for the task undertaken here, and I doubt whether it is of any importance at all: in each case we are speaking of the right to other people acting in certain ways. To say that a man has a right to play golf on Sundays is to say that he has a right to expect others not to interfere with his doing so. To say that I have a right to civil treatment is to say that I have a right to others treating me civilly. To say that we have a right to our lives and property is to say that we have a right to others not taking our lives nor appropriating our property. In each case, a right is a right to other people acting in certain ways: a right to non-interference if we choose to play golf; a right to civility from others; a right to others not taking our lives or property. The expression 'a right to others acting in certain ways' is in many cases less natural than, and in all cases less elegant than, 'a right to expect others to act in certain ways'. It is adopted because it avoids a confusion to which the use of the more elegant expression may lead. It is unwise to render '*A* has the right to *B*'s doing *x*' as '*A* has the right to expect *B* to do *x*'. The latter expression tends to become confused with, '*A* has the right to expect *that B* will do *x*'. This in turn may be confounded with, '*A* has the right to believe that *B* will do *x*' and this with, '*A* has good reason for believing that *B* will do *x*'. This process of easy transitions leads to a sentence whose meaning is totally different from that with which we started. For this reason the less elegant expression will be adopted in general. I shall speak of a man's right to, for example, other people returning kindnesses he has rendered to them; other people doing what they have promised him to do; other people not causing him physical harm; other people not soiling his reputation, and so on. This is not to say that I shall not also speak of a man's right to his property, his life, his reputation and so on. It is often most convenient to do so.

There is a distinction between rights and deserts. A man can

---

[1] *Generalisation in Ethics* (Eyre and Spottiswoode), p. 312 note.

properly be said to deserve punishment but not to have a right to punishment (a right to others punishing him). More generally, he may be said to deserve blame, but not to have the right to be blamed. The proposition that a man has a right to something is not implied by the proposition that he deserves something. If a man falls below certain standards in any field of activity, he deserves blame. Similarly, if he rises well above those standards, he deserves praise. But by the same token, it does not follow that he has the right to be praised (the right to others praising him). A desert does not imply a right. Hardy's mathematician (1, 11) deserves praise for his elegant and economical proof of a theorem; he has done something uncommonly well; his achievement surpasses the standards acceptable among mathematicians. But it does not follow that he has the *right* to be praised. It may indeed be urged on independent grounds that he has. For example, it may be said that the facts adduced constitute good reason for praising him, and suggested that his having the right to our praising him does follow from our having good reason for praising him. The fact is that there being good reason for one man's doing something does not imply that anyone has the right to his doing it. There may be very good reason for my keeping butterflies, but it does not follow that anyone has the right to my keeping butterflies. It is indeed true, as we shall see, that there is a kind of reason for acting such that if a man has good reason of this kind for doing *x*, it does follow that at least one other man has the right to his doing *x*. But this is a very long way from saying, in general, that good reason for one's doing something implies a right for another. If anyone wishes to say that a proposition which constitutes good reason for *A*'s doing *x* implies that someone else has a right to his doing *x*, the onus is upon him to show that it does.

At this point it may be suggested that if *x* is an action such that *B* has the right to *A*'s doing it, no proposition can count as *good* reason for *A*'s doing it unless it does imply that *B* has the right to his doing it. I do not need nor wish to object to this. But I must stress that anyone who holds this position cannot say, 'This proposition is a good reason for *A*'s doing *x*. Therefore a right is implied'. He has to show that the proposition implies a right to establish his claim that it constitutes good reason.

Finally, a minor point: a right is not to be confused with a privilege. It may be my privilege to pay no taxes, but it does not follow that I have a moral right in the matter: the privilege may have been conferred by an arbitrary despot upon a favourite. Again, I have the right to my life, but this need not be a privilege. In England at the present time, it is not through privilege that individuals retain their lives.

This completes the preliminary study of the concept of a right. I have argued (1) that it is not a purely legal concept; (2) that there is no distinction of importance among moral rights; (3) that a right is distinct from a desert; (4) that the proposition that A has good reason for doing something does not imply that anyone has the right to his doing it, except in special cases; and (5) that a right is distinct from a privilege.

2. BASIC OBLIGATION AND RIGHTS

I argued in the last section that A's having a right to his life consisted in his having a right to others not taking his life; that A's having a right to play golf on Sunday consisted in his having the right to others not interfering with his playing golf on Sunday; and that A's having a right to civility consisted in his having a right to others treating him civilly. The point may be generalized by saying that A's having a right to x consists in his having the right to others according him x. Now the proposition that A has the right to others according him x implies that others have an obligation to accord him x. This point has, so far as I know, never been disputed. If A has a right to B's acting in a certain way, it follows that B has an obligation to A to act in that way. A right implies an obligation.

The implication does not hold in reverse provided we do not discriminate between two modes of the concept of obligation. But there is a class of obligation propositions such that, once it is established that A has an obligation of that class to B, the question is no longer open whether B has a right against A. It is no longer open because precisely the same factors are involved in establishing the one as in establishing the other. This is the class of basic obligations: the proposition that A has a basic obligation to B does imply that B has a right against A; the implication between a basic obligation and a right is a mutual implication. Suppose *A* killed *B*. We may think at first that *B* had a right to his not doing so and that *A* had an obligation not to do so. But if it turns out that *A* killed in self defence, and this is sufficient to establish that *B* had no such right, it is also sufficient to establish that *A* had no such obligation. There is not one way of finding out whether *B* had the right and another way of finding out whether *A* had the obligation. Anything which is a reason for giving either answer to the first question is also a reason for giving the same answer to the second. Again, suppose a man has told me a lie, and I charge him with violating an obligation. He replies, 'Look here! A couple of weeks ago you told me a lie. You gained as a result just about as much at my expense as I've gained this time at yours. I guess that makes us quits'. We do not have to decide whether this is a consideration which deprives me, on this occasion, of the right to be told the truth. The point is that, if it is, it is also a consideration which, on this occasion, nullifies his obligation to tell the truth. There is not one set of considerations which establishes the first point, and another distinct set which, granted the first, may either establish or fail to establish the second. There is one set of considerations which either establishes both or fails to establish either. We cannot say without self contradiction that, in these circumstances, he had an obligation to tell me the truth but that I did not have the right to be told the truth. Basic obligation and rights are opposite sides of the same coin.

Whenever we say that a man had a basic obligation to act in a certain way we are logically committed to saying that someone had a right to his acting in this way. If a man beats me up in circumstances in which he had an obligation not to beat me up, then I had a right to his not beating me up in those circumstances. If a man tortures my cat and we are justified in saying that he ought not to have done so, then it follows that I had a right to his not torturing it. A man who says I am a liar in circumstances in which he has an obligation not to necessarily violates my right not to be called a liar in those circumstances. And another who drives a car when drunk, in such a situation that he has an obligation not to, has of necessity violated the right of those who stand to suffer by his action. In each of these cases, a basic obligation is involved. In chapter 4, I shall argue that there is a distinct class of ought propositions which are undoubtedly moral but which do not have any logical connection with the concept of a right. They will be called, as already stated, propositions of ultra obligation.

3. ABSTRACT OBLIGATION

The ground of propositions of basic obligation, i.e., the proposition corresponding to P in the schema (1, 8) when a proposition of basic obligation corresponds to Q, is contractual in a sophisticated sense. The argument to establish this will need as a premiss the following: that the conjunctive proposition that A promised to do x and that A can do x implies that A has an obligation to do x, the obligation being basic and abstract. 'Implies' is used in the strong sense explained earlier. To many this will seem a highly implausible claim, and the greater part of the remainder of this chapter will be devoted to arguing for it. Before this can be done, more must be said about abstract obligation. As we shall be concerned throughout with basic, and never with ultra obligations, the word 'basic' will usually be omitted.

I need to be able to speak of an abstract obligation in regard to a class of actions. To facilitate this, the symbol 'X' will be used to refer to any class of actions, and 'x' to refer to individual actions which are members of that class. The proposition that A has an abstract obligation to do X implies that he has an abstract obligation to do x if he can. As used here 'can' refers to physical possibility—it has the sense in which some men can jump six feet into the air without assistance and in which no man can jump a hundred feet. 'Physical impossibility' can be interpreted more or less rigorously. The example given is of a rigorous interpretation, but it is also a natural use of 'can' to say 'I couldn't do it' when it was merely very difficult to do it, or when doing it would have been repellent or would have had seriously adverse effects. The rigorous interpretation will be understood here. If it is physically impossible for a man to do x, then he has no abstract obligation to do that individual action even though he has an abstract obligation to do actions of the class X. For example, suppose I have an abstract obligation to help blind men to cross the road. My abstract obligation in regard to the class of actions is independent of the fact that on a particular occasion it may be physically impossible for me to do an individual action of that class—because, perhaps, I am being carried on a stretcher with a pair of broken legs. But in this situation I do not have an abstract obligation to do that individual action.

To accommodate discussion of obligations in regard to *classes* of actions, the Reason-for-Acting/Obligation schema has to be extended. In setting out this extension, I shall refer to a certain proposition as the contract ground. This proposition is the ground of basic obligations and I have ultimately to show that it is capable of doing the job allotted to it in the schema:

> The contract ground
> implies
> *A* has an abstract obligation to do actions of the class *X*
>
> *A* has an abstract obligation to do actions of the class *X* and
> *A* can do the individual action *x*
> implies
> *A* has an abstract obligation to do the individual action *x*
> implies
> There is a reason for *A*'s doing *x* which is better than any in terms of his overall *independent* interest for doing either *x* or not-*x*.

The obligations referred to are, of course, basic. As applied to abstract obligations of this mode of the concept everything before the antecedent of the final implication takes the place of the proposition *P* in the schema for the prudential mode of the concept.

If *A* ought (abstractly) to do *x* it follows that there is a reason for his doing *x* which is better than any in terms of his independent interest. Such a reason could only be in terms of the interests of other people, or, as I shall in fact argue, in terms of his interest assessed in conjunction with the interests of other people and not independently of them. This is why an abstract obligation is a moral obligation: because it implies that there is a reason for acting in terms of the agent's interests assessed in conjunction with the interests of others which is a better reason than any in terms of his interests assessed independently of the interests of others. But although the proposition that *A* ought (abstractly) to do *x* implies this, it does not imply that there is not a still better reason for not doing x. A man may have an abstract obligation to do x because it is an action of a certain class, but x may also be a member of another class by virtue of which he has an abstract obligation not to do it; and the reason for acting implied by the latter obligation may be better than that implied by the former. In this case there is a better reason for his not doing x. If the reason for acting implied by one abstract obligation is better than the reason for acting implied by another, I shall say that the former is a superior obligation. Criteria for determining superiority among obligations will emerge later.

The final implication of the schema for actual obligation (1, 10) is:

> A has an actual obligation to do the individual action x
> implies
> there is a reason for A's doing x which is better than any other reason of the same kind for doing either x or not-x

Where the obligation is basic, the reason referred to is of the same kind as the reason referred to in the final implicandum of the schema for abstract obligation, this obligation also being basic. Both implications are mutual provided the reasons are specified as being of this kind, but without this stipulation they are not: for without it the consequent could be true while the antecedent asserted A to have an ultra obligation. Given that these implications are mutual, it follows that if A has an abstract basic obligation to do x and x is not also a member of a class of actions by virtue of which he has an abstract basic obligation not to do it, then A has an actual basic obligation to do x. The same relation holds for the same reason for ultra obligations. Thus, without discriminating between basic and ultra obligations, we may say (incorporating a proposition asserting an abstract obligation in regard to a class of actions):

> A has an abstract obligation to do actions of the class X
> and
> A can do an individual action x falling under that class
> and
> x does not also fall under any class of actions by virtue of which A has an abstract obligation not to do it
> implies
> A has an actual obligation to do x.

At present we are concerned only with basic, and not with ultra, obligations. Conflicts between abstract obligations of these two kinds will be considered later. It will become obvious later that there cannot be a better reason for acting than the best reason of the kind referred to in the implicanda of propositions of basic obligation.

The account given of abstract obligation makes it a close relation of Ross's *prima facie* obligation. It is difficult to say how close a relation, because it is difficult to be clear how Ross would have answered some questions which might be put to him. There is however one point upon which Ross has often been misunderstood. When he said that a certain class of actions was *prima facie* obligatory he did not mean that actions of that class ought (actually) to be done as a general rule. It may be true that they ought to be done as a general rule, but this is not what it means to say that they are *prima facie* obligatory.[1] Similarly, when I say that a class of actions is abstractly obligatory I do not mean that actions of that class are actually obligatory as a general rule. The notion of abstract obligation to be employed here is determined by the logical relations which have been set out.

4. THE PROMISING FUNCTION

The remainder of this chapter will be devoted to examining the relation between *having promised* and *having an abstract obligation*, the obligation being basic. A man may promise to do a class of actions X or an individual action x. It will be argued that the propositions that A promised to do X and that A promised to do x both imply that A has an abstract obligation to do x if he can. 'Implies' is used in the strong sense explained, and 'can' refers to the physical possibility of A's doing x, as explained at the beginning of the previous section. If this implication is to hold when the implicans refers to an individual action, the innocuous premiss that A has not already done x is needed. And the premiss that A has not been released from his promise is needed in the case of both classes of actions and individual actions. These premisses are not interesting, and it would encumber the text unnecessarily to keep repeating them. I ask that they are understood whenever I claim the implication in question. Further economy is

[1] *The Right and The Good* (Oxford), p. 19.

effected by writing 'obligation' for 'abstract basic obligation'. As ultra obligations will not be in question at all, 'basic' may be omitted. 'Abstract' may be omitted also except in contexts in which both abstract and actual obligations are being discussed.

The concept which is of importance for this work is in fact that of contracting, not promising, but I shall argue in terms of promising to align myself with the substantial literature on the subject. A contract is a mutual promise in which each party promises to do something upon the condition that the other does something. Thus the promise involved in a contract is of a more specific kind than a gratuitous promise, and no harm will result from discussing the more general case.

I shall argue that promising is the function of placing oneself under an obligation and that the proposition that A promised to do x implies that A has an obligation to do x if he can. In speaking of promising as a function, I am following the late Professor J. L. Austin on a point of cardinal importance: that to promise is to do something rather than to say something; that when a man says 'I promise to do x' he says nothing which has a truth value, and in consequence makes no assertion. To accept this view, for which I shall argue in a moment, is not to deny that the sentence 'I promised to do x' (past tense) expresses a proposition, for plainly a truth value is involved here. Consequently, we are free to talk about the implications of this proposition. The position to be taken up here is not identical to that adopted by any other philosopher, but it has some affinity to the views of Professor D. W. Hamlyn,[1] Professor J. R. Searle[2] and Professor John Rawls.[3] The views of these philosophers are different among themselves, and the position adopted here differs from each of them on points of more or less significance. It may seem at some points in this chapter as if we are heading for a deontological position, but if it does the appearance is deceptive. The most I will admit is that some quasi-deontological elements have to be absorbed if a teleological system of morals is to prove satisfactory. As we go on, a system will emerge which will be seen to accommodate the truths on which both deontologists and teleologists have been insisting.

---

[1] 'The Obligation to Keep a Promise', *Proceedings of the Aristotelian Society* (1961–2).
[2] 'How to Derive an "Ought" from an "Is"', *Philosophical Review* (1964).
[3] 'Two Concepts of Rules', *Philosophical Review* (1955).

It is not sufficient to say that to promise is to place oneself under an obligation, for there are many ways of doing that. We do it when we accept a kindness, incur a debt or hit someone on the head. We have to say that promising is the function of placing ourselves under an obligation. This formulation meets with the objection that we sometimes promise to do what we already have an obligation to do, e.g., a young offender sometimes promises the magistrates in the juvenile court not to steal again as a condition of being placed on probation instead of being sent to Borstal. As he antecedently had an obligation not to steal, his promising would be otiose if promising were a matter of placing himself under such an obligation. I shall nonetheless argue that promising is *primarily* the function of placing oneself under an obligation, and *secondarily* a related function, which is involved in cases of the kind just considered. But that both primary and secondary functions are such that the proposition that A promised to do x implies that he has an obligation to do x if he can, i.e., that it is self contradictory to assert the former and deny the latter. The truth of this view becomes evident, it seems to me, in examining objections of three different kinds which may be brought against it:

(1) The claim that promising is exhaustively analysed in terms of making assertions, from which it does follow that 'A promised to do x' does not imply 'A has an obligation to do x'

(2) Apparent counter examples

(3) The Utilitarian view that the ground for judging that a particular promise ought to be kept is that better effects are produced by doing so than by not doing so.

5. THE ASSERTION THEORY

The question, 'How do promises oblige?' has been discussed again and again in the history of philosophy. It has often been understood, clearly or unclearly, as 'Whence the motive to keep promises?'; but it is to be understood here as, 'What is the ground of the proposition that we ought to keep promises?' By contrast, the question, 'What is it to make a promise?' has received fairly scanty treatment. It seems often to be thought that it presents no important difficulty, the main problem residing in the earlier question. And there is no hint, until quite recent times, that perhaps the two questions cannot be handled independently. We can only conjecture why it should be so. It may have been uncritically assumed that promising just is saying the words 'I promise' or some equivalent. Such an account does not stand up to a moment's scrutiny; but, as an assumption, it may have passed unscrutinized. And it would, I think, be rash to say that it has never been at work in a philosopher's pages. More probably, however, it has been generally thought that in promising we are making assertions; saying that something is the case. It is very easy to suppose that in saying 'I promise to do *x*' I am asserting that I have the intention to do *x* and in addition asserting something else, the additional assertion distinguishing an expression of intention from a promise. What the additional assertion would have to be is not obvious. But it is not difficult to suppose that philosophers, so far as they have asked themselves the question at all, have thought that the additional assertion would soon be revealed to anyone sufficiently interested to look for it, and have addressed themselves to the apparently more important question, 'How do promises oblige?' It has not been realized that this question arises only through neglect of the other.

If, in promising, we are making assertions, then 'I have an obligation to do *x*' plainly does not follow from 'I promised to do *x*'. Suppose, for example, that in promising to do *x*, I am asserting (i) that I intend to do *x* and (ii) that I am placing myself under an obligation to do *x*. From (i) it does not follow that I intend to do *x*, and from (ii) it does not follow that I am under an obligation to do *x*. It no more follows than 'George is cold' follows from 'George said he is cold'. Whatever assertion I make, whatever I state to be the case, it does not follow that it is the case; and whatever I may state to be the case in regard to *x*, it does not follow that I have an obligation to do *x*. Hence the question arises, 'How *do* promises oblige?'

If the assertion theory is correct, the account for which I argue is mistaken. But the assertion theory is not correct. Against it Austin argued that in promising we are doing something other than making assertions; a point he expressed by writing that we are not *saying* something but *doing* something. In this, he is, I believe, right, and the question immediately arises, 'What are we doing?' Or, since that question may elicit only the perfectly correct answer, 'We are promising', we should ask, 'What is the point of what we are doing?' 'What is the purpose of promising?' It shall be my thesis that the only possible answer to this question is that promising is the function of placing ourselves under (abstract) obligations. And moreover a function such that 'I promised to do x' implies 'I have an obligation to do x'. I shall now argue briefly, following Austin, that it is a mistake to think that in promising we are making assertions; briefly because I believe the position is now generally accepted.

If A says to B, 'I promise you I'll do x' it would be proper for an onlooker to say, 'That's sincere' or 'That's insincere'. But he cannot say 'That's true' or 'That's false' in the sense in which he could if A had made an assertion; if A had stated that something was the case. When we speak of a promise as false, as we sometimes do, we mean that it is insincere. And to say that it is insincere is to say that the promiser does not have the intention of doing what he promises to do. But to say that a sincere promise is one in which an intention accompanies the utterance of the words 'I promise' is very different from saying that when a man promises, sincerely or insincerely, he makes an assertion of intention or any other assertion. In another context, I may say, in an appropriate tone of voice, that my wife is heavily overworked, and I may intend you to think that I help her a good deal. But I have not asserted that I help her a good deal. If the words 'I promise to do x' did make an assertion, then it would be proper to ascribe truth or falsity, whereas we have just seen that it is not. Promising cannot consist in making assertions.

Many philosophers, as I have said, seem to take it uncritically that promising is to be analysed in terms of making assertions and, showing no further interest in the matter, turn their attention to what they take to be the more important question, 'How do promises oblige?' But when we look at philosophers who have asked seriously, 'What is it to make a promise?' we find the element of doing, as distinct from saying, recognized. Even when it is thought that promising includes an assertion of intention, it is recognized that what distinguishes a promise from such an assertion is not that it makes some further assertion. Hume and Sidgwick provide good examples. Hume writes,

When a man says *he promises any thing*, he in effect expresses a *resolution* of performing it; and along with that, by making use of this *form of words*, subjects himself to the penalty of never being trusted again in case of failure.[1]

We need not concern ourselves with the expression of resolution or intention; it is the second part of Hume's account which is interesting. In promising, Hume says, a man is doing something, viz., subjecting himself to something. He uses the word 'penalty' which is unfortunate for, understood literally, it is connected with the provision of a motive for keeping promises whereas the question which Hume is discussing is, 'What is it to make a promise?' The blemish is, however, easily removed by writing '. . . subjects himself to the charge of untrustworthiness in case of failure'. I think this is a fair rendering of Hume's meaning, and he is now seen to be saying that in promising, over and above the expression of resolution, a man is doing something of such a kind that the proposition that he promised to do x implies that if he does not do x, he is untrustworthy. 'Implies' is too strong but it does not matter. We shall see later that there is a perfectly good implication relation between having promised, trustworthiness and some other concepts, and Hume's view could well be expressed in this way. Thus Hume is saying that promising is doing something such that having promised has logical relations with trustworthiness. So far he is perfectly correct, but he has not gone nearly far enough. For, as we shall see, it also has logical relations with the notions of rights, reason for acting, moral good and blame; and there is no reason to suppose that any of these is more central than the other. We shall also see later that the relations of all these concepts to having promised are identical with their relations to having an obligation. And given that promising is doing something, we are eventually left with no alternative but to say that the purpose of promising is to place the promiser under an obligation.

Sidgwick writes:

If I merely assert my intention of abstaining from alcohol for a year, and then after a week take some, I am (at worst) ridiculed as inconsistent; but if I have pledged myself to abstain, I am blamed as untrustworthy. Thus the essential element of the Duty of Good Faith seems to be not

---

[1] *Treatise of Human Nature*, ed. Selby-Bigge, p. 522.

conformity to my own statement, but to expectations that I have intentionally raised in others.[1]

Like Hume, Sidgwick recognizes that in promising we are doing something other than making an assertion; we are raising expectations in other people. But Sidgwick knows he cannot answer the question, 'How does a promise differ from an expression of intention?' by saying that in promising we raise expectation in others; we also do that in expressing an intention. Nor can he say that the function of promising is to raise expectations: as such it would be redundant, for we already have a way of doing that by expressing our intentions. He holds instead that in promising we raise expectations in such a way that we are correctly judged to be untrustworthy if we fail to fulfil them. Like Hume, he draws our attention to a logical connection between promising and trustworthiness. He is perfectly correct to do so. But why stop there? There are also logical connections between promising and rights, moral good, blame and reason for acting, i.e., the central concepts of morals. And these concepts are identically related to having promised and having an obligation. The recognition of these relations eventually commits us to accepting that promising is the function of placing the promiser under an obligation. When it is worked out fully, Sidgwick's account, like Hume's, turns into the account to be offered here. It is not surprising that promises should usually give rise to expectations of performance: in promising a man places himself under an obligation, and there is a widespread and justified expectation that people will, for the most part, respect their obligations.

It is worth keeping open and pressing against a Utilitarian like Sidgwick the question, 'What is the *point* of this activity of promising?' 'What purpose does it fulfil?' He cannot, I believe, give any answer; and, although it forms only a part of what has to be said against such accounts of promising, his failure to do so must increase sympathy for the position defended here. This question cannot be pressed against the objection from counter examples. The thesis I want to maintain is that promising is (primarily) the function of placing ourselves under an obligation; *and* a function such that '*A* promised to do *x*' implies '*A* has an (abstract) obligation to do *x* if he can'. Now the first part of this thesis can be

[1] *Methods of Ethics*, 1907, p. 304.

admitted and the second denied, just as it can be admitted that the function of the throttle pedal is to make the car go faster and denied that 'I pressed the throttle' implies 'The car went faster'. The linkage may have been broken. Apparent counter-examples can be brought against the thesis that a promise implies an obligation; but anyone bringing forward such objections may still admit that promising is the function of placing ourselves under obligations. He has only to say that, like the throttle linkage, it sometimes breaks down. Consequently, the question, 'What is the point of this activity of promising?' cannot be pressed against him. He will give the same answer as we do. But his apparent counter-examples are designed to show that there is no implication. I shall now argue that his counter-examples are indeed apparent.

6. APPARENT COUNTER-EXAMPLES

'G' will be used to refer to the man who gives the promise and 'R' to the one who receives it. Constant repetition of the ugly words 'promiser' and 'promisee' is thus avoided.

To suppose that G promised to do x implies that G has an abstract obligation to do x if he can is to suppose that the trio of propositions: G promised to do x; G can do x; and G's doing x does not involve violating a superior obligation, jointly imply that G has an actual obligation to do x. It is important to remember that the claim made here about the relation between a promise and an abstract obligation commits me to a claim about the relation between a promise and an actual obligation. It does so by virtue of the relation between abstract and actual obligation set out previously (2, 3).

The argument against me from counter examples consists in producing cases—of which there are many kinds—and saying 'Here is a case in which G has promised but in which he is not under an obligation'. Some of the cases to be discussed are the following:

   (i)   G's keeping the promise would have disastrous effects upon him
   (ii) R extracted the promise by fraud
   (iii) G's keeping the promise would have ill effects upon G and R

(iv) In the case of a mutual promise, R broke his part of the bargain

(v) G's keeping the promise would have undesirable effects on R

(vi) R does not want G to keep the promise.

(The case of promises extracted by threats is considered later.)

Let us grant that in these cases G has no obligation. The apparent strength of the objection lies in the assumption that of any of them we can say *simpliciter* that G promised; and therefore that, granted he has no obligation, the proposition that he promised cannot imply that he has. This would be in order if promising were merely uttering the words 'I promise', or if these words made an assertion. For, *ex hypothesi*, G did say 'I promise' and, on the assertion interpretation, he did make an assertion; the assertion alleged to be made by saying 'I promise'. But the former of these is an absurd view, and the latter is false. I shall now argue that it is a gross over-simplification of cases of this kind to say, without qualification, 'Here's a case in which G promised but . . . therefore . . .'

Consider the first case. G has said to R of a given action, 'I promise you I will do *x*', but it so turns out that it would be absolutely disastrous to himself to do it. G did not foresee this situation, and no one could have foreseen it. Suppose now that R, fully aware of the position, complains to G because he did not do *x*. I think it will be agreed that it would be a perfectly natural reaction on G's part to say, 'But surely R, you didn't think I was promising to do it in those circumstances!' The fact that this is a natural reaction shows that the expression 'I promise' is not normally used to promise to do an action under any circumstances whatever. To catch the normal use we should have to see 'I promise to do *x*' as a truncated version of 'I promise to do *x* provided . . .' the sentence being completed by a set of conditions. The conditions are not normally made explicit because it would make the promising function unwieldy. They are understood by people who make promises. In saying this, I do not mean to say that it would not also be a natural reaction for G to reply, 'Surely you didn't expect me to do it in those circumstances!' i.e., surely you did not expect even an obligation-respecting person to do it in those circumstances. This is also a perfectly natural reaction and is tantamount to saying there is no obligation in these circumstances. But it is, of course, not in conflict with anything I am saying.

Consider now the second case, in which R extracts a promise by fraud. He particularly wants G at a party but knows G is reluctant to go. He also knows that if he tells G that Miranda will be there he will go like a shot. But Miranda is not going to be there and R knows it. Suppose that having been misled by R, G says 'I promise' but later finds out that R was lying and, duly angered, does not go to the party. If R complains that G did not come, G's natural reply would be, 'But you told me Miranda was going to be there when you knew perfectly well she wasn't!' Why is this relevant? Because G promised on the condition that R was telling him the truth about Miranda. His 'I promise' was again a truncated version of 'I promise to come provided . . .' The condition does not need to be made explicit because it is quite obvious from the context that the promise is made upon that condition.

In the third case, G promises to do such and such but as it turns out it would have undesirable effects upon both R and himself to do it. R is not likely to complain in these circumstances, but suppose someone else does. 'You broke your promise!' he says, in an appalled tone of voice. G's natural reply is, 'But don't you see, it would have been thoroughly stupid to do it in the circumstances'. This reply is relevant because a promise to do x is made upon the condition that it will not be thoroughly stupid to do it. Again, there is no need to specify this condition; no need unless one of the parties to the promise is indeed stupid.

It is obvious that the same kind of treatment can be applied to the fourth case; in a mutual promise each party promises upon the condition that the other keeps his part of the bargain. But the fifth and sixth cases are superficially different because the disadvantage which results from doing the promised action lies on the side of R. Talk of conditions seems inappropriate here because it suggests safeguards to G's interests. But this difference is only superficial. For a promise to be made, it has to be accepted as well as offered. The point is obvious in the case of mutual promises. It is concealed in the case of gratuitous promises because they are usually so plainly to the advantage of R that the acceptance does not need to be voiced by him. But it is always open to him to reject any promise which he is offered. He may say, for example, 'But I don't want you to do x' or 'I'm sorry G, but I don't believe you are to be trusted' or 'No, no, to do x would be immoral'. If he rejects the promise in one of these ways, no promise is made. The point is missed by Sidgwick[1] when he argues that a promise to do an immoral act is not binding because '... otherwise one could evade any moral obligation by promising not to fulfil it, which is clearly absurd'. Sidgwick ignores the fact that no moral person would accept such a promise, and that it is only in special circumstances that an immoral person would be interested in accepting. If I were to select the name of a criminal from the newspapers and write to him, 'Sir, I hereby promise you that I will steal, rape and commit arson whenever possible', he would probably not reply—and in this case, unlike many others, his silence could not be taken as acceptance. In a case like this, I may have tried to promise but I would have failed. The situation would be different if I were one of a band of criminals. And the fact is that criminals do make promises to each other and that they are not simply doing something which does not bind them. More explanation is needed. Whatever may be said of moral sympathy, logical sympathy for the criminal classes is not out of place, and any adequate account of promising must be able to cater for the function of promises to do immoral actions. On this point I maintain—consistently—that to promise is to place oneself under an abstract obligation whether the promised action is moral or immoral; but that the abstract obligation to do an immoral action can never be actual. I reply later to the obvious question, 'What is the point of promising to do an immoral action if the resulting obligation can never be actual?' (2, 12). For the moment I want only to point out that a promise can only be given provided it is accepted by R, and that this makes it perfectly natural to speak of the conditions of the promise in the fifth and sixth cases as in the others. For now we speak of the conditions upon which R accepts the promise; he accepts G's promise upon the condition that G's doing x does not, as it turns out, have undesirable effects upon him (R).

The interpretation I wish to maintain for cases like these is that it is correct neither to say that G did promise nor that G did not

[1] *Methods of Ethics*, 1907, p. 305.

promise; that it is correct to say only that he promised upon certain conditions. It is only when these conditions are satisfied that we can say that G did promise, simpliciter. From the proposition that G promised upon certain conditions it follows, so I maintain, that he is under an obligation if those conditions are fulfilled. And this is the same as saying that from the proposition that G promised it follows that he is under an obligation—for we can say that he promised only if the conditions upon which he promised are fulfilled; and if the conditions upon which he promised are fulfilled, the conditions upon which he placed himself under an obligation are fulfilled and he is under an obligation.

I will justifiably be asked how the conditions spoken of are determined. The complete answer to this question has its place in the general theory to be developed and will be stated later (3, 15). For the present it is enough to say that promising is a function; and that as such it can be exercised rationally or irrationally. By an exercise of the function I mean the activity of counting an offer and acceptance of a promise as having made a promise. An offer and acceptance may be so counted by someone when the circumstances are such that it is stupid to do so. For example, it may as it turns out be disastrous to the promiser, or to the disadvantage of the promisee, that the action in question should be done. Such an exercise of the promising function is, as I think will be agreed, an irrational exercise of it. It is not, I admit, clear at this stage just what is involved in speaking of an *irrational* exercise; but despite that, since promising is a function, it obviously can be exercised rationally or irrationally; and despite our lack of complete understanding of what we are saying, we have enough understanding of the concept of rationality to enable us to take the argument further. I have previously spoken of the conditions under which promises are understood to be given. Let us speak instead of conditions controlling the promising function. The conditions may be so determined that counting an offer and acceptance of a promise as having made a promise is a rational exercise of the function if and only if all the conditions so chosen are satisfied. When, from now on, I speak of conditions, or of conditions under which promises are understood to be given, I shall be speaking of conditions determined in this way. Our understanding is skeletal; but we need no more for the argument of this chapter.

One loose end has to be tied up before we can go on. Promises extracted by threats seem to provide another counter-example. This objection cannot be dealt with in the same way as the previous cases. Nor can it be dealt with at the present stage, for its adequate consideration revolves round what I have called the secondary function of promising. The matter must therefore be postponed.

7. UTILITARIANISM: THE PARTICULAR CASE

In examining the Utilitarian account of the obligation to keep a promise in a particular case, I shall have in mind the late W. A. Pickard-Cambridge's sustained defence[1] of the position against the different account of Sir David Ross. In this section the concept of an abstract right will be employed, but the term 'a right' will generally be used to refer to it. Abstract rights are related to abstract obligations as actual rights are related to actual obligations; and abstract rights are related to actual rights as abstract obligations are related to actual obligations. If A has an abstract right to B's doing actions of the class X and the individual action x is a member of the class X, then A has an actual right to B's doing x provided (i) B can do x and (ii) x is not a member of another class of actions from which B has a superior abstract obligation to desist.

A Utilitarian denies that the proposition that A promised to do x implies that A has an abstract obligation to do x and thus denies that, with the appropriate additional premisses, it implies that A has an actual obligation to do x. His actual obligation, he asserts, is to do the action which has the best effects. According to this account, a promise is one thing—though what it is we are not told. When a man has promised that is over and done with. The question then arises, 'Ought he to keep his promise?' and the answer is determined by balancing the total effects of doing so against the total effects of not doing so. Whichever action produces the more good, that is the action which ought to be done. I shall now argue that this account is mistaken. The important point which will begin to emerge in the discussion, and be fairly clear at the end of it, is that there is a logical connection between the notions of having promised and a right.

[1] *Mind* (1932).

Suppose I have promised A that I will do x but that when the appointed time arrives it is evident that my doing x will prevent my doing some good to another man B. For the moment, let us assess the good I can do to A by keeping the promise, and the good I can do to B by breaking it, independently of the fact that I have made a promise to A. It may be that the amount of good I can do for them is exactly the same. But it would be a naïve mistake to suppose that the Utilitarian is committed to saying that it does not matter which I do. For he will correctly reply that it is absurd to assess the relative good independently of the fact that I promised. Changes that A has made in the pattern of his life on the strength of the promise have also to be taken into account. For example, he may have refused an invitation to the cinema. And although A's pleasure in going to the theatre may not outweigh the pleasure B would obtain by my breaking the promise, we have also to remember that, on the strength of the promise, A has deprived himself of an alternative pleasure. Thus, by breaking my promise I not only deprive him of the promised benefit—the pleasure of the theatre. I also deprive him indirectly of the pleasure of the cinema; a pleasure which he would have obtained had it not been for my promise. Moreover, if I break my promise, I disappoint him, and this disappointment is another bad effect which has to be taken into account in deciding what I ought to do.

In determining whether the promise ought to be kept or broken, a Utilitarian holds that the following factors (at least) have to be taken into account:

> the good effects upon A of keeping it, viz., the benefit he obtains from the promised action
>
> the good effects upon B of breaking it, viz., the benefit he obtains from the alternative action
>
> the ill effects upon A of breaking it, viz., his disappointment and his deprivation of benefits he would have obtained had the promise not been made

It is also held that other factors have to be taken into account, e.g., the ill effect of breaking a promise upon the promiser's reputation for trustworthiness; the ill effect upon his character; and the ill effect upon the general system of good faith in society. These last three factors will be left on one side for the moment. I shall argue later that, even on the Utilitarian's own showing, they are irrelevant in determining whether a particular promise ought to be kept on a particular occasion. And that even if they were relevant, it would not affect the point I have to make.

Suppose then that the only relevant Utilitarian factors are those inset above and that as far as we can tell after careful study the effects of keeping the promise exactly balance the effects of breaking it, so that the resultant good done by both courses of action is the same. If these are the only relevant factors, a Utilitarian is committed to saying that it does not matter which course of action is adopted, for the ground for saying that the promise ought to be kept is no better and no worse than the ground for saying that it ought to be broken. I shall now argue that this result is not false but conceptually absurd.

Let us suppose that the benefit A would obtain from the promised action is enjoyment, that the benefit B would obtain from the alternative is also enjoyment, and that the production of enjoyment is a good effect. It is plain that if the total good effects resulting from keeping the promise and breaking it are to be the same, the enjoyment which comes to B from breaking the promise must be greater than the enjoyment that comes to A from keeping it: there are other good effects which have to be added to the enjoyment A would obtain in order to balance the enjoyment B would obtain. But we suppose that, taking everything into account, I can do as much good for B by breaking the promise as I can do for A by keeping it. In this situation, a Utilitarian is committed to saying that it does not matter which I do. It seems to me that this result is transparently absurd and that it is quite obvious that in these circumstances the promise ought to be kept. I know there are many who will agree with me, but there are also others who will not, and I must therefore show that there is a factor which is relevant in deciding what ought to be done which cannot be taken into account by a Utilitarian.

Enjoyment, we must remember, is the benefit which was promised to A; and the benefit which B obtains if the promise is broken is also enjoyment. Enjoyment by A and enjoyment by B are two elements in the total good done by the alternative actions, and not the whole of it. We are supposing that the same amount of total good is done whichever course is adopted. The factor which a Utilitarian cannot take into account is that if the promise is kept A gets the enjoyment while if it is broken B gets it. This is independent of the fact that the total good done by both courses of action is the same. It is a fact about *who* actually enjoys himself; it is the fact that the promisee enjoys the promised benefit in the one case and another enjoys a benefit he was not promised in the other. As such it is plainly relevant to determining what ought to be done because the benefit was promised to one of them and not to the other. But a Utilitarian cannot take it into account because everything which his theory allows to be relevant is already taken into account in determining that the total good done by the alternative courses of action is the same.

The point may be emphasized by considering a simplified case in which the *only* effects to be taken into account are the enjoyment which A would obtain if I acted in one way and the enjoyment which B would obtain if I acted in another. Suppose I have promised A that I will do x with him. If I do he will enjoy himself. On the other hand, if I do not he will not be disappointed because he is not the sort of person who allows himself to be. He will do something else which does not depend upon my acting as I promised. He will enjoy the alternative but enjoy it *less*. Moreover, he has not done anything on the strength of my promise which interferes with his doing this alternative. Suppose, on the other hand, that by breaking my promise to A I can do something with B which he would enjoy but that he has an alternative which he would also enjoy but enjoy less. It may be that the enjoyment A would obtain if I keep my promise is no greater and no less than the enjoyment B would obtain if I break it. And that there is nothing to choose between the lesser enjoyment which A would obtain if I break it and which B would obtain if I keep it. Thus, if I keep my promise A benefits in a certain degree—he enjoys himself more; if I break it B benefits in the same degree. The case has been designed so that this is the only Utilitarian factor to be taken into account. Thus a Utilitarian is committed to saying that it does not matter what I do. His theory does not allow him to recognize as relevant the fact that if I act in one way it is A who benefits in a certain degree while if I act in the other it is B who benefits in the same degree. It allows him to recognize only that both benefit in the *same* degree whichever course I choose. But the fact that if I act in one way A benefits while if I act in the other B benefits is relevant to determining what I ought to do: A is *entitled* to benefit whereas B is not; and A is entitled to benefit because the promise was made to *him*. If I made a promise to A, and the conditions upon which I promised are satisfied, A has an (abstract) *right* to the extra enjoyment which he would lose if I broke my promise; and if the appropriate additional premisses[1] are true, he has an actual right to it. B, on the other hand, does not have a right in the matter. No promise was made to him.

It does not matter how minutely the goods and ills resulting from keeping and breaking promises are analysed—and how minutely and at what length it can be done may be seen from Mr. Pickard-Cambridge's articles: whatever may be the outcome of such an investigation, we may always suppose that the total good to be done by breaking the promise exactly balances the total good to be done by keeping it. In such a case a Utilitarian must say that it does not matter whether the promise is kept or broken. He is mistaken because his theory does not allow him to take account of a factor which is relevant. The total good done by keeping the promise, including the good done to A, may indeed equal the total good done by breaking it; but the fact remains that if the promise is kept one element of the good done, viz., the enjoyment of the promised benefit, *goes to* A. The factor is relevant because the promise was made to A. It is because *he* enjoys the benefit if the promise is kept, and because he has the *right* to enjoy it, that the promise ought to be kept.

I mentioned earlier additional effects which a Utilitarian also thinks ought to be taken into account, viz., the ill effect of breaking a promise upon the promiser's reputation for trustworthiness; the ill effect upon his character; and the ill effect upon the general system of good faith in society. Thus Mr Pickard-Cambridge writes:

... the maker of a promise ... has as a rule a direct personal interest in its fulfilment unless for some obviously sufficient reason. Breach of it is likely to hang round his neck a reputation for untrustworthiness, which will very seriously hamper his power to co-operate with others and thereby his power to do good ... and the self-paralysis thus sustained and tending to endure may easily entail a more serious loss of good than the momentary disappointment or loss caused to the promisee.[2]

---

[1] See p. 57. [2] *Mind* (1932), p. 153.

And

We have ... to consider the value of the fidelity to A as tending to maintain, and of the infidelity as tending to disintegrate, the whole system of good faith in society.[1]

These factors, and others which may be brought forward as having a claim to be considered, do not affect the point made earlier. However many and various the effects may be which have to be taken into account, we may still suppose that the total good done by breaking the promise is equal to the total good done by keeping it. And we can still point out that there remains a relevant factor in determining what ought to be done which cannot be accounted for on Utilitarian principles, viz., that if the promise is kept, one element of the good done by that course of action—the enjoyment of the promised benefit—is enjoyed by the promisee. And that as he has the right to enjoy this benefit provided certain conditions are satisfied, this factor determines what ought to be done.

The factors just brought forward are in any case irrelevant in determining whether a particular promise ought to be kept in particular circumstances. The point is indeed obvious: these ill effects do not result from breaking a promise unless it is antecedently wrong to break it. I do not hang round my neck a reputation for untrustworthiness and nor do I damage the system of good faith in society by breaking a promise which it was right to break. These factors therefore cannot enter into determining whether it is right or wrong to break a promise: they are ill effects which result from breaking a promise if it was wrong to do so. Whether, on the Utilitarian's showing, it is right or wrong to break a promise must depend upon the factors indented a few pages back. There may indeed be some others, but the factors discussed in this paragraph cannot be involved.

The important point which emerges from this and the previous section is that if A has promised B simpliciter to do x, then it cannot be denied that B has the right to A's doing x. If A said 'I promise to do x', or used some equivalent expression, and the conditions controlling the promising function are satisfied, then B has the right to A's doing x. The right is indeed abstract, but given appropriate additional premisses, it becomes actual. The

[1] *Ibid.*, p. 312.

claim is independent of Utilitarian considerations, except in so far as such considerations are relevant in determining the conditions under which promises are made. It holds because there is a logical connection between the concepts of having promised simpliciter and having a right. In the section which follows the point will be argued independently.

8. OBLIGATION, PROMISING AND OTHER MORAL CONCEPTS

A short while ago (2, 5) we considered Hume's account of what it is to promise and saw that it contained a grain of truth, viz., that there is a logical connection between having promised and trustworthiness. While it is true that there is such a connection—it will be set out precisely in this section—it is also true that there are connections between having promised and the notions of rights, blame, moral good and reason for acting. The connection with trustworthiness is no more central than any of the others. It will turn out in this section that having promised and being under an obligation are identically related to these five notions; that they are identically related to the central concepts of morality. The following discussion forms the heart of the argument that promising is the function of placing oneself under an abstract obligation and a function such that 'A promised to do x' implies 'A has an abstract obligation to do x'.

Rights

In this sub-section, the notion of an abstract right, as explained at the beginning of the previous section, will be employed, but the term 'a right' will be used to refer to it. The sentence 'A promised to do x' will be used to say that A *has* promised to do it, i.e., that the conditions upon which promises are made are satisfied. If they are not we cannot say, simpliciter, that the promise was made, and such cases are not under discussion.

It is obligatory in most of the societies we know to tell the truth and return kindnesses, a point which may alternatively be expressed by saying that in the societies we know people have the right to be told the truth and to have kindnesses returned. There may, however, be a religious group within the society for whom it is an insult to return kindnesses within three days. To such a suggestion, it may be objected that returning a kindness implies doing a kindness, and that as insulting someone is not doing a kindness, it cannot be returning a kindness. To meet this difficulty, I use 'returning a kindness' in a technical sense: in the technical sense, 'returning a kindness' is the name of a class of actions which would be returning kindnesses, in the ordinary sense, were it not for the foible of this particular religious group. In view of what I am about to say, this move might appear illicit, but it will turn out later on that it is not.

Suppose one member of this group, B, did a kindness (in the technical sense) for A on Monday and that on Tuesday an opportunity arose for A, by doing the action x, to return this kindness. If an outside observer remarked that B had the right to A's doing x, we should have to explain to him that he was mistaken. We should have to point out that among these people it was an insult to return a kindness within three days and therefore against their interests to do it. And that it was absurd to speak of the individuals of a group having a right as members of that group to anything which was against their interest. We have pointed out to him that the proposition that B has the right to A's doing x cannot be deduced from the proposition that A's doing x is returning a kindness to B. To obtain this conclusion the additional premiss is needed that people of the group to which A and B belong have the right to having kindnesses returned. This premiss is false of the group considered unless it is qualified by a three day clause. Thus, the argument:

A's doing x is returning a kindness to B
implies
B has a right to A's doing x

is not valid.

I will now show that the same conclusion cannot be established by the same method for the argument:

A promised B to do x
implies
B has a right to A's doing x

Suppose the particular foible of the religious group is that it is an insult among them to promise to do anything within three days and that on Monday A says to B, 'I promise you I will do x for you on Tuesday'. There are three possibilities: (1) B rejects the promise offered to him; (2) B accepts the promise, judging the insult to be worth the candle; (3) B accepts the promise thinking the insult is worth the candle when it is not. We consider the present argument in the light of these three possibilities. (1) We cannot establish that the conclusion does not follow from the premiss in the same way as before because, although the conclusion is false, the premiss is also false. If B rejected the promise, no promise was made, and the proposition asserting that one was made is false. (2) In this case B accepts the promise because he judges the benefit promised is worth the insult in obtaining it. In this case the premiss is true, but so is the proposition that B has the right to A's doing x: the only ground we had for saying it was false, viz., that it was against B's interest that A should do x, has been removed. Consequently we cannot deduce that this proposition does not follow from the premiss. Both are true. (3) This case reduces to the first, for it is a case in which one of the conditions controlling the promising function is not satisfied, and in which we cannot say, simpliciter, that A promised. Consequently the premiss is false and we can form no conclusion about the deducibility from it of the proposition that B has the right to A's doing x. Thus one method of establishing that the first premiss of the kindness argument cannot by itself imply the conclusion cannot be used to establish the same point about the promising argument.

Consider now a corresponding argument in terms of truth-telling. We shall see that it is in the same position as the kindness argument. Suppose that on Tuesdays a group within a society play a game. It consists in each member of the group guessing whether or not another has told him the truth. If he guesses rightly he receives a tick and if he guesses wrongly a cross. It is an all embracing game played for the whole twenty-four hours of each Tuesday, and this is all that happens. At the end of the day, the man with the most ticks is the winner. Suppose one member of the group, A, meets another, B, and says to him something which is false. An outside observer, not knowing about the game, may say that B had the right to A's doing x, where A's doing x consists in his telling the truth to B. If he did we should have to explain to him that he was mistaken. We should have to explain that constant truth-telling would spoil the game and was against the interest of this group on Tuesdays. And that it was absurd to speak of individuals of a group having the right as members of that group to anything which was against their interest. In doing this we have pointed out that the proposition that B has the right to A's doing x cannot be deduced from the proposition that A's doing x is telling the truth to B. To obtain this conclusion the additional premiss is needed that people of the group to which A and B belong have the right to be told the truth. And this premiss is false of the group considered unless a clause is added excepting Tuesdays. The argument

A's doing x would be telling the truth to B
implies
B has the right to A's doing x

is not valid.

We now have to see if it can be established in the same way that the premiss of the promising argument does not imply its conclusion. We will try to imagine a group which plays a game with promising like the game played by the previous group with truthtelling. The game is played, as before, on Tuesdays, and consists in individuals saying to each other, 'I promise to do x'. Thereafter the practice is for the hearer to guess whether or not the speaker will do x. If he guesses correctly he receives a tick and if incorrectly a cross. The winner at the end of the day is the one with the most ticks. This is all that happens. We suppose now that two members of the group, A and B, meet on a Tuesday, and that A says to B, 'I promise to do x'. We have to consider the proposition that B has the right to A's doing x. It must be judged false on the same ground as before: constant promise keeping would spoil the game and be against the interest of the group, and it is absurd to speak of individuals of a group having the right as members of that group to something which is against their interest. If we now consider the promising argument, viz.,

A promised B to do x
implies
B has the right to A's doing x

it may seem that we have a proposition about B's rights which does not follow from the premiss—for the proposition about B's rights is false and the premiss is true. But the fact is that the premiss is not true, for the game imagined does not involve the promising function. We imagined that A said to B, 'I promise to do x' and that all that happened thereafter was that B received a tick if he guessed rightly about what A would do and a cross if he guessed wrongly. Apart from the expression used, the game would have been precisely the same if A had said to B, 'I will do x'. The function of promising does not enter into it. The words 'I promise to do x' are being used by A purely to make an assertion, true or false, about his future actions. And if one thing is certain it is that promising is not purely making an assertion about one's future actions. The second game reduces to a special case of the first.

Thus a method of showing that the first premiss of the truth-telling argument does not alone imply the conclusion of that argument fails to establish the same point about the promising argument. The situation found with the kindness argument repeats itself. The reason for this is not far to seek. To deduce the proposition that B has the right to A's doing x from the proposition that A's doing x is returning a kindness or from the proposition that A's doing x is telling the truth, we need the extra premisses that members of the group have the right to kindnesses being returned and have the right to be told the truth respectively. And these extra premisses are needed because, as the cases discussed have shown, they may be false. But the proposition that members of a group have the right to promises being kept cannot be false. To describe a group and a situation which provides a ground for saying that B does not have the right to A's keeping his promise is to describe a group and a situation which provides a ground for saying that A did not make a promise to B. It may look at first sight as if he did because the words 'I promise' are used. But this must not mislead us. It may be that the promise was rejected or that the words are being used simply to make an assertion.

But—the objection may be lodged—surely we can describe a group in which the function is so exercised that, in some circumstances, it is against the interest of the group that promises should be kept; that 'I promise to do x' counts as having made a promise even when, for example, doing x is disastrous to the promiser or to the disadvantage of the promisee. The possibility—the objector continues—shows that if B's right to A's keeping his promise is to be deduced from the proposition that A promised, an additional premiss will be needed to exclude such cases: if a right implies an obligation, and an obligation to do x implies that there is a reason better than any in terms of independent interest for doing x, then a promise does not imply a right, for it is obvious that in a case such as that imagined there is no reason of any kind for doing x. To answer this objection, we have to ask on what basis it is said that an utterance of 'I promise to do x' by a member of this group counts as having made a promise under such a circumstance. The answer must be that the group act towards a man who fails to do x under this circumstance in the same kind of way as they act towards people who omit to keep promises in other circumstances. But if acting in these ways in this case is a contribution to an irrational exercise of the promising function, then there is every reason for their not acting in these ways; there is every reason, that is, for their not acting, in this case, in ways which are appropriate when a promise has been broken. But if this is so we cannot say that a promise has been broken. We cannot say that there is every reason for not acting in ways appropriate when a promise has been broken and still insist that a promise has been broken. And if we cannot say that a promise has been broken, we cannot say that a promise has been made.

It is not always obvious whether an exercise of the promising function is irrational or not, and we shall see later what is involved in a judgement of irrationality in this sphere (3, 15). But the examples cited quite obviously are irrational exercises of the function. Consequently we must say that, although the group are unanimous in their judgement that a promise has been made in the circumstances described, they are mistaken. When the group we are considering judges, at time t, that one of their number promised to do x at this time on the basis of his having said at an earlier time, 'I promise to do x at t', they are, if it is disastrous to him to do x or to the disadvantage of the promisee, making a false judgement. In consequence, the argument we have been considering, viz.,

A promised B to do x
implies
B has a right to A's doing x

is not shown to be invalid by the case discussed. In the circumstances in question, the conclusion is not true. But nor is the premiss. I should stress that we have been discussing an irrational exercise of the promising function in a society. Nothing that has been said commits us to the view that an individual man cannot make a stupid promise. It will turn out eventually that there is a perfectly good use for the expression 'This man has promised stupidly'. But its correct use is such that there is no ground for saying that, having done so, he is not under an obligation.

I argued previously (2, 2) that 'A has an obligation to B' implies 'B has a right against A'. I have now argued that 'A made a promise to B' also implies 'B has a right against A'. In other words, the notions of having promised and having an obligation stand in the same relation to the notion of a right. Now since we have shown that a promise implies a right and that a right implies an obligation (2, 2), we could deduce immediately that a promise implies an obligation. But it is better, I think, to complete the picture by setting out the relations between having promised and the notions of blame, moral good, trustworthiness and reason for acting. Having promised and having an obligation stand in the same relations to each of these concepts. If in any case it is doubted whether having promised stands in the relation stated to the concept in question, arguments parallel to those employed in discussing rights may be devised to show that it does. In the four sub-sections following, I shall be stating rather than arguing. The symbol 'C' will be used to represent the conjunctive proposition that A can do x and that his doing x does not violate a superior obligation; and 'obligation' will be used for abstract obligation throughout.

Blameworthiness

This and the next two points I shall despatch quickly and then spend more time on reason for acting which is more important. 'Blame' is being used as a shorthand here. It is a loaded word and it is not really blame that I wish to discuss. What needs to be said is this: If A promised B to do x and C is true and A did not do x, then it follows that B is justified in trying to get him to act differently in future. ($C = A$ can do x and his doing x does not violate a superior obligation). Similarly, if A has an obligation to B to do x and C is true and A did not do x, then it follows that B

is justified in trying to get him to act differently in future. The antecedents cannot be true and the consequents false.

The point made here—that B is justified in trying to get A to act differently in future if C is true and A did not do x—is purely logical. It is only to say that there is *something* which B is justified in doing. Once we begin to say *what* he is justified in doing, e.g., blaming him, we make a moral judgement. But the point actually made is purely logical and not a judgement based upon, say, Utilitarian considerations. Having promised and having an obligation stand in the same relation to the notion discussed.

Moral Good

If A has promised B to do x and C is true, then it follows that it is morally better that A should do x than an alternative. Similarly, if A has an obligation to B to do x and C is true, then it follows that it is morally better that A should do x than an alternative. The antecedents cannot be true and the consequents false. Having promised and having an obligation stand in the same relation to the notion of moral good.

Trustworthiness

At this point we come to the logical relation which Hume thought was sufficient to explain what it was to give a promise once he had said mistakenly that promising included expressing an intention (2, 5). We are in the process of seeing that it is just one of many relations, and there is no reason for thinking it is more central than any other. The term 'trust' has moral and non-moral uses. Non-morally we say that a dog can be trusted not to bite, that a child can be trusted on the road and a man can be trusted to get his facts right. In the moral use, we tend to say not that a man can be trusted to do such and such but that he is trustworthy. When an employer writes to another recommending an apprentice as trustworthy, he is making a moral point about him. After such a recommendation the new employer would be surprised if the apprentice stole 10/– from the till. He would also be surprised if he broke a promise to work late one evening. As a first approximation, we may say that the knowledge that a man is trustworthy is a reason as good as we could have for judging that he will do what is obligatory or what he has promised to do provided C is true.

We must add, however, that we have better reason if we know he also wants to do the action for its own sake, because even trustworthy people sometimes fall victim to counter desires. The correct formulation is that both the proposition that A has an obligation to do x and that A promised to do x imply that there is a reason as good as there could be for judging that A will do x if they are conjoined with the propositions C, A does not want to do x for its own sake and A is trustworthy. Having promised and having an obligation stand in the same relation to the notion of trustworthiness.

Reason for Acting

In this section I argue that, given the final implication of the Reason-for-Acting/Obligation schema, the propositions that A promised to do x and that A has an abstract obligation to do x imply the same proposition about reason for acting, i.e., that if a man has promised to do x, it is implied that there is a reason for his doing x which is better than any in terms of his independent interest. If a man said, 'I promised to do x, but that's no reason for doing it if it's against my interest', we should have to conclude that he had not understood part of what was involved in the notion of having promised. The point is a tricky one to make, for we should not wish to say the same of a man who said, 'I promised to do x, but that's no reason for doing it if it's disastrously against my interest', and there is plainly no sharp dividing line between what is disastrously against his interest, and what is against it but not disastrously so. There could be no simple rule of thumb for reading off an answer to the question, 'Is it disastrously against his interest?' which could be applied in all cases. In many it must be a matter for judgement. But this provides no objection to what I am saying. The absence of a sharp dividing line does not imply the absence of a distinction. If anyone objects that the latter case is one in which a man has promised but does not have a reason for acting better than any in terms of his independent interest, the answer is that the objection has already been met. The promising function is controlled by certain conditions. If it is disastrously against a man's interest to do the action of which he said 'I promise', one of these conditions is not satisfied and we cannot say simply that he has promised. Thus, his not having a reason better than any in terms of his independent interest in these conditions leaves untouched the claim that the proposition that G promised to do x implies that he has a reason for doing x better than any in terms of his independent interest. The claim is made only when we can say simpliciter that G promised, and apparent counter-examples involving cases in which we cannot say it obviously provide no objection.

Thus, having already seen that having promised and having an obligation stand in the same relations to rights, blame, moral good and trustworthiness, we now see that they stand also in the same relation to the notion of reason for acting: the propositions that G promised to do x and that G has an obligation to do x both imply that there is a reason for G's doing x which is better than any in terms of his independent interest for doing either x or not-x. Having promised and having an obligation stand in the same relations to the central concepts of moral thought. When this conclusion is considered along with the other points established in this chapter, we are left with no alternative but to say that promising is the function of placing ourselves under an abstract obligation; and a function such that 'A promised B to do x' implies 'A is under an abstract obligation to B to do x'.

Promising is not unique in the respect that 'A promised to do x' implies 'A has an abstract obligation to do x'. Consider the argument:

> A's doing x would be telling the truth to B
> implies
> A has an abstract obligation to B to do x

In discussing the equivalent argument in which the conclusion was in terms of rights (B has a right to A's doing x), we saw that it was not valid without the additional premiss that the group to which A and B belong have the right to be told the truth. The additional premiss was needed because it may not be true; we imagined a group of whom it was not true unless a clause excepting Tuesdays was included. Let us now suppose that this group have the expression 'telling the frut' in their language. 'Telling the frut' means the same as 'telling the truth, except on Tuesdays . . .', the sentence being completed by clauses excluding all other circumstances which provide a reason for denying validity to the argument without an additional premiss. The argument:

A's doing *x* would be telling the frut to *B*
implies
A has an abstract obligation to *B* to do *x*

is then valid without any additional premiss. It is valid because the expression 'telling the frut' is so tailored that any additional premiss which would otherwise be needed is stated in the premiss we already have. There are numerous expressions in our language which have the property we have bestowed upon 'telling the frut'. 'Murder' is an excellent example. 'Murder' stands to 'killing' as 'telling the frut' stands to 'telling the truth', except that in the former case the implied obligation is actual and not only abstract:

A's doing *x* was an act of murder
implies
A had an actual obligation not to do *x*

Cases in which an actual obligation is implied are, I think, rare, but the implication of an abstract obligation is not at all uncommon. I suspect that 'returning a kindness', employed in its ordinary sense, and not the technical sense used earlier, is such that:

A's doing *x* is returning a kindness to *B*
implies
A has an (abstract) obligation to *B* to do *x*

It was for this reason that, in introducing the technical use, I guarded against the charge of misdemeanour. Sometimes,

A's doing *x* is an act of . . . to *B*
implies
A has an obligation to *B* to do *x*

because the expression filling the vacancy in the premiss is so tailored that any additional premiss which would otherwise be needed is already stated in the premiss given.

I suggested in the *Introduction*,[1] by considering the case of murder, that while pointing to an implication in such cases establishes, given the premiss, that the action referred to in the conclusion ought, or ought not, to be done, it does not *explain* why it ought or ought not to be done; why it is right or wrong.[2] To obtain an explanation, we should have, as a first step, to extract

---

[1] Introduction 1.

[2] I use '*x* ought to be done' and '*x* is right' synonymously throughout; and so for '*x* ought not to be done' and '*x* is wrong'.

the premiss or premisses which are concealed in the premiss given, and, as a second step, show how it or they explain the rightness or wrongness of the action in question. This programme has yet to be undertaken for the general case; but it has already partly been done for promising. If a man says, 'I promise', he offers to place himself under an obligation under conditions which control the rational exercise of the function. If the offer is accepted, and such conditions are satisfied, there can be no *reason* for denying that he *is* under an obligation. The premiss '*A* promised *B* to do *x*' is the conjunction of the propositions '*A* offered to place himself under an obligation to *B* to do *x*', '*B* accepted' and 'The conditions controlling the rational exercise of the function are satisfied'. The wrongness of failing to do a promised action is thus explained. The explanation is, it is true, not complete, for we have not yet a clear understanding (2, 6) of what it is to exercise the promising function rationally. And that cannot come until later (3, 15). But, if I am right, taking the promising case this far is a necessary condition of setting out the general ground of judgements of basic obligation.

9. UTILITARIANISM: THE GENERAL RULE

We discussed earlier the Utilitarian account of the obligation to keep a particular promise in particular circumstances, and found it wanting. One of the points noticed was that the effect of promise breaking upon, to use Mr Pickard-Cambridge's words, 'the whole system of good faith in society' could not be relevant in determining whether a particular promise ought to be kept. I shall now argue that this effect can have no bearing on the proposition that we have an abstract obligation to keep our promises. The point will be approached by discussing the propositions that we ought, as a general rule, to keep our promises, i.e., that we ought usually to keep them. These two propositions are not equivalent (2, 3), but I shall acquiesce in Mr Pickard-Cambridge's assumption that they are and allow the distinction between them to emerge. The account of the obligation to keep promises given by Rule Utilitarianism is not under discussion in this section. General promise breaking would have the effect that the promising function would become less useful to us and, in the limit, disappear. This would be a disastrous effect: the promising and contracting functions are of inestimable value. That they are of such value, and that general promise breaking would decrease their value to negligible proportions, certainly looks like a good reason for keeping promises as a general rule, and certainly looks like a ground for saying that we ought to keep them as a general rule. This Utilitarian argument appears powerful, and to understand its weakness, we must start at the beginning: that the promising function is useful. On this basis we may say that there is good reason for acting in ways necessary to preserve it: for instructing our children in its exercise, for example, and, so it seems, keeping our promises as a general rule. And, on this ground, we may be tempted to say that we ought to keep our promises as a general rule.

One of the many weaknesses of this argument is that the ought proposition which it establishes does not imply that others have the right to our keeping promises as a general rule. It is not a proposition of basic obligation. Its ground is simply that there is good reason for keeping promises as a general rule; but it was argued earlier (2, 1) that the proposition that there is good reason for A's doing X does not imply that anyone has the right to his doing X, and consequently the proposition that we have good reason for keeping promises as a general rule does not imply that others have the right to our doing so. It is obvious in any case that good reason for acting does not imply a right: we may all have good reason for cleaning our teeth three times a day, but it does not follow that anyone has the right to our doing so. If anyone wishes to hold that a particular proposition which is a good reason for acting does imply a right, the onus is on him to show that it does. The demand is fair because the implication does not in general hold; and it is a demand which it not satisfied by the Utilitarian argument.

The point may be made in a slightly different way. The inference rests on the principle that we ought to act so as to preserve useful functions, i.e., on the assumption that

> F is a useful function
> implies
> We ought to act so as to preserve F.

If the conclusion is taken to be a proposition of basic obligation, this implication does not hold. For, in that case the conclusion implies that others have the right to our acting in such ways, while the premiss has no such implication. The implication does hold if the implicans is taken to constitute good reason for acting so as to preserve F and the implicandum to assert only that there is good reason for so acting. In other words the implication upon which the Utilitarian inference rests, is valid if the implicandum is understood in terms of one of the residual uses of 'ought' (1, 11), but not if it is taken to assert a basic obligation.

In holding that the right to general promise keeping rests upon the usefulness of the promising function, the Utilitarian sets the cart before the horse. It is not because promising is a useful function that we have a right to promise keeping as a general rule. We have the right as a general rule just because promising is the function of conferring rights and the conditions required for its rational exercise are, as a general rule, satisfied. And it is just because promising is the function of conferring rights that it is a useful function.

In discussing the Utilitarian account of the obligation to keep a particular promise, we saw that the theory ignored the right of the promisee. When the total good to be done by breaking a promise is equal to the total good to be done by keeping it, Utilitarian theory commits its supporters to the absurd conclusion that it does not matter whether the promise is broken or kept. The theory cannot accommodate the fact that in this situation the promisee has the right to enjoy the benefit which was promised to him nor the consequence that the promiser has a basic obligation to accord it to him. With the Utilitarian account of the obligation to keep promises as a general rule, the story repeats itself: the rights of promisees are nowhere to be found. No one can deny that we have the right to promise keeping as a general rule; but Utilitarian theory fails utterly to account for it. It is a theory which looks satisfactory because it provides a ground for an ought proposition. But it is an ought proposition of the wrong kind. It is totally innocent of any implication about promisees' rights. The failure to provide the ground of propositions about rights is a general defect of Utilitarian theory. Not only promisees' rights but human rights in general are supplied with no decent foundation. It is for this reason that Utilitarians are often shy of the notion (2, 1). Their theories look plausible so long as a selection of the concepts of moral thought are considered. The selection does not include the concept of a right which is either ignored completely, as by Moore and Rashdall, or taken up as an afterthought, as in Mill's *Utilitarianism*.

I said I would show that considerations about the effect upon society of general promise breaking were irrelevant to the question: Have I an abstract obligation to do *x* given that I have promised to? This has now been done, for the proposition that *A* has an abstract obligation to *B* to do *x* implies that *B* has the abstract right to *A*'s doing *x*. All the Utilitarian argument establishes, if it establishes anything at all, is an ought proposition which has no such implication. The argument is irrelevant to the question.

10. THE REASON FOR KEEPING A PROMISE

We now ask whether 'Promising is a useful function' is a reason for keeping promises as a general rule. Having, in the last section, challenged the validity of an argument if the conclusion is taken to assert a basic obligation, we now challenge the truth of the premiss. It is, it must be admitted, almost irresistibly tempting to concede that the premiss is true. Cars and lawn mowers are useful to us, and it would be hard to deny that their usefulness constitutes good reason for acting, as a general rule, so as to preserve them. It is not immediately obvious that promising is in a different position. But the fact is that the utility of the function is otiose as a reason for acting. It is not because promising is a useful function that we have, as a general rule, a reason for doing what we have promised to do. We have such a reason because promising is, *inter alia*, the function of giving ourselves such a reason. Promising is the function whereby the promiser places himself under an abstract obligation, i.e., among other things, gives himself a reason for acting; a reason which is better than any in terms of his independent interest. And it is because promising is this function that it is a useful function.

The question, '*What* function is being said to be useful; what is its purpose and what is its point?' must be pressed against anyone who holds that its utility constitutes a reason for keeping promises as a general rule (2, 5). He must be pressed for an answer to the question, 'What *are* we doing when we promise?' And if he cannot answer, his case collapses. The present argument, unlike those employed earlier, constitutes an objection to Rule Utilitarianism. This theory applies the criterion of the best effects producible to the adoption of rules rather than the commission of particular acts. An Act Utilitarian holds that we ought always to do that act which will produce the best effects of all those open to us. A Rule Utilitarian holds that we ought to act in accordance with those rules whose universal adoption would have the best effects. The rules of which he speaks may be very complicated but they have no exceptions. His thesis is very different from the thesis that we ought as a general rule, i.e., usually, to act in certain ways because acting in those ways usually has the best effects, exceptions arising as particular actions of the kind in question do not have better effects than alternatives to them. His thesis is that we ought to act in accordance with rules whose universal adoption has the best possible effects, and such a rule, although it may indeed be very complicated, cannot have exceptions. This is no place to extol the merits of Rule Utilitarianism as against Act Utilitarianism.[1] Our concern is with the Rule Utilitarian's account of the obligation to keep promises. He holds that there is some rule such as: Keep promises unless, e.g., it is quite disastrous to yourself, or against the interest of the promisee, or . . ., whose universal adoption has better effects than its rejection. And that this is the reason for doing actions which fall under it. Now a Rule Utilitarian must be able to answer the question, 'What is this rule about?' And the obvious reply, 'It is about keeping promises', raises the further question, 'Keeping *what*? What are promises? What is a man doing when he makes a promise?' If the reply is that he is making assertions, it will be generally agreed that it is false. What then is he doing, and what is the purpose of doing it? The Rule Utilitarian is, so far as I can see, in no better position than any other kind of Utilitarian in regard to providing an answer to this question. Once it is seriously tackled, it becomes transparent that the only answer to it is the answer given in these pages. And if that is so, any rule of the kind envisaged by a Rule Utilitarian is otiose as a reason for keeping promises.

I am saying that the reason for keeping our promises is, quite

---

[1] In discussing Rule Utilitarianism I rely, here as elsewhere, on the account of the theory given in John Hosper's *Human Conduct* (Harcourt, Brace and World), pp. 311–37.

simply, that we promised: that we promised simpliciter. We promised simpliciter only if the conditions which ensure that the promising function is rationally exercised are satisfied. But if we have promised, there is a reason for doing the promised action which is better than any in terms of independent interest for doing either that action or any action incompatible with it. The account is consistent with the Reason-for-Acting/Obligation schema:

A promised to do x and he can do x
implies
A has an abstract obligation to do x
implies
There is a reason for A's doing x which is better than any in terms of independent interest for doing either x or not-x

Our account of the obligation to keep promises is thoroughly down to earth and conformable to common sense. The simple fact is that, for our greater convenience, we have the function of placing ourselves under abstract obligations to others. Provided the function is exercised rationally, its exercise places us under abstract obligations to others. And placing ourselves under abstract obligations is, *inter alia*, giving ourselves reasons for acting which are better than any in terms of our independent interest. Nothing could be more earth bound than this.

II. PROMISES EXTRACTED BY THREATS

It is usually said that promises extracted by threats do not oblige. I do not know of any reason that has ever been given for saying so, but there is no doubt that it is the standard reaction among philosophers. It will be plain by now that I am not going to concur. A promise implies an abstract obligation. It remains an open question whether the obligation is actual in the circumstances obtaining at the time for fulfilment, but this is a quite general point about promising. The important question about 'promises extracted by threats' concerns their relation to abstract obligation. Given that a promise implies an abstract obligation the alternatives are:

(1) that putative promises extracted by threats are not promises
(2) that they are promises and do place the promiser under an abstract obligation

Anyone who wishes to take the former alternative has (1 *a*) to explain how there could be any point in extracting 'promises' by threats; (1 *b*) to account for certain apparent counter-examples of which it seems absurd to say that the promiser is not under an obligation and equally absurd to say that his 'promise' is no promise. The second alternative provides the problem of explaining the spontaneous and universal reaction of philosophers that promises extracted by threats do not oblige. It is not likely to be simply wrong.

I shall deal with (1 *b*) first and describe two cases—out of a large number which can be imagined—which fall under this heading.

(i) A man says to an acquaintance, 'I know you've been carrying on with my wife. It's been going on for months, and it's got to stop. If it doesn't I shall tell your wife what's going on. I mean that. If you don't leave Joan alone, I'll break up your marriage. I want a solemn promise that you'll keep right away from her for the future, and if you give it to me, I'll lie low and say nothing to your wife'. The second man is appropriately disconcerted by the first's knowledge, but soon replies, 'All right, That's fair enough. I give you my word.'

(ii) It often happens in the juvenile court that the magistrate says to an offender, 'I have given careful consideration to your case, and I have decided to give you another chance. Instead of sending you to Borstal, I am going to put you on probation provided you promise me not to get yourself into trouble again. This is your final chance. Will you promise me that you will keep out of trouble in future?' We suppose that the promise is given.

In both these cases the promise is extracted by threats: if you do not promise, I will tell your wife; if you do not promise, I will send you to Borstal. But no one would wish to say in these cases that the promiser was not under an obligation. The cases are however both peculiar in that the promiser antecedently had an obligation to do what he has now promised to do—not to have an affair with another man's wife and, let us say, not to throw bricks through shop windows. In these cases we cannot simply say of promising that it is the function of placing ourselves under an obligation, for as such it would be redundant. It was cases like these which led me to talk earlier (2, 4) of a secondary function of promising. It is a function which is included in the primary function but is more restricted than it. In cases like these we cannot say that the promiser gives the promisee the right to his doing x, for he already has the right. But we can say that the promiser gives himself reason for doing x better than any in terms of his independent interest; for although he already has such a reason, it is a different one. What it is will be discussed in chapter 3, but it certainly is not that he has promised. But if he promises he also has the reason that he has promised. The recognition of the secondary function of promising does not affect the claim that a promise implies an obligation, for it only comes into play when there is an antecedent obligation to do what is now promised. Consequently, one cannot have given a secondary promise to do x and yet have no obligation to do x.

There is then no problem about secondary promises, i.e., promises to do what one already has an obligation to do, which are extracted by threats. They are perfectly good promises and are such that if a man promises to do something it follows that he has an obligation to do it. So far it looks as if we must come down on the side of the second of the alternatives stated at the beginning of this section; it looks so far as if we must say not that promises extracted by threats are not promises, but that they are perfectly good promises and do, in the restricted sense explained, place the promiser under an obligation. If we were to do this without more ado, we should have to provide answers to the problem which the second alternative poses: the universal philosophical reaction that promises extracted by threats do not oblige—or, as I should wish to put it— that such 'promises' are not promises. The line of thought followed here suggests that this reaction might derive from considering cases of primary promising only, and that there may be something about primary promises extracted by threats which should lead us to say, not indeed that they are promises which do not oblige, but that they are not properly understood as promises at all. To investigate this suggestion, we consider the following case:

(iii) The son and heir of a rich man has become infatuated with a girl who, as is plain to any impartial observer, is interested not in him but in his father's money. All the father's attempts to persuade his son of this truth fall upon stony ground. The boy is completely under the woman's spell. Eventually, in desperation, the father says, 'All right, if you won't listen to sense, perhaps threats will work. Unless you promise not to see this woman any more, I will cut you off without a penny. I mean that. Not a single penny out of my estate will come to you'. The boy may or may not give his promise, but let us suppose that he does. 'All right,' he says feeling bitter and angry, 'I promise'.

I shall take it that he now has an obligation to abandon the woman. I know that some people may dispute this, but those who do are asked to invent a case for themselves to which what I am about to say will apply and in which they would agree that an obligation is created. I have no doubt they will be able to do so. I think further that what follows will remove any inclination there may be to deny that there is an obligation in this case. Here we have a case of an obligation arising out of a promise which was extracted by threats. To guarantee that we are discussing the right problem, we must ensure that it is a case of primary and not secondary promising. We must ask whether the boy had an antecedent obligation to discard the woman. No doubt he has obligations to his parents, but they can hardly be supposed to extend to his choice of wife. But whether this is so or not, it does not matter. For it is plain that what is in question here is not the boy's obligations to his parents but his own interest. He is not being asked to promise because he has violated or is about to violate his obligations to his parents. He is being asked to promise because it is in his own interest to wean himself of the woman's fascination. So we are safe in concluding that it is a case of primary promising.

This is a perfectly good case of a primary promise extracted by threats, and there is no inclination to say that it is not completely in order as a promise. The interesting point is that although it is extracted by threats, it is in the boy's interest to make it. The suggestion is that it is not threats in themselves which are the nigger in the woodpile, but promises obtained by threats which it is against the promiser's interest to make. It suggests that the promise just discussed is all right because it is in the boy's interest to make it, but that another promise extracted by threats which it is not in the promiser's interest to make might be far from all right. This is, I think, an important element in the truth of the matter. I shall go on to argue that it is primary promises of the latter kind which philosophers have in mind when they send up their universal cry, 'Promises extracted by threats do not oblige!'

But they are, of course, mis-stating their position when they express it in this way. They should be saying that such putative promises are not promises because it would be an irrational exercise of the promising function to count them as such.

It is, in general, against people's interests to be forced into doing things. There are many exceptions, but the general truth is guaranteed by the fact that force is usually exerted in the interest of the man forcing rather than the man forced. People who wish to make and receive promises are a sub-class of people in general, and promising is a sub-class of things done. Thus, in general, it is against the interest of people who wish to make and receive promises to be forced into making them. In giving a promise we confer a right upon another, and it is, as a rule, against a man's interest to be forced into a position in which others have rights against him. In general, then, it would not be a rational exercise of the promising function to count utterances of 'I promise' extracted by threats as having made promises; and so far as we employ the function rationally, we do not do so. Cases like that discussed a moment ago provide exceptions to the rule. In that case, it was in the boy's interest to bid the girl farewell, and this was the action he promised to do. He was forced into making the promise, but it was in his interest to do the action which was its subject. In such cases it is not an irrational exercise of the function to count his utterance of 'I promise' as having given a promise; and when we employ the function rationally, we do so count it. Further light will be thrown on these points at a later stage in the argument (3, 15).

At the beginning of this section I stated two alternative views which might be adopted about promises extracted by threats. Instead of adopting either, we have arrived at a compromise between the two. Secondary promises extracted by threats, i.e., cases in which the promise concerns an action which the promiser antecedently had an obligation to do, are perfectly in order. Primary promises extracted by threats are generally not in order, but they sometimes are. Whether they are or not depends upon whether or not it is a rational exercise of the promising function to count them as promises. I think it is plain without labouring the point that the compromise position proposed meets the difficulties stated at the beginning of the section, while neither of the bolder answers could meet them if it were offered by itself as the whole truth of the matter. We have no difficulty in explaining the point of extracting promises by threats—they are sometimes perfectly good promises. Where they are not, the explanation of what is going on will no doubt vary from case to case and be of a psychological nature. The account given accommodates counter-examples to the view that promises extracted by threats do not oblige. And the universal inclination of philosophers to say they do not oblige is explained: it is the position at which one would arrive by considering only the general case; for in general the promising function would be exercised irrationally if utterances of 'I promise' extracted by threats were counted as having made promises.

12. CRIMINAL PROMISES

I referred earlier (2, 6) to Sidgwick's saying that a promise to do an immoral act is not binding. His claim is necessarily true; it is logically impossible to have an obligation to do an immoral act. But we cannot leave it at this, as Sidgwick does. We have to be able to explain what criminals are doing when they make promises to one another; when, for example, one undertakes to look after the night watchman while the other cracks the safe. They are not binding themselves, for that is logically impossible. Nor are they pretending to bind themselves, for that means something different; it means saying 'I promise' without having the intention of acting accordingly. Perhaps a Utilitarian would say that they think they are binding themselves. But on his own account, this means that they think keeping their promises does more good than harm, and we can hardly hold that promises among criminals have a job to do only so long as they see themselves as devoted to moral works. The only alternative which appears to remain to a Utilitarian, that they are making meaningless noises at each other, is no less absurd.

The following account is, I think, an improvement. I have argued at length that a promise implies an abstract obligation. A criminal promise is no different from any other in this respect. When a criminal promises to do an immoral act he places himself— just like a decent man promising to do a decent act—under an abstract obligation. It is true that this obligation cannot be actual. That is a logical impossibility, for the action which he promises to do falls also under a class which he has a superior abstract obligation not to do. What then is the point of his promising if the abstract obligation can never be actual? Are we in any better a position than the Utilitarian? I shall argue that we are in a much better position, a position, in fact, which is completely satisfactory.

In promising, a criminal A places himself under an abstract obligation. It follows that criminal B has an abstract right against him. This is to say that he has the right provided other moral factors in the situation are discounted, i.e., disregarding the fact that the action falls under another class which is abstractly obligatory (or the reverse), B has the right to A's doing it. Now it is precisely this that criminals do disregard. They disregard the fact that what they are doing is immoral. Thus the relation between the criminals A and B is exactly the same as the relation between two moral people one of whom has made a promise to the other. The only difference in the situations is that in the one case the immorality of the action is discounted and in the other it is not immoral. The fact that the relation is the same between the two pairs of people shows that a promise between criminals works in just the same way as a promise between decent moral agents.

The point can be brought out slightly differently by dealing with reasons for acting instead of rights. The proposition that A has an abstract obligation to do x implies that there is a reason for his doing x better than any in terms of his independent interest. If the abstract obligation is to do something immoral there is a better reason still for his *not* doing it. But still his reason *for* doing it is better than any in terms of his independent interests for doing anything. Thus, if instead of looking after the night watchman while his companion cracks the safe, he, following his inclination, consorts with a lingering female, he has acted against better reason. And when he later visits his confederate in prison to apologize, the bitter recriminations which he receives are fully justified. We thus see in a different way how being under an abstract obligation which logically cannot become actual allows for the operation of promises in the criminal world.

The fact that we are able to account for this is a merit of our view against the Utilitarians' which, it seems, can only make nonsense of the brute fact that criminals do make promises to each other and that promises do work among them. It is worth noticing that the previous paragraph shows quite clearly that '*A* has a better reason for doing *x* than any in terms of his independent interest' does not mean the same as the Utilitarian sentence '*A*'s doing *x* does more good than his following his own interest'. In the case considered, a Utilitarian would say that *A* did more good by pursuing the female, for a bank was not robbed and a criminal was apprehended. But he nonetheless had a reason better than any in terms of his independent interest for not pursuing her.

CHAPTER 3

THE GROUND OF BASIC OBLIGATIONS

The problems to be solved in this chapter will be approached by discussing first the ground of obligation principles, i.e., the ground of propositions asserting individuals to have an obligation in regard to a class of actions, where the obligation is basic and, in the first instance, abstract. This ground is social in a sense in which the ground of principles of ultra obligation is not. The notion of a society thus has a central role, and in thinking of societies I shall have nations primarily in mind so that I can comment at a later stage on positive law; I think of a nation as the range of application of a particular, more or less constant, set of laws. It goes without saying that many obligation principles transcend the largely artificial boundaries between nations. From this unit, the nation, we shall eventually move upwards to more general principles and downwards to more specific ones. We shall be concerned in the first instance only with the most general obligation principles in any given society, i.e., only with principles which apply to every member of the society to which such principles can apply. The earlier and greater part of the argument of this chapter is designed to establish the first implication of the Reason-for-Acting/Obligation schema for the basic mode of the concept. The second implication is established independently later. Thus the method of argument to be employed is different from that used to establish the schema for the prudential mode of the concept (1, 8).

I. THE PROGRAMME

It will be assumed in this section, for it was established in the last, that the proposition that A has made a promise to B implies that A is under an abstract obligation to B. Let us suppose that every member of a society is under an abstract obligation to every other member in regard to a certain class of actions, an obligation which does not arise out of any promise. The relations in which each stands to the other by virtue of being under this obligation are identical to the relations which would hold between them if they had each made a promise to the other; except, of course, that in the one case they would have promised and in the other they would not (2, 8). These relations include the rights the individuals have against each other; the justification they have for trying to get each other to act in certain ways; and the reasons they have for believing that others will act in certain ways, given the trustworthiness of the others. Further, in both cases, each has a reason for acting better than any in terms of his independent interests. If everyone is under an abstract obligation to everyone else (which does not arise out of a promise), the relations which hold between them are identical with those which would hold if everyone had made a promise to everyone else. This suggests—I will say no more—that the ground of the most general obligation principles has something to do with the reasons which everyone would have for making promises to everyone else in certain circumstances. It suggests that the ground of such principles is *in some sense* contractual. I shall argue that this is true and in doing so make it plain what the sense is.

The position which I am about to take up is, I think, sufficiently novel to be open to numerous misunderstandings. It is important to stress at this stage what I shall not be maintaining. In the first place, I do not hold that the individuals of a society have *in any sense* made contracts with each other. The claim would be historically false, and it would be inept to suggest that it was true in some more tenuous sense. Nor shall I make any appeal to the notion of implicit contracts. This notion, as it stands, is not sufficiently clear to be useful. Nor am I going to say that our abstract obligations are to act *as if* we had all made promises to each other. Nor—though it can hardly be necessary to emphasize this—am I going to do anything which could be described as 'starting from' a group of people in a 'state of nature' and showing how their obligations arise. That is an anthropological question which is of no interest to us here. On the contrary, our programme is to take any society we like as it is *now* and to ask what is involved in establishing that a certain class of actions is obligatory in that society, the obligation being, in the first instance, abstract.

We consider any society we like as it is now. For the sake of concreteness, it might as well be the people of the United Kingdom.

We suppose that there is widespread disagreement upon whether a certain class of actions is abstractly obligatory. This is a situation which often obtains in fact: at the present time, for example, there is widespread disagreement in the United Kingdom about whether adult homosexuals ought to have private relations with each other, and there is widespread disagreement on whether unmarried girls who conceive ought to have abortions. At other times disagreement has centered round other questions: Ought people to own slaves? Ought people to be persecuted for their religious opinions? Ought a man to be hanged for stealing a sheep? Ought people to appropriate the rent of land for their private advantage? Ought women to be treated as the property of their husbands? It will not be disputed that such questions arise and are important. It ought not to be disputed that it is also important to understand clearly what is involved in giving either one or the other answer to them. It is this that I try to bring to light here. The discussion is thoroughly earthbound. Our programme is to consider any society in such a condition of doubt and to show that there is a proposition in terms of the notions of contract, of people's interests and a certain class of actions, which implies that actions of this class are abstractly obligatory in that society. But I must repeat that the first proposition does not assert that contracts have actually been made and does not contain any notions such as implicit contract, or 'acting as if', which are, I believe, too weak to bear a heavy load. It is in fact a pretty tough-minded proposition and just what we need at the foundations of practical reason.

I must guard against another possible misunderstanding. In saying that I will put forward a proposition which implies that actions of the class specified in it are abstractly obligatory, I must not be understood as claiming that we shall thereby be able to 'read off' what is abstractly right or wrong. Once it is established that the first proposition is true, it will be possible to do that, but it will often be extremely difficult to establish that it is true. In such cases the hard work begins where the philosophy ends; and it certainly cannot be described as 'reading off the answer from a principle'. Nor must it be forgotten that even when it is decided what is abstractly obligatory, the question of what is actually obligatory in particular circumstances remains. It is perhaps not necessary to say that a philosopher cannot make moral problems easy to answer if the nature of the case makes them difficult to answer. The discovery of the ground of obligation principles could not be the discovery of a magical decision procedure which makes further effort unnecessary. The most a philosopher can do is to establish what, in the end, is relevant to the solution of a moral problem, and to explain why it is relevant.

2. EDICTS AND OBLIGATION PRINCIPLES

I shall now consider an important characteristic of obligation principles by contrasting them with positive law; but to avoid any possible confusion with natural law, I shall speak of edicts issued by an authority. We consider a society incorporating an authority with power to issue edicts governing the actions of individuals; power which has force as its instrument. Such edicts require that individuals refrain from doing some actions they want to do and do some actions which they do not want to do. So far their purpose is like that of obligation principles, for these too require that individuals refrain from some actions and do others whatever their desires may be. The *way* in which edicts require may indeed be different from the way in which obligation principles require, but what they require is the same so far as it has been described: both require that some desired actions are not done and that some undesired actions are done. But here the similarity ends, and the differences begin. It is plain that the requirements of edicts need not be in the interests of the individuals of the society; it need not be in the interests of the individuals that their actions should be restricted in these ways. The restrictions may be in the interest of the authority alone or in the interest of the authority and a favoured class. By contrast, we could make nothing of the suggestion that the restrictions required by obligation principles were in the interest of an authority or a favoured class or both. Obligation principles are moral principles and such principles logically cannot cater for selective interests. Anyone who maintained that they could would show that he did not know what a moral principle was; he confuses it perhaps with a law or an arbitrary decree issued by some authority. That obligation principles cannot cater for selective interests is the important truth perceived and insisted upon by Bentham and other Utilitarians with their formulae of the greatest happiness for the greatest number and 'each to count for one and none for more than one'. Witness Bentham:

. . .'the greatest happiness principle. . .(said Wedderburn) is a danger-ous one'. So saying, he said that which, to a certain extent, is strictly true: a principle which lays down, as the only *right* and justifiable end of Government, the greatest happiness of the greatest number—how can it be denied to be a dangerous one? Dangerous it unquestion-ably is, to every government which has for its *actual* end or object, the greatest happiness of a certain *one*, with or without the addition of some comparatively small number of others, whom it is a matter of pleasure or accommodation to him to admit, each of them, to a share in the concern, on the footing of so many junior partners. . . . In a Govern-ment which had for its end in view the greatest happiness of the greatest number, Alexander Wedderburn might have been Attorney General and then Chancellor: but he would not have been Attorney General with £15,000 a year, nor Chancellor, with a peerage with a veto upon all justice, with £25,000 a year, and with 500 sinecures at his disposal under the name of Ecclesiastical Benefices, besides et ceteras.[1]

It will be plain from what follows that Utilitarianism cannot succeed as a theory of morals, but its failure does not detract from the importance of the truth the early Utilitarians perceived. The requirements of obligation principles cannot cater for selective interests. There appear to remain two alternatives: either they are in the interest of no one; or they are in the interest of the individuals of the society severally. I take it that the first alternative is too absurd for discussion, and that we are compelled to accept the second.

The preceding argument supports the conclusion, but an appar-ently powerful counter argument has to be considered: it is as plain as can be that obedience to an obligation principle often prevents a man catering for his own interest. How then can we hold that the requirements of such principles are in people's interests severally? The facts seem stubbornly to oppose any such claim. But the opposition is only apparent. Our conclusion is not that it is in every man's interest to act, in any individual situation, as an obligation principle relevant to the situation requires. And it is not that the requirement upon him *alone* is in his interest. Our conclusion concerns the requirement in regard to a class of actions: and it is that such a requirement, not upon *A* alone, but upon

[1] *Principles of Morals and Legislation*, 1879, p. 5 note.

everyone, including A, is in A's interest, whoever A may be. The claim is not incompatible with the truth upon which the counter argument insists: that it is sometimes, or often, against a man's interest that he should be required to act, in an individual situation, as an obligation principle requires. 'Doing x is against my interest', is not incompatible with, 'The requirement upon everyone, including me, to do X, is in my interest'.

Moreover, the counter argument, if it is to pass unchallenged, must be taken to refer to people's interests, independently assessed (1, 9). Now certainly the requirement of an obligation principle may not be in the interest of an individual, or of a group within the society, if their interest is assessed independently of the interest of others. Why should it be? An obligation principle is a moral principle, and moral principles have nothing to do with people's interests so assessed. But the claim made is not, and could not be, that the requirements of such principles are in the independent interest of the individuals severally. It is that they must be in everyone's interest assessed *in some other way*. I shall use the formula that the requirements of obligation principles must be, *in some sense*, in the interest of the individuals of the society severally, i.e., since we are dealing only with principles which apply to everyone in the society, that it is, in some sense, in the interest of the individuals severally that every individual, including himself, should be required to act as obligation principles require. I do not say that the requirements must be equally in everyone's interest, a remark to which clear sense will be given at a later stage, but only that they must be in everyone's interest in some natural sense of this expression. It is clear that the claim made about obligation principles would be patently untrue if made of edicts issued by an authority.

At this point, it may be suggested that the requirements of obligation principles are in the interest of that class alone which respects its obligations, the remainder being subject to the various penalties attached to breaking them. 'How can you say', I may be asked, 'of a man who has spent most of his life in prison for stealing that the requirement not to steal is in his interest in any sense? Wouldn't he have been better off in a property free-for-all in full possession of his liberty?' I have not so far said that the requirement to submit to a penalty upon infringing an obligation principle must be, in any sense, in everyone's interest. But, although it is not necessary to insist upon it for the argument immediately following, I believe in fact that it must be: that just as the requirement placed upon everyone by an obligation principle must be in everyone's interest in some sense, so the requirement upon everyone to submit to an appropriate penalty in the case of infringement is in everyone's interest in the same sense. The argument just brought forward does not show that this claim is false: if the facts it alleges are substantiated, it shows either that there is something wrong with the principle or, more likely, with the penalty which attaches to it. It is not necessary to insist upon this point at this stage of the argument; and it will become evident later that it is true.

On the basis of this section, I shall take it to be true that it is in everyone's interest, in some sense, that everyone should be required to act in the ways which obligation principles require. There is no implication that the requirements are equally in everyone's interest. It may be suggested that although there is no class of people of whom it can be denied, there are nonetheless individual exceptions. But the fact is that the argument presented excludes the latter possibility just as it excludes the former. I must admit however that there are two apparent exceptions, one provided by a kind of individual and one by a possible state of affairs, and I must also admit that the claim I am making does require a qualification to accommodate the latter. It is a defect which I can see no way of overcoming that I cannot at this point deal with these apparent exceptions. It cannot be done because the sense in which it is in everyone's interest that everyone should be required to act as obligation principles require cannot be made clear until after the next section. The situation is such that I can only ask indulgence and go on to the next section as quickly as possible.

3. THE CONTRACT ARGUMENT

Henceforward I shall use the expression 'X is obligatory in the society S' as an abbreviation for 'A general principle of obligation enjoining a class of actions X is true of the society S, the obligation being basic and abstract'. We leave open the possibility that a class of actions which is obligatory in one society is not in another; and we are concerned, in the first instance, only with the obligations of individual members of any society to one another; not with the obligations of one society to another nor with the obligations of an individual of one society to an individual of another. We consider a class of actions, represented by X, of which it is not known whether actions of that class are obligatory or not.

Formally, the contract argument is very simple, but the matter of it is not. I shall first present its bare bones, and then deal with the numerous ancillary questions which clamour for attention. The contract argument consists of two deductive chains which have inconsistent conclusions. As the subject matter is complex, it is well to keep the two chains clearly separated.

First Deductive Chain (A)

We suppose that we can say of the society with which we are dealing:

Some classes of action are obligatory in this society

The status of this proposition is not obvious, nor is it plain precisely what it comes to. But in pursuit of the policy of setting the heart of the argument down first, I shall leave the elucidation of these points until later. For the moment we notice only that if we can say of the society that some classes of action are obligatory, we are free to suppose that Not-X is obligatory. ('Not-X' is used, instead of 'X', for later convenience: X and Not-X may be, for example, blackmailing and not blackmailing, or helping the poor and not helping the poor.) Thus we may suppose that

(A, 1) Not-X is obligatory in the society

I argued in the previous section that (A, 1) implies that it is in everyone's interest, in some sense, that everyone should be required to do Not-X. It implies it because Not-X is the subject of an obligation principle applying to everyone, and the discussion of *Edicts and Obligation Principles* has shown that the requirements of such a principle must be, in some sense, in everyone's interest. Thus, (A, 1) implies:

(A, 2) It is in everyone's interest, in some sense, that everyone should be required to do Not-X

(A, 2) is the conclusion of the first deductive chain. Before setting out the second, it is necessary to make several points about the proposition which lies at its head; the proposition to be called 'the contract ground'.

The Contract Ground

I have promised to state a proposition, in terms of the notions of contract, people's interests and a certain class of actions, which implies that that class of actions is obligatory in a society. The proposition is the contract ground:

> It is in everyone's interest to make a contract with everyone else to do X

It is not at all obvious that it implies the conclusion claimed, and it is my job to show that it does. But before setting out the second deductive chain and completing the argument, several points must be made about the contract ground itself.

First, it asserts nothing about any contract having been made; it asserts only that it is in everyone's interests to make a contract. Nor does it assert that everyone would, in his present circumstances, make a contract if invited to do so. People sometimes do not know where their interests lie. Secondly, we are not concerned at present with the truth of the contract ground for any X. It may be said, for example, that it will not be true of any X unless everyone has good reason for believing that most other people—not everyone, but most other people—respect the contracts they make. The point is conceded, and will be taken up (3, 10). Thirdly, and this point apart, it may still be doubted whether there is any class of actions of which the contract ground is true. I shall return to the point (3, 8) with an answer which is, I hope, satisfactory. But for the moment our concern is with the implications of the contract ground and not with its truth for any X. Fourth, the distinction should be noticed between, 'Doing X is in everyone's interest', and 'It is in everyone's interest to make a contract to do X'. It may be in everyone's interest to clean his teeth three times daily, but it does not follow that it is in everyone's interest to make a contract to do so. The propositions are distinct and should not be confused.

Second Deductive Chain (B)

The first proposition of the second deductive chain is the contract ground:

> It is in everyone's interest to make a contract with everyone else to do X

From this proposition it follows, by the argument of chapter 2, that:

(B, 1) It is in everyone's interest to be under an abstract obligation to do X provided everyone else is

It follows because, as the argument of chapter 2 has shown, the proposition that A promised to do X implies that A is under an abstract obligation to do X, and therefore the proposition that it is in A's interest to promise to do X implies that it is in A's interest to be under an abstract obligation to do X. We have to add to (B, 1) the clause, 'provided everyone else is', because we are talking about a contract, i.e., a mutual promise, and not about a gratuitous promise. I think it is plain that the implication holds also in reverse; a point which is important in elucidating the sense, of the previous section, in which it is in everyone's interest that everyone should be required to act as obligation principles require.

Now (B, 1) says that it is in everyone's interest to be under an obligation to do X provided everyone else is. But the sense in which it is in everyone's interest to be under an obligation can only be the sense in which *being under an obligation is in everyone's interest*. It was the sense in which this italicized proposition is true which eluded us in the section *Edicts and Obligation Principles*: the sense in which *this* proposition is true while it is false that subjection to the edicts of an authority must be in everyone's interest. It is the truth we expressed in that section by saying that the requirement placed upon everyone by an obligation principle must be, *in some sense*, in everyone's interest. Thus the proposition (B, 1) implies:

(B, 2) It is in everyone's interest, in some sense, that everyone should be required to do X

(B, 2) is the conclusion of the second deductive chain. It must now be compared with the conclusion of the first deductive chain:

(A, 2) It is in everyone's interest, in some sense, that everyone should be required to do Not-X

In a short while, we shall be able to understand what the sense, referred to in (A, 2) and (B, 2) is. But for the moment it is irrelevant. For whatever it is, it is the *same* in both propositions: it is the same because it is the sense, whatever it may be, in which everyone's being under an obligation is in everyone's interest.

Conclusion

The first chain of the contract argument has the conclusion:

(A, 2) It is in everyone's interest, in some sense, that everyone should be required to do Not-X

The second chain has the conclusion:

(B, 2) It is in everyone's interest, *in the same sense*, that everyone should be required to do X

These propositions may both be false because X may be a class of actions which, done by one person, does not have any effect upon others, e.g., X may be reading novels. But they cannot both be true. Thus, the propositions from which they are respectively deduced cannot both be true. If the contract ground is true of a class of actions X, then the supposition that Not-X is obligatory in the society is false. The alternatives remain that either X is neutral or that X is obligatory. To show that the contract ground asserted of X implies that X is (abstractly) obligatory, we need a complementary proof that it implies that X is *not* (abstractly) neutral.

Complementary Proof

The required proof is short. I shall argue that the proposition that X is abstractly neutral implies that it is *not* in everyone's interest to make a contract or do X; a claim which must not be confused with saying that it implies that it is not in everyone's interest to do X. The latter claim is distinct and false. For example, going to bed in the afternoon is abstractly neutral, but it could be in everyone's interest not to do it: it may be that the sun is at its best in the afternoon and that everyone likes the sun. But saying so is very different from saying that it is in everyone's interest to make a contract not to do it. It is the contradictory of the latter which is implied by the proposition that X is abstractly neutral, and it is for this claim that I shall now argue.

When we say that X is abstractly neutral, part of what we are saying is that neither x nor not-x, done by one person, adversely affects others by virtue of x's being a member of the class X. Either x or not-x may indeed adversely affect others, but only by virtue of x's being also a member of another class. For example, playing golf is abstractly neutral; it is a class of actions which does

7   G G O

not adversely affect others. But a particular act of playing golf may affect others adversely because it is also a member of another class which is not abstractly neutral, e.g., neglecting one's wife, cheating or failing to do one's job. Thus, from 'X is abstractly neutral' it follows that people are not adversely affected by the commission or omission of actions of that class; and it follows, as is obvious, that it is *not* in everyone's interest to make a contract to do X or to do Not-X. Consequently, if it *is* in everyone's interest to make a contract to do X, it follows that X is not abstractly neutral.

Thus, so far as the bare bones go, the proof is completed that the contract ground asserted of a certain class of actions implies that that class of actions is abstractly obligatory. With the proviso that further elucidation is to come, and that the whole scheme has to be subjected to one qualification, we have set out the ground of the most general obligation principles, where the obligation is basic and, so far, abstract. The conclusion as to the ground of such judgements should not be surprising. We saw in chapter 2 that if A has an abstract obligation to B, not arising out of a promise, the relations between him and B are identical with those which would hold if he had promised, except that in the latter case he would have promised while in the former he would not. It is not then surprising that the ground of the most general principles should be connected in the way found with the reasons which everyone would have for making a contract with everyone else, viz., that it is in everyone's interest to do so.

An Objection

It has been suggested that the contract argument has the consequence that there cannot be any such thing as a conflict of obligations because it implies that X and Not-X cannot both be abstractly obligatory. But the mistake lies not with the contract argument; it lies with the critic's analysis of a conflict of obligations as a matter of both X and Not-X being abstractly obligatory. The correct analysis is as follows: In talking about X being abstractly obligatory, we are talking about a class of actions taken in abstraction from particular circumstances. A conflict of obligations arises when an action which is open to a man in particular circumstances falls under two different classes of actions both of which are abstractly obligatory or the reverse. For example, the action of telling a man where a gun is is abstractly neutral. Considered in abstraction from particular circumstances it is neither right nor wrong. But we can imagine circumstances in which this action falls under the class described as aiding a murderer and in which the alternative falls under the class described as telling a lie. Both these classes of action are abstractly wrong and so a conflict of obligations results. A conflict of obligations does not consist in both X and Not-X being abstractly obligatory, 'X' being, it will be remembered, a symbol for a class of actions. To say this is like saying that it is abstractly obligatory both not to kill and to kill our neighbours, which is absurd. This is sufficient to show that my account does not make a conflict of obligations impossible and that the appearance of its doing so results from a faulty analysis of the possibility of such a conflict.

4. CONTRACTUALLY HARMONIZED INTERESTS

I have argued for, and been operating with, the following implication:

X is abstractly obligatory in the society
implies
It is in everyone's interest *in some sense* that everyone should be required to do X

This implication was involved in the contract argument. The fact that we did not know what the sense was did not matter because it was evidently the same in the conclusion of both deductive chains. But it is now time to make clear what the sense is; and the answer is, in fact, already implicit in the argument. We saw earlier that, by the argument of chapter 2, the contract ground is logically equivalent to the proposition:

(B, 1) It is in everyone's interest to be under an abstract obligation to do X provided everyone else is

It is plain that it is since (B, 1) asserts that the state of everyone's being under an obligation to everyone else is in everyone's interest; and the contract ground asserts that the state of everyone's being contracted to everyone else is in everyone's interest. Now, the sense in which it is in everyone's interest to be under an obligation can, as we have seen, only be the sense in which being under an obligation is in everyone's interest. And this is precisely the sense we were after, in *Edicts and Obligation Principles*, with the formula, 'It is in everyone's interest, in some sense, that everyone should be required to do X'. But as the proposition (B, 1) is logically equivalent to the contract ground, it follows that the sense in which it is in everyone's interest that everyone should be required to do X is this: that it is in everyone's interest to make a contract with everyone else to do X, i.e., that it is in everyone's interest to *place himself* under an obligation provided everyone else does; that it is in everyone's interest contractually to place the requirement upon himself along with everyone else. Thus the sense in which the requirement upon everyone is in everyone's interest may be expressed by saying that it is in the *contractually harmonized interests* of everyone. Thus we can write the implication at the head of this section:

X is abstractly obligatory in a society
implies
It is in everyone's interest to make a contract with everyone else to do X

The implication between the contract ground and the obligatoriness of the class of actions specified is a mutual implication. Apparent material objections can be brought against this claim, i.e., objections of the form, 'Here is a class of actions of which the antecedent is true and the consequent false'. To anyone who wishes to object on such a ground, I can only plead that he suspends judgement. I believe it is possible to answer him given time.

It is very important that this *is* the sense in which the proposition that X is abstractly obligatory implies that it is in everyone's interest that everyone should be required to do X, i.e., that the implicandum is that it is in everyone's interest to make a *contract* with everyone else to do X. And it is very important that the implication does not hold if the implicandum is: It is in everyone's interest that everyone should *do* X. If this implication held, then its negation would imply the negation of the proposition that X is abstractly obligatory in the society. And with a modified version of the complementary proof, the contract ground and the contract argument would be condemned as otiose. An obligation proposition would be implied by a proposition in terms of everyone's interest, and the notion of contract would not be involved.

The truth is that the implication does not hold if the consequent is understood in this way for, with this understanding, the antecedent may be true and the consequent false. The point may be brought out by considering a man of such ingenuity and cunning that, for any class of obligatory actions we care to take, he may neglect to do actions of that class without incurring any of the penalties attached to doing so. Such a man is of some interest in this inquiry, and he deserves a special name. I shall call him the Master Criminal. Now a man with the exceptional talents of the Master Criminal may indeed be happier if he does not exercise them. He may be more at ease with himself if he conforms along with other members of his society. But he may not. He may find life most satisfactory in exercising his talent on numerous occasions. Under this circumstance, the putative consequent of the implication is false: it is not in everyone's interest that everyone should do X because it is not in the Master Criminal's interest that he should do X. It may indeed be in his interest that everyone else should, but not that he should. The consequent of the alleged implication is false and the antecedent is true. Thus, with the consequent understood in the way under discussion, the implication does not hold.

By contrast, the Master Criminal is not an exception if the consequent is understood in the way proposed, viz., that it is in everyone's interest to make a contract with everyone else to do X. For, even with the talents at his disposal, it is in his interest to enter into the contract with everyone else; it is an effective way of ensuring that other people do X, a state of affairs which suits him well. It can be in his interest to make a contract to do X without its being in his interest to do X. This particular threat to the contract argument is chimerical. It may however be suggested that in arguing that it is not in the interest of the Master Criminal to do X, I have been taking it that his independent interest is in question; and that while it is true that doing X is not in his independent interest, it by no means follows that it is not in his interest assessed non-independently. The objection, I am afraid, carries no weight. The fact is that it is *against* the Master Criminal's interest to do X; it is not *in* his interest assessed either independently or non-independently. *Doing* X is against his interest. There is indeed a sense in which the *requirement to do* X is in his interest. But the sense in which the requirement is in his interest is, as will be seen (3, 14) just this: that it is in his interest to make a contract with everyone else to do *X*. And it is with the consequent understood in this way, and in this way only, that the implication at the head of this section is claimed to hold.

The Master Criminal is one of the apparent exceptions mentioned at the end of the section *Edicts and Obligation Principles*. I said that he was an apparent exception because the consequent of the implication might have been understood by a reader of that section in the way now rejected. If it is understood in that way, then he is an exception. But it is now clear that it cannot be understood in that way if the implication is to hold.

5. ENTRENCHED LEGAL INSTITUTIONS

The first apparent exception to the claim made in *Edicts and Obligation Principles* arises from the possibility of a certain kind of individual, the Master Criminal; the second from the possibility of a certain state of affairs. A society may be imagined in which it is not in everyone's interest to make a certain contract only because there is a law which has a bearing upon the question; in which, that is, it would be in everyone's interest if there were no such law. Consider, as an example, a society in which Group *A* are legally bound to give four-fifths of their income to Group *B* for the latter's pleasure. They have a legal obligation to do so, but the question arises whether they have a moral obligation in the matter, the mode of the concept involved being basic and abstract. According to the thesis developed here, the question is answered by asking whether it is in everyone's interest to make a contract whereby Group *A* give four-fifths of their income to Group *B* for the latter's pleasure. The answer may well be that it is not: it is not in the interest of Group *A* and therefore not in everyone's interest. So there is no moral obligation. Suppose we now ask whether it is in everyone's interest to make a contract whereby everyone is left in full possession of his income—apart, of course, from contributions, such as taxes, which are needed to run the society. The answer to this question may also be negative—because under the *status quo* Group *B* are already assured of receiving four-fifths of the income of Group *A*. As the law stands, part of Group *A*'s income already comes to them, and it is hardly in their interest to make a contract whereby they lose it. Thus, according to the thesis presented here, there is no obligation to leave others in full possession of their income. And as there is no obligation that Group *A* give part of their income to Group *B*, we have the conclusion that both classes of action are morally neutral.

This is a result which no enthusiasm for a theory would render palatable. Moreover, the case discussed reveals a rule for constructing limitless numbers of cases in which the contract argument will break down in the same way: it is necessary only to imagine an unjust law which favours one group in a society at the expense of another, and which has a bearing on the question of whether it is in everyone's interest to make a contract about a given class of actions. The outcome in every case will be moral neutrality for the class of actions. But the fact that this rule works shows what has been left out of the contract argument as so far stated. The assessment of a law as just or unjust is logically posterior to the assessment of a class of actions as right or wrong. But in the case just discussed, an unjust law has been allowed to enter into determining whether a class of actions is right, wrong or morally neutral. For it has been allowed to bear upon the question of whether it is in everyone's interest to make a contract in regard to that class of actions. This is a logical mistake which has been brought to light by an unacceptable conclusion. In applying the contract argument, any law which affects the truth of the contract ground has to be discounted if this error is to be avoided. This is not to say that any *unjust* laws have to be discounted, for that would beg too many questions. It is to say that *any* law which bears upon the truth value of the contract ground for a given class of actions has to be discounted. It must not be asked simply whether the contract ground is true of a class of actions *X*, but whether it is true under the condition that no law and no entrenched legal institution has a bearing on the question. As an example of such an institution, I have given that whereby individuals of one group are legally obliged to make over four-fifths of their income to others for the latter's pleasure. Other examples are the institutions of chattel slavery, monopoly, hereditary privilege and race discrimination, legally backed. To say that laws authorizing such institutions have to be imagined away before we can properly ask whether the contract ground is true of a class of actions is not to say that these institutions and the actions involved in them are *ipso facto* wrong. It is to say that laws which authorize them have to be discounted before we can properly ask whether they are. Nor is it to say that we have to imagine away all laws and legal institutions; any attempt to do so would result only in bewilderment. Those only which bear upon a particular question have to be discounted.

This completion of the contract argument does not imply that classes of action are obligatory in a society only if there is no law which has a bearing upon the question of whether it is in everyone's interest to make a contract. If it did the world would be largely denuded of morals. All it implies is that if we wish to find out whether a class of actions is obligatory we have to consider the society with relevant laws and legal institutions removed, i.e., imagine a situation in which no group of individuals is already favoured by the legal *status quo*.

6. THE TYRANT

A society may be ruled by a tyrant of immense power. It may be in the interest of each of his subjects to become a party to numerous contracts. But it may not be in the tyrant's interest to do so for he has at his disposal a more powerful means of securing for himself any of the advantages to be gained; he has at his command the instruments of force. Should it seem implausible to say that it is in his interest to become a party to no contracts, at least we may suppose that there are many of which it is so. Thus, for many classes of action of which we ask whether it is in everyone's interest to make a contract concerning them, the answer is positive if the tyrant is left out of account, but negative if he is included. We may seem to be committed to saying that such a society can have only a sparse set of obligation principles—only a small number of the principles it would have in the absence of the tyrant; or that it has the full set of principles appropriate to the interests of the subjects, but that the tyrant is substantially outside morality—that many of the principles, although they apply to the subjects, do not apply to him. The second alternative might involve us in saying, for example, that although each of the subjects had an obligation not to take the wife of another subject to his bed, the tyrant had no such obligation, but was morally free to demand any woman. And the first alternative might involve us in saying that everyone was morally free to take the wife of another even though, in the absence of the tyrant, he would not be.

Something again plainly is wrong. In fact, the mistake is the same as that which we learned to avoid in the previous section. States of affairs, such as that in which a tyrant of immense power rules over a society, are assessable as just or unjust in the same way as laws are assessable under these concepts; and the assessment is logically posterior to the assessment of classes of actions as right or wrong. The tyrant operates by issuing edicts and ensuring that they are obeyed by force and threats of force. A quasi legal system operates in the tyrant ruled society. Except in degree, the situation is not different from that discussed in the previous section. The difference is that we must consider the possibility that most of the rules the tyrant makes are unjust, whereas in the more usual kind of society some, but not most, of the laws are unjust. Now if the assessment of a tyrant's rules as just or unjust is logically posterior to the assessment of classes of actions as right or wrong, it is a logical mistake to allow the existence of an unjust rule to play a part in determining the truth value of the contract ground. It is a mistake of the same kind as that which we avoided earlier by refusing to allow an unjust law to play a similar part. But as we could not say in the previous case, that unjust laws must be discounted without begging too many questions, so in this case, we cannot say that unjust rules enforced by the tyrant must be discounted. In determining the truth value of the contract ground for a class of actions, any rule of the kind considered must be discounted if it bears upon the question.

Neither of the unacceptable alternatives with which the conception of a tyrant ruled society seemed to present us is a consequence of the thesis advanced. The contract argument stands, with suitable emendations, in the face of such considerations. But at this stage it has become obvious, I think, that the search for the grounds of judgements of obligation will not provide us with any simple and easily applied decision procedure for the truth value of such judgements.

7. SOCIETIES AND BASIC OBLIGATION

In stating the contract argument, it was assumed that we could say that some classes of actions were obligatory in the society with which we were dealing. This enabled us to suppose that Not-X was obligatory. We were then able to show that this could not be true if the contract ground was true of the class of actions X. It followed that X was either abstractly neutral or obligatory. A complementary proof to show that, given the truth of the contract ground, the first alternative could not be true left us with the conclusion that the second was. The argument enables us, given that some actions are obligatory, to answer the question 'Which?'

The proposition that some classes of actions are obligatory in the society is essential to the argument, and it is now time to look at it more closely. It is easily seen that it is not a necessary proposition. We can imagine a society in which any restrictions upon people's actions are pointless simply because they do by nature what, if their nature were different, they would have to be guided into doing either by reasons or sanctions. Kant conceived of such a society under the title of holy wills. As any restrictions are pointless, obligation principles are pointless, and we could not say of such a society, 'Some classes of actions are obligatory here'. We must now see what it comes to to say it of a given society. In chapter 2 the notion of A's being under a basic obligation to B was elucidated in terms of its implication relations to B's rights, the justification of blame, A's trustworthiness, moral good, and the reason there is for A's acting in the way enjoined. The elucidation is readily extended to the case of general principles which we have been discussing. To say that some classes of action are basically obligatory in a society is to say that this conceptual structure is employed in their thought about certain kinds of practical problem. And this is to say that the individuals of the society have the concept of basic obligation, and that they apply it over a wide range of problems. The latter qualification is needed because the members of the society of holy wills may have the concept of basic obligation; they may make promises which would be impossible otherwise; but there would be no point in their applying it over a wider field. Indeed, they have no problems to which it could be applied.

It is worth looking at another society in which the concept of basic obligation is not employed on the range of problems in question. We can imagine a people among whom all the restrictions needed if they are to exist as a society are provided by the edicts of an authority. Unlike the tyrant, the authority may be supposed benevolent, and we may suppose that the only reason ever given for doing or refraining from an action is that the authority commands it and that he is benevolent. In such a society we could not say that some classes of actions are basically obligatory. We could say that they are commanded by a benevolent authority, and as this proposition has no implication about anyone's rights, the complementary notions of rights and basic obligation are still not involved in their thought about practical problems. Moreover, the reasons which the individuals of such a society give are quite different from those given in a society of which we can say that some classes of action are basically obligatory. The reason which they give is that the action is commanded by a benevolent authority. But in a society in which some classes of action are basically obligatory, the reasons given are, I should maintain, reasons which support the contract ground as asserted of the class of actions in question. If it is suggested that 'X is commanded by a benevolent authority' does support the contract ground asserted of X, the answer must be that 'benevolent' is a very commodious term and that for the purposes of the example it must be understood in such a way that it does not. The authority may, for example, issue edicts on the principle that the actions enjoined improve everyone's lot but the lot of his friends most of all. He is still benevolent, but such a principle would not yield the same results as the contract ground. The term 'a right' may indeed be used in such a society. But if a friend of the authority were to claim a right to one of the unfavoured doing an action enjoined by this principle, it is manifest that his claim would be a very different thing from a right claimed on the basis of the contract ground.

It has sometimes been said that the recognition of obligation principles, and therefore obligation principles themselves, are necessary conditions of the existence of societies. But the two cases just discussed show that it is not so. It is true that if most of the people most of the time do not do actions of those classes which would be basically obligatory given that some classes were, the society to which they belong would soon cease to be a society. But it does not follow that any classes of action are basically obligatory. A society of holy wills is an obvious exception; and we can imagine an edict ruled group, constituting beyond doubt a society, in which no actions are basically obligatory. Of such a society, we might indeed say that they ought to recognize obligation principles or that the restrictions upon their actions ought to be provided by such principles. In such judgements we use the word 'ought', but we use it in one of the residual ways to which attention has already been drawn (1, 11). We are to be understood as saying that there is good reason for their recognizing obligation principles. The judgement could no doubt be defended, but it is not a judgement in which the basic mode of the concept of obligation is involved.

The contract argument has no application unless some classes of action are obligatory in the society to which we seek to apply it; unless, that is, the individuals of the society have the concept of basic obligation and apply it over a wide range of practical problems. Saying this of the society goes hand in hand with saying that for the most part certain classes of action are done, and that the reasons given for the judgement that they ought to be done are reasons which support the contract ground, i.e., reasons of a kind which are not given in an edict ruled society. If it were not so, it is plain enough that the concept of basic obligation would soon be lost. The pattern of our argument by no means consists in deriving obligations from some Cartesian bedrock, a procedure which has been attacked often enough. We could by no means apply it to a group of people in a state of nature and prove that they had this or that obligation. They have no obligations. The pattern of the argument is quite different from this. We consider any society as it is now of which we can say that some classes of actions are obligatory; a society which already has a more or less flourishing moral existence. We then show that the supposition that Not-X is obligatory is incompatible with the contract ground asserted of X. If the latter is true, it cannot be consistently held that Not-X is obligatory. Complementary argument then shows that all that can consistently be held is that X is obligatory.

The contract ground asserted of X may be true of a society S, but it may still be false that X is abstractly obligatory in that society. It may be a society in which no classes of action are obligatory. The implication of the contract ground is that a certain class of actions is obligatory in a society in which some classes are. Its merit is not that it enables us to pass from a state of nature to a full-blown moral system. Its merit is that it enables us to determine *which* classes of action are obligatory in a society in which *some* are.

8. MATERIAL OBJECTIONS

I must now consider an important type of objection to the theory I have been advancing. It consists in taking a class of actions which practically everyone thinks is abstractly obligatory and saying that it does not satisfy the contract ground. It is admitted that it would be in the interest of the majority of people to make a contract, but it is maintained that there are quite large numbers of exceptions whose interest would not be served by doing so. Consider stealing as an example. I think it is easy to argue that the interest of the majority of people would be served by making a contract with others not to steal—that they would be better off by being bound in this way than by being 'free' to purloin each other's goods and chattels and have others purloin theirs in return. This is not to say that it is equally in the interests of each to make it. There is a clear sense in which it is not, for the well-endowed have more to lose by its absence than the relatively poorly endowed. But, provided we are still speaking of the majority, it is easy to argue that it is in the interest of all to make the contract in the sense that they all stand to be better off with it than without it. At this point the objector moves in with his big guns and asks: What about the destitute and the starving? Can you seriously maintain that it would be in their interest to make a no-stealing contract when they could to some extent alleviate their misery by stealing as opportunity arose? Surely not!

This pattern of objection can be repeated in case after case as brief reflection will show. It is plain enough that people are vastly unequal in natural endowments—in intelligence, in qualities of character, in looks, tastes and so on; that they are vastly unequal in the human relations they enjoy, their capacities for pleasure and the experiences they are able to appreciate. It may seem that when we approach the bottom of the scales, we arrive at people of whom the contract ground is not true even though it is true of the same classes of action for all people above certain points on the scales.

Returning to our example of theft and the destitute, I think that what the objector says very probably is true. I do not know for certain because it is a complex contingent question about what best satisfies the interests of classes of people. But let us suppose for the sake of argument that it is not in the interest of the destitute to make a contract with everyone else to forgo stealing. It may seem that this quite destroys the contract argument; and that as the same pattern of objection can be repeated over and over again for other classes of action, the poor thing lies shattered at our feet.

The fact is quite otherwise. The contract argument is untouched by this pattern of objection. All it shows is that when we think of our abstract obligation not to steal, we are failing to specify completely the subject of that obligation. The fact is that if it is not true that it is in everyone's interest to make a contract to forgo theft, some compensatory class of actions must be included in the terms of the contract, the compensatory class being such that, when it is included, it *is* in everyone's interest to make the contract. If 'the destitute' is the name applied to those whose interest is not served by becoming a party to the contract when its terms do not include a compensatory clause, then the compensatory clause must be to the effect that those who are not destitute will help those who are. This, of course, is not a precise formulation. It shows only the way such a formulation would have to go. Such precision as is possible will be achieved by so specifying the class of compensatory actions that it is in everyone's interest, including the interest of the destitute, to become a party to the contract.

The philosophy of morals advocated here, when taken in conjunction with certain facts about the interests of human beings, yields substantial moral consequences. This makes possible the kind of objection we have been considering—a material objection—and also lays upon the theory a certain burden. Any such theory would be damned outright if it came up with the consequences that it was perfectly in order to rape on inclination, eat your neighbour's children, embezzle the funds, steal as you please and drive a car only when intoxicated. But it is a very different matter for such a theory to come up with the consequence that many of the classes of action which we believe to be abstractly obligatory are not specified as fully as they ought to be. Against this there can be no complaint, and it is all that is shown by the objection just discussed.

It shows that we must not take so simple a view of our abstract obligations. Some of the judgements we make about them are no doubt true without qualification, and some are no doubt wholly false. Between these two extremes, they provide a vast body of coarse grained truth in need of systematic refinement. Material objections of the kind discussed consist in offering an element of this crude truth as an objection to a theory which provides the means for refining it.

9. THE TIME OF CONTRACT AND COMPLEMENTARY CLASSES

In this section, and sometimes subsequently, I shall use language which might suggest that the individual members of societies have actually made contracts with one another. Such language avoids verbiage and is adopted solely for that reason. Its adoption is in no way a withdrawal from the earlier insistence that the contract theory advanced here makes no such claim.

If we are to assert that it is in everyone's interest to make contracts concerning certain classes of actions, we must be armed with an answer to the question, 'When? At what time in each individual's life?' It is plain that the answer cannot be, 'When he reaches the age of maturity' or 'At the age of 21'; for later in his life, when he is say 70, he will stand in relations of obligation to people who are then 21, and to explain these relations we should have to suppose that it made sense to say that, when he was 21, it was in his interest to make contracts with people who were not yet born. A more promising answer is that in asserting the contract ground we are saying that it is in every individual's interest to make certain contracts at any time in his mature life, the contracts applying to all subsequent times in his life. But this suggestion meets the objection that it may be in a man's interest to make different contracts at different times in his life; so that at some times he may be morally required, by virtue of a contract which was in his interest at an earlier time, to do actions of classes in regard to which it is not in his interest, at a later time, to make a contract. The suggestion is self contradictory. But the difficulty may be avoided by introducing the idea that contracts become renewable when the interests of any party change in such a way that a contract which was previously in his interest is no longer so. We suppose that the contracts apply not to all subsequent times in the lives of the parties, but to all subsequent times prior to any change in interest which makes them revisable; and that a covering clause to this effect qualifies any contract of which we say that it is in everyone's interest to make it. In speaking of its being in everyone's interest to make a particular contract we are to be understood as saying that it is in everyone's interest to make the contract at any time in his life, the contract applying to all subsequent times so long as his interests remain unchanged. It is vitally important not to confuse the assertion that it is in a man's interest to make a contract to do X with the assertion that it is in his interest to do X. Obviously, a man is often required by the contract ground to do actions which it is not in his interest to do, his interest being assessed independently. But the fact is no basis for claiming that the contracts which were in his interest previously are renewable. Such a claim, if allowed, would defeat the object of the entire exercise. The contract is due for revision only if a man's interests so change that there is a change in the contracts which are in his interest, i.e., only if it is not true now that it is in his interest to make such and such a contract although it was true at an earlier time. For example, he may in later life come to enjoy some activity which is ruled out by a contract which was in his interest earlier because, at that earlier time, he did not enjoy that activity. Under such a circumstance the contract is due for revision, not perhaps to the extent of permitting the activity, but to the extent of including some compensatory class of actions in the subject of the contract. In practice no change is likely to be required by such a change in interest. The probability is that, at the earlier time, some other member of the society will have enjoyed the activity he now enjoys, and that the new element in his interest will be allowed for in the existing contract. But it need not be so. The thesis advanced is clearly different from saying that a contract is due for revision when a man is required by that contract to do an action which it is against his interest to do, his interest being assessed independently. The latter suggestion is absurd; the former is, I hope, correct.

It may seem that the contracts which are in a man's interest are not the same when he is old and feeble as when he is young and virile. To take an extreme case as an example, it may be said that it is in the interest of the young to kill off the old as a burden upon them; and that it is in the interest of the old to curb all those activities in the young which, in many cases, they find so irksome. It may seem that the contracts which are in their interest reflect these interests. But we have to remember that any contract which is to be the ground of an obligation principle must be in the interest of every member of the society; the young and the old, geniuses and fools, the halt and the lame, the courageous and the cowardly. When we ask what contracts it is in everyone's interest to make, we are asking the question of any time in any man's mature life. Whatever time we may select, 'everyone' will cover an enormous variety of people, and the content of the contracts is determined accordingly. It may indeed be in the interests of the young to kill off the old people, but it is hardly in the interest of the old to be killed off. And if it seems that the young have the overwhelming bargaining power, we have to remember that any contract which may be in the interest of the young while they are young will apply to them at all subsequent times in their lives. One day they will be in the position of the old people with whom they seek so hardly to bargain. One day they will be old too; a reflection sufficient to show that, while they are young, it is not in their interest to drive a bargain which is in their interest only while they are young.

To say that the contract determines obligation principles which apply to all subsequent times in people's lives requires qualification against possible changes in interest in a way we have already seen. We have to say that it applies only so long as changes in interest do not occur which require its revision. But it does not require qualification against changes in interest which are a consequence *only* of growing old. Any qualifications of that kind will be included in the subject of the contract and will not require a covering clause to the effect that the contract applies only while interests remain unchanged. They will be included by virtue of the bargaining power of the old people who are a party to the contract and by virtue of the fact that the young people who are a party to it will one day be old people.

The consideration of people who differ in the way the young differ from the old shows that an extension of the notion of compensatory clauses, introduced in the last section, is required. Some of the contracts will require the young to do certain kinds of action for the benefit of the old and the old to do certain kinds of action for the benefit of the young; and the consequent obligation principle requires actions of the one kind from the young and actions of another kind from the old. This is another case in which an obligation principle does not enjoin a single class of actions, but enjoins one class of actions upon one section of the community and another upon another section. This is likely, I think, usually to be the case; and I shall mark it by saying that, in general, an obligation principle enjoins *complementary* classes of action.

It may seem that to speak of bargaining power in the way I have is to put forward a thoroughly egoistic theory. But we are talking of the *reasons* which can be given for acting in certain ways; no comment whatsoever is being made about the *motives* from which people act. There is no doubt whatsoever that when young people act for the benefit of old people they very often do so from purely altruistic motives. But we are not concerned with motives at this point. We are speaking of the reason which can be given for acting in certain ways. And a reason has to be such that no man can reject it without forfeiting his claim to rationality. It has to commend itself as a reason to a man who has no good will towards his fellows, provided only that he understands what is being said to him. The fact that people very often act from altruistic motives is irrelevant to the questions discussed here, and an irrelevant comment upon the theory proposed.

It will be worth giving another example of an obligation principle which enjoins complementary classes of action. It may be in the interest of every member of a society to make a contract whereby a sub-class in the society, e.g., parents with children under 18, undertake to treat third parties, e.g., their children under 18, in certain ways; and the remaining sub-class undertake not to impede them. Most parents want to bring up their own children and it is usually in their interest to do so. But they have no 'natural' right to. From the fact that Master *A* was sired by Mr *A* out of Mrs *A* it does not follow that Mr and Mrs *A* have the right to nurture him. 'Rights' do not come from 'is's' that easily. They are deducible from the contract ground. Some members of the society are not parents, and some are parents whose children have grown up. It is in the interest of these classes that there should be a healthy rising generation, and it is in their interest also that it should be reared by its progenitors. The alternative is that the burden falls upon society at large with a consequent rise in taxation. It is also, as a rule, in the interest of parents to rear their own children. Thus it is in the interest of both parties to make a contract whereby parents nurture their offspring in certain ways and others do not impede their doing so. This, in outline, is the application of the contract ground to this case. From the contract ground asserted of these complementary classes of action it follows that parents have the right to bring up their own children in certain ways (not, for example, as pickpockets), and that others have the right to their doing so. The contract ground explains also the foundation of the right, which society has at large, to remove children from parents who neglect them or otherwise lead them into bad ways. In regard to the nurture of children, a basic obligation principle again enjoins complementary classes of action: that parents bring up their children in certain ways, and that others do not interfere provided they do so.

We have been speaking of rights and basic obligations only. Most parents also have ultra obligations in relation to their children, and the ground of such obligations is quite different.

10. PUNISHMENT

The contract ground will not be true of any class of actions unless people have reason to believe that others will respect the contracts into which they enter. We cannot assert that it is in everyone's interest to make a contract with everyone else in regard to any class of actions unless there is reason for everyone to believe that the majority of people will respect their contracts. This is a matter of concern, for if the contract ground is not true of any class of actions, or of any complementary classes of actions, the thesis for which I am arguing commits me to the absurd view that all obligation principles are false.

If I am right in holding that 'A promised, or contracted, to do X' implies 'There is a reason for A's doing X which is better than any in terms of his independent interest for doing either X or Not-X'; and if people were such that they always did actions of classes for which there was better reason; then there would be no problem facing us at this point. If these two propositions were true, we should no longer be able to deny the contract ground asserted of any class of actions on the basis that there was no reason for anyone to think that other people would respect their contracts. For, given the truth of these two propositions, there would be reason to think just this. But the lamentable fact is that the second of these propositions is not true: people manifestly do not always do actions of those classes for which there is better reason. It is this fact about human nature which presents us with our problem.

How then do we make it possible for the contract ground to be true of some classes of action? The only possible answer is obtained by attaching a penalty to each of the classes of action specified in it; a penalty which will provide a motive for doing actions of that class. The contract ground has to be modified so that it reads:

> It is in everyone's interest to make a contract with everyone else to do X and to submit to an appropriate penalty if he does not do X

The appropriate penalty has to be such that, given a suitable X, (*a*) the contract ground is true, i.e., it *is* in everyone's interest, including the interest of those who are most likely to be offenders, to make a contract which includes the requirement to submit to that penalty upon failing, in appropriate circumstances, to do actions of the class X; and (*b*) it has to be such that it does provide a motive for the majority of people. The consequent principle is that everyone has an obligation to do X and that, if he does not, he has an obligation to submit to the appropriate penalty. His obligation to submit to the penalty if he does not do X is the correlative of the right of others to submit him to that penalty. The contract ground as modified to include a penalty clause is the logical source of the right to punish offenders.

I do not much like the word 'punishment'. It suggests to me that those who are due for punishment are at the mercy of those who are not. It suggests that the rights of those who have offended are a small thing beside the rights of those who have not. These barely articulate views appear to be quite widely accepted in practical life. It is of course agreed that every man has a right to a fair hearing; but once condemned, his rights are thought to recede into the background. So far as this view is articulate, it is false. In offending, a man does not forfeit any of his rights save the right not to be submitted to an appropriate penalty; and in determining what is an appropriate penalty, his interests are just as much to the point as anyone else's; for the penalty attached to a class of actions X is appropriate if and only if it is in *everyone's* interest to make a contract whereby actions of the class X are done on pain of submission to that penalty. There is no question of the interests of the offender being subordinate to the interests of those who have not offended; and there is no question of his rights being insignificant beside the rights of the virtuous. If justice is to be done, the penalties—if that is the right word—must be so designed that it is in everyone's interest to make a contract specifying them.

But they have also to be such that they provide a motive against offending for anyone who is likely to offend. These two requirements are not irreconcilable for a man who is likely to offend once or twice, even if we have available only the institutions of punishment we have at the moment. It is not obviously false to say, for example, that it is in everyone's interest to make a contract not to embezzle the firm's funds and to submit to a five year prison sentence if one does. The disadvantages of spending five years of one's life in prison are, it seems, far outweighed by the advantages of spending the remainder of one's life in an obligation bound society. This is not to say that any contract would take precisely this form provided no one was likely to offend more than once or twice, but it might. The case appears to be otherwise when we turn to the recidivist. It is by no means obvious that his contractual interest is satisfied in being forced to spend virtually the whole of his life in prison; it is by no means obvious that it is in his interest to become a party to a contract not to thieve and to submit to a prison sentence of up to so many years *every time* he is convicted of doing so. It is of course the business of a moralist, and not of a moral philosopher, to pursue questions of this kind. But the suggestion is plain: that a society which inflicts such a penalty is guilty of moral error.

11. THE LAW GIVER AND THE GENESIS OF MORALITY

We have just seen that if the contract ground is to be true of any class of actions the contract referred to must require not only that actions of that class are done but also that a penalty is submitted to in the event of failure. I shall waive the point that 'penalty' may not be the right word in all cases. The necessity for penalty clauses provides the first explicit hint of the need for what the classical social contract theorists called a Contract of Government. We are speaking here of the practical necessity of laws in a society and of the practical necessity of a Law Giver. In a nation, the Law Giver is the legislative function of government; in a tennis club it is the committee; in the Roman Catholic Church, it is the Pope, standing in for God. I shall assume that, in any society with which we have to deal, it is in the interest of everyone to make a contract whereby the law giving function is invested, upon strict conditions, in a subgroup. I shall assume also that it is in the interest of everyone to make a contract to obey the laws provided the law giving function is exercised substantially within these conditions. These assumptions are not large; anything which is controversial would hinge upon the interpretation of the phrases 'strict conditions' and 'substantially within these conditions'. The Law Giver has a job within the society. How well he does his job is measured by the justice of the laws he makes.

The presence of a Law Giver in a society appears to be a causal condition of the genesis of morality. Consider again the content of the contracts which it is in everyone's interest to make. It might be tempting to think that the contracts between people take the form: to do X for your benefit provided you do X for mine; this contract being entered into by each individual with each other individual. For example, we might think of the contract in relation to theft as taking the form: not to steal from you provided you do not steal from me; this contract being made throughout the society. In most cases, though not in all, it would be a mistake to think in terms of this pattern, for it leaves no room for a penalty clause. The only penalty would be retaliation, and the fact is that, in general, people's interests are better served by a different kind of penalty; effected in practice, in the case of theft, through a legal system. We should think of the content of the contract rather as: to do X provided most others most of the time also do X, with an appropriate penalty clause added, e.g., not to steal provided most others most of the time also do not steal, and to submit to an appropriate penalty in the event of doing so. We should think of a contract of this form being made throughout the society, i.e., entered into by each individual with each other individual. Now if a man steals from me, I still have an obligation not to steal from him, for to say that one man has stolen from me is not to deny that most people most of the time do not steal. It is not my business to deal with the offender by retaliating; the penalty clause is designed to serve that function. There may indeed be cases in which, when a man has offended against me, I do not have an obligation not to retaliate. But these will be cases in which retaliation is the most effective form of penalty; cases in which it is in everyone's interest to make a contract which includes retaliation as the appropriate penalty. Examples would perhaps be cases in which property has been borrowed and not returned or, more generally, in which kindnesses have been done and not returned.

The content of the contract ground is then, in general, of the form: to do X provided most others most of the time also do X . . . The consequent abstract obligation has that form too; an obligation principle requires us to do actions of a certain class provided most other people most of the time also do actions of that class. Consider now a society in which the contract ground is true of a class of actions X, but in which it is not recognized to be true; the consequent obligation principle is not recognized; and actions of the class X are not, for the most part, done. In this situation, if you or I came to recognize the truth of the contract ground for X, we still would not have an obligation to do actions of that class. For what we should have recognized is that it is in the interest of everyone in the society to make a contract whose content is: to do X provided most others most of the time also do X. But we are members of a society in which X is not for the most part done, and we should not have an obligation, in this circumstance, to do X. This is to say that in this circumstance there would be no obligation upon Tom, Dick and Harry. It is not to say that there are not some people who, in this situation and given this knowledge, would not think, and correctly think, that *they* ought to do X. But their judgement is one of ultra obligation, a judgement which depends, in ways to be seen, upon their character. A reason can be given for saying that they ought to do X. But no reason can be given for saying that Tom, Dick and Harry ought to; it is no more possible to give them a reason than it is possible to give A a reason for doing an action by pointing out to him that it is in B's interest that B should do that action. If we were to tell them that they ought to do actions of the class X, actions that is, of a class of which the contract ground is true but not recognized to be true, their justifiable retort would be, 'Induce most of the others to do such actions and then we will accept that we have an obligation to do them'.

As this is so, how does a hitherto unknown moral truth ever come to be known and respected? Well, it may just come to pass. But it is more likely that it will be proclaimed by a Law Giver who has greater insight than the general run of the society or, failing it himself, the advice of others who have. The law proclaimed will include a penalty for infringement with the consequence that the greater number of people in the society will soon come to obey it. The condition that most of the people most of the time do actions of the class enjoined is now satisfied, and, supposing the law is sanctioned by the contract ground, everyone has in consequence an obligation to do actions of that class. The Law Giver functions as a catalyst. This function no doubt explains why a Law Giver is the apparent source of all historical moral systems, but I think enough has been said to show where his function, in this respect, begins, and where it ends. There is no question of the command of a Law Giver being the logical ground of obligation principles; and, as goes without saying, the position is not different if he happens to be God.

For simplicity, I have omitted in this section any discussion of complementary classes of action. Such a discussion would be cumbersome, and it poses no problems which cannot be solved on the basis of what has already been said.

12. SPECIFIC OBLIGATION PRINCIPLES AND
ACTUAL OBLIGATIONS

So far I have considered only principles which are directly deduced from the contract ground. Some of the principles place the same requirement upon all individuals of a society; others, which enjoin complementary classes of action, place different requirements upon different classes of people, e.g., the principle relating to the nurture of children places different requirements upon parents and those who are not parents. Such principles could be said to be specific on the ground that what they require of an individual depends upon the specific class to which he belongs. But if so they should not be confused with another kind of specific principle which is simply the form taken by a general principle when applied to specific classes of people; as, for example, the obligation of owners of motor vehicles to keep their silencers in good order is one of the forms taken by the general principle to avoid causing unnecessary annoyance when applied to the owners of motor vehicles; and as the obligation of men not to rape women is the form taken by the general principle not to use violence upon others as it applies to men.

Such specific obligation principles present no difficulty. They are not deduced directly from the contract ground, but require also some premiss about the specific class of people to whom they apply, e.g., a premiss about a way in which motor vehicle owners can cause unnecessary annoyance or a way in which men can act violently towards women. There is nothing interesting for discussion here, and I shall move on to consider the application of general and specific principles to concrete cases, i.e., the question of actual obligation. Two major topics arise for discussion. They will be dealt with under the headings *Conflict of Obligations* and *Interpretation*.

Conflict of Obligations

In this chapter we have been concerned, except for occasional remarks about ultra obligations, with basic obligations only, and, up to this point, we have considered only basic obligations which are abstract. We have been concerned with the implication of the contract ground, and this implication is in terms of the abstract mode of the concept. It is now time to look at judgements of actual obligation. Abstract and actual obligations are related in the following way (2, 3): the trio of propositions (i) A has an abstract obligation to do X; (ii) A can do x; (iii) x does not also fall under another class of actions which A has a superior abstract obligation not to do—these three propositions imply that A has an actual obligation to do x. I ignore for the moment cases, which may well be the most numerous, in which the abstract obligation relates to a class of complementary actions. A simple extension of the present argument will enable us to deal quite briefly with these later. The questions to be answered are: how is our actual obligation determined when the condition (iii) is not satisfied; and what determines whether one obligation is superior to another? They are easily answered in principle. Suppose a particular action x falls under the classes X_1 and X_2 which are such that (a) X_1 satisfies the contract ground; (b) Not-X_2 satisfies the contract ground; and (c) x does not fall under any other class of actions Z such that either Z or Not-Z satisfies it. These stipulations ensure that (a') x is abstractly obligatory on the ground that it falls under the class X_1; (b') not-x is abstractly obligatory on the ground that it falls under the class Not-X_2; and (c') neither x nor not-x is abstractly obligatory on any other ground. If it is in everyone's interest to make a contract to do x (and not not-x) when x falls under the class X_1 and X_2, then X_1 is the superior abstract obligation, and the condition (c, c') ensures that it is actually obligatory to do x. And if it is in everyone's interest to make a contract to do not-x (and not to do x) when x falls under the classes X_1 and X_2, then, Not-X_2 is the superior obligation, and the condition (c, c') ensures that it is actually obligatory to do not-x. The account given of what counts as a superior obligation is obvious, but the role of the premiss (c, c') is perhaps not quite so obvious. The contract ground implies only an abstract obligation, but with the addition of the premiss (c, c') an actual obligation is implied (provided A can do x). The reason for this is that the condition (c, c') ensures that over and above x's falling under X_1 and X_2 no *further* question of abstract obligation is involved, i.e., once we have taken into account its falling under X_1 and X_2 the condition (iii) given at the beginning of this section is satisfied, and A therefore has an actual obligation to do x. The case of abstract obligations in regard to complementary actions is now easily dealt with. We simply say that the specification of a complementary class as obligatory must contain a clause, which may be complex, enjoining one or the other of the actions should there be a conflict between them. So far, this account applies when there is a conflict of *basic* obligations. Conflicts between a basic and an ultra obligation are considered later.

It may seem perversely mistaken to say that the interests of everyone in the society are relevant in determining what a man's actual obligation is in a concrete situation, and more plausible to say that only the interests of those affected by the various alternatives are to the point. 'Surely', it may be said, 'In deciding what I ought to do I should consider the effects upon A of my doing this, upon *B* of my doing that, and so on. The interests of those who are not touched by any of the alternatives are not relevant'. There are several potential confusions in this objection. In the first place, the objector must be reminded that basic obligations only are being discussed, and that what is basically obligatory may be only one of the factors involved in determining what ought to be done. The question at issue at this point is what can be demanded as a *right*. I return to other factors which may be involved later. For the moment, it must be noticed that although general principles of abstract obligation are determined, as explained, by the contractually harmonized interests of everyone in the society, other factors enter into determining which principles apply, in concrete cases, and into determining the specific action required by the principle. These factors are the relations in which the agent stands to other people, and the interests of those affected by the alternatives open to him. For example, if the agent has incurred a debt of gratitude or reparation, and an alternative open to him discharges such a debt, principles apply which would not otherwise apply. Again, a schoolmaster, physician and public relations executive stand in different relations to other people, and different forms of the obligation to do one's job properly apply to them in concrete situations. Thirdly, in certain concrete situations, the obligation covering, for example, theft and help for the destitute enjoins actions upon a rich man which it does not enjoin upon a poor one; and different actions are enjoined by general principle upon parents and non-parents. General principles of abstract obligation do indeed depend upon the contractually harmonized interests of everyone in the society; but in deciding in a concrete situation which principles, or which form of a principle, applies, or which of complementary actions are enjoined by a principle, a man is taking account of the relations in which he stands to others. For example, if he decides in a certain situation that the general obligation to return kindnesses applies and that he ought to do such-and-such for *A* he is taking account of his peculiar relation to *A*; and he is, *ipso facto*, taking account of the effects of his action upon *A* in a perfectly straightforward sense in which he is not taking account of its effects upon Tom, Dick and Harry. Again, if I find a man in a coma and can tell that he is a diabetic who needs an insulin injection, two of the alternatives open to me are to telephone for a physician or to carry on with whatever I was doing before. If I judge that I ought to call the physician, I have taken into account the interests of the sick man in a perfectly straightforward sense in which I have not taken into account the interests of those in remote corners of Ireland, Scotland and Wales. And I have taken into account the effects of the alternatives upon him in a perfectly straightforward sense in which I have not taken into account the effects upon them. Neither alternative has any effect upon them. Again, it is the interest of the sick man which determines the specific action which ought to be done: that I ought to call the physician and not, for example, sprinkle him with water or fan him with my handkerchief. But the fact remains that the proposition that I have an abstract obligation to give to another man *this* measure of help, as balanced against the trouble caused to myself, is determined by the truth of the contract ground asserted of actions of this class; it is determined, that is, by the contractually harmonized interests of everyone in the society. Suppose on another occasion I am on my way to the cinema and chance upon a man whose car has broken down. He is already covered in oil and grease, and it is plain that I can only help him by getting myself filthy. Besides, there is a garage only a few yards down the road. If I judge that I have no obligation to help him, I have again taken account of the effects of the alternative actions upon myself and upon him in a perfectly straightforward sense in which I have not taken account of their effects upon others, for they have no effect upon others. But if the judgement which I make is true, this is because there is no abstract obligation to give to another man *this* measure of help, as balanced against the trouble caused to myself. And this is to say that the contract ground is not true when asserted of actions of this class, i.e., actions which consist in giving this measure of help. If I am to have an actual obligation to do a particular action x, this action must be a member of a class X which is abstractly obligatory upon me—and it must also be true that I can do x and that doing it does not involve violating a superior obligation. I have an actual obligation because these conditions are satisfied. The proposition that X is abstractly obligatory is true if and only if the contract ground is true of that class of actions, i.e., it depends upon the contractually harmonized interests of everyone in the society. But if x is a member of the class X it must be an action which affects somebody. If it affects A and A only, then in judging that I have an actual obligation to do x I am taking account of the effect of my action upon A in a perfectly straightforward sense in which I am not taking account of its effects upon anyone else.

If it is now objected that the *measure* of help which ought to be given depends only upon the interests of those concerned, the objector must again be reminded that basic obligations only are under discussion. It is true that if a situation calls for help to another not in excess of a certain measure, then the help which ought to be given depends only upon the interests of the man affected: it depends upon the help needed. But the important point is that the measure of help required by basic obligation is limited. It is limited because it is plain that the contract ground is true of some degrees of help, such as telephoning a physician to save the diabetic's life in the case considered, and it is false of some greater degrees of help such as helping the other man with his broken down car at the expense of getting filthy. In speaking of the degree of help, it is the differential between the benefit to the patient and the disbenefit to the agent which is in question. And it is plain enough that the contract ground is true of some degrees of help and false of some others, though it is not plain where the line is to be drawn. We may say that we have a basic obligation of *limited beneficence*, and that we have the right to limited beneficence, the limit depending upon the contract ground. An individual may, of course, have the right to a greater degree of help from another because he has previously done a greater service for the other. But if he has it is because we have an obligation to return kindnesses; and this obligation too is a consequence of the truth of the contract ground asserted of that class of actions; it arises out of the contractually harmonized interests of everyone.

I have tried to explain the ways in which the interests of everyone in the society, on the one hand, and the interests of those affected, on the other, are relevant in determining an actual obligation in a concrete situation. I must stress again that basic obligations and rights alone have been under discussion. It will be argued in the next chapter that many people have ultra obligations which require them to do more for others than those others are entitled to by right. It must not be forgotten that in many moral situations we are not directly concerned with basic obligations and rights at all. Sometimes we are concerned with determining what is ultra obligatory upon ourselves or upon someone we have been asked to guide. Such questions, as will be seen, require the deepest insight into character and are, on that score, the most difficult. More often still the problem is a technical one. A man has decided, say—as a matter of ultra obligation—that he ought to do his best for his son or his ageing mother or a friend tragically paralysed while quite young. Given this, the remaining problem is the technical one of determining what course of action *is* best. In doing this, he has to be mindful that he does not violate the rights of others, but in neither of these cases are the rights of others anywhere near the heart of the problem. Consequently, the contractually harmonized interests of everyone in the society are irrelevant to the problem which engages him, and only the interests of those concerned are relevant. But it would be a mistake to argue by false analogy that the same holds for problems of basic obligations and rights. In the most complex moral problems all factors, basic, ultra, prudential and technical are likely to be involved; but we should not conclude that because the contractually harmonized interests of everyone are irrelevant to three of these factors, they are irrelevant to the fourth also.

Interpretation

It is assumed throughout this section that no conflict of abstract obligations is involved in the cases discussed. In the statement of general and specific principles words like 'avoidable', 'unnecessary', 'negligent', 'reasonable care', 'harmful', 'properly' and so on repeatedly occur. For example, we have abstract obligations to refrain from causing *avoidable* annoyance or *unnecessary* suffering, to drive with *reasonable* care, to do our jobs *properly* and not to *harm* others. The question is: What is involved in determining what is to count as avoidable, unnecessary, reasonable, etc.? We have, let us say, an abstract obligation to refrain from causing avoidable annoyance. A building contractor and a highway engineer have the more specific obligation to refrain from using pneumatic drills so as to cause avoidable annoyance. One fine morning the workers move onto the site outside my study window, and the pneumatic drills start their ear splitting din; there is an enormous slab of concrete to be removed, and it is plain that drills are the only effective means of dealing with it. Work for me is impossible unless I transfer everything to a room on the other side of the house, and this is a great annoyance to me. Has the contractor caused me avoidable annoyance? Has he violated his obligation? I think it would be agreed in this case that he has not. Yet there is no doubt that he has caused annoyance, and there is certainly an interpretation of 'avoidable' in which he could have avoided doing so: he could have turned down the job or instructed his men to use pick and shovel. But the fact is that these interpretations of 'avoidable' do not support the claim that he has violated his obligation. To say that the annoyance he caused was avoidable in these ways is not to the point in supporting that claim.

In law the expression '"such-and-such" within the meaning of the act' is used. By analogy, I shall use the expression '"avoidable annoyance" within the meaning of the principle' i.e., the principle that we ought not to cause avoidable annoyance; and I shall say that the contractor has violated his obligation if and only if he has caused '"avoidable annoyance" within the meaning of the principle'. This is the way to label our understanding of 'avoidable annoyance' as it is used in determining whether an obligation has been violated. But it is only a label borrowed from another field and so far not illuminating. I shall now explain how our understanding of '"avoidable annoyance" within the meaning of the principle' is dependent upon a series of applications of the contract ground.

The contractor could have avoided causing annoyance by refusing the job. To avoid it in that way would involve giving up his livelihood—for he would have to refuse practically all the jobs he was offered. We ask

> Is it in everyone's interest to make a contract to avoid causing annoyance to others by giving up one's livelihood?

If the answer is No, it is thereby determined that annoyance which could be avoided only in this way does not count as 'avoidable' within the meaning of the principle. Again, the contractor could have avoided causing annoyance by instructing his men to use pick and shovel. This would be hopelessly inefficient. We ask:

> Is it in everyone's interest to make a contract to avoid causing annoyance to others by doing one's job with this measure of inefficiency?

If the answer is again No, it is thereby determined that annoyance which could be avoided only in this way does not count as 'avoidable' within the meaning of the principle. Suppose silencers were available for pneumatic drills and that the cost was a small fraction of the cost of the drills. The contractor could then have avoided causing annoyance by fitting silencers, and we ask:

> Is it in everyone's interest to make a contract to avoid causing annoyance to others at this sort of cost to oneself?

If the answer is 'Yes', then it is determined that annoyance caused by not fitting silencers is 'avoidable' within the meaning of the principle. The process could be repeated for endless pages, but there is no need. Enough has been said to show that our understanding of 'avoidable' as it occurs in this obligation principle is determined by a series of applications of the contract ground. It is not, of course, suggested that the noise which counts as avoidable annoyance could be determined to the last decibel. The application of the contract ground does not allow for that kind of precision. The treatment applied here to 'avoidable annoyance' can be applied to all the other words mentioned earlier—'unnecessary', 'reasonable', 'properly', 'harmful' and so on.

There is an idea abroad that behind the proposition that an act was negligent or that a man did not take reasonable care there lies a mode of inference which is neither inductive nor deductive. The fact is that behind such a proposition there lies a series of questions, 'Is it in everyone's interest to make a contract to take this degree of care in this kind of situation?' The question is asked over a range of degrees of care. At a certain point in this range, and at all points below it, the answer will be 'Yes', i.e., that it is in everyone's interest to make a contract to take this degree of care and all lesser degrees. Now if 'taking *this* degree of care' satisfies the contract ground it follows that we have an obligation to take this degree of care. It is this degree of care which is called '"reasonable" within the meaning of the principle'. When we judge that a man did not take reasonable care or was negligent, where these judgements have the implication that he ought to have taken more care, this is the kind of inference involved. But there is nothing new about it. Whether the contract ground is true or false of a certain degree of care is a question of evidence about people's interests, and of balancing that evidence; it involves no hitherto unknown kind of inference. And given that the contract ground is true of a certain degree of care, the step to a true judgement of abstract obligation is a purely deductive step. I do not say that there are not kinds of inference that are neither evidential nor deductive, but only that this kind of case does not involve any.

In the last paragraph, I said in passing that the proposition that A acted negligently *implies* that A ought to have taken more care, the 'ought' signifying a basic obligation. This is true, but it is important to see how it looks when more work is done upon it. Suppose the proposition that A acted negligently is equivalent to the proposition that A took less care than degree D. Then the implication to be looked at is:

A took less care than degree D
implies
A ought to have taken more care

This implication holds if and only if the degree of care D is that degree which satisfies the contract ground. Otherwise a basic obligation cannot be implied. It is this degree of care which counts as reasonable care, and what counts as reasonable care is determined by the contract ground just as what counts as avoidable annoyance is so determined. Thus the implication holds if and only if the antecedent is:

A took less care than that degree of care which it is in everyone's interest to make a contract to take

Now this implies

A ought to have taken more care

because the antecedent implies that he took less care than he ought to have taken. But the antecedent is equivalent to the proposition that A acted negligently: and it is this equivalence which makes for the implication of a basic obligation by a judgement of negligence.

This pattern lies behind all cases in which an evaluative concept implies a basic obligation. The use of some of the words in our language is so tailored that some judgements in terms of them do imply basic ought judgements (2, 8). 'Negligent' is one example. 'Murder' is another. 'A did murder' does indeed imply 'A ought not to have done as he did'. The claim that this implication holds might be defended by saying that if the consequent were false, we should not call the action named in the antecedent 'murder'. Alternatively, it might be said that 'murder' is defined as unjustifiable killing. But in defending the implication in these ways we do not *explain* the wrongness of murder.[1] We explain it by pointing out that the contract ground is true of not doing actions of certain classes, and that 'murder' is the name of one such class. Innumerable cases can be brought forward to show that the contract ground is not true as asserted of never *killing* another man. But if we change the content of the contract to 'not to kill another man in such and such circumstances', the contract ground is true for some specifications of the circumstances. And 'murder' is the name we give to killing in some of the sets of circumstances for which it is true. The contract ground, and the work we have done upon it, bears the explanatory load; and the explanation is enhanced when we see (3, 13–14) that the truth of the contract ground as asserted of Not-X is a *reason* better than any in terms of independent interest for not doing actions of the class X.

Whenever a word such as 'negligent' or 'murder' is used only in such a way that its correct application is in conformity, in the way explained, with the contract ground, then there will be judgements in terms of the word which imply a basic ought judgement. 'Negligent' and 'murder' are, I think, correctly used only in this way. 'Avoidable annoyance' is not only so used. As we saw earlier, the contractor could have avoided causing annoyance with his pneumatic drills by turning down the job or instructing his men to use pick and shovel. And thus there is no corresponding implication. It would be pointless to go through the whole series of expressions which could be discussed—'harm', 'unnecessary suffering', 'avoidable inconvenience' and so on, to decide whether a corresponding implication holds. The fact is that if the only correct use of the expression is to name a class of actions of which the contract ground is true, then the implication does hold; but if there are other correct uses, it does not.

In speaking in this way about the contract ground, I do not of course mean that it is actually employed in moral discussion. It evidently is not. I mean that it is a proposition which implies, in the strong sense used throughout, basic ought judgements. But

[1] Introduction, I.

unlike other propositions which imply such judgements, it also explains, as they do not, the rightness or wrongness of the actions in question. It explains, in a way to be enhanced in the two sections following, the demand which morality makes upon us. Furthermore, it is a proposition which the reasons given in day to day moral argument are seen, so far as they are good reasons, to support: it explains our discrimination between some reasons as good and others as bad; between some considerations as relevant and others as irrelevant. In this sense, it explains moral argument.

13. REASON FOR ACTING AND BASIC OBLIGATION

I have now completed my argument for the first implication of the Reason-for-Acting/Obligation schema as it applies to basic obligation. We have seen that a certain proposition, which has been called the contract ground, implies a general principle of abstract obligation; and we have seen how this proposition is related to more specific principles and to judgements of actual obligation. The next task is to establish the second implication of the schema, i.e., the implication of the general form,

A ought (   ) to do X
implies
There is a reason for A's doing X which is better than . . .

The point will be argued only for the case of a general principle of abstract obligation, i.e., I shall argue that 'Class of actions X is abstractly obligatory in the society' implies 'There is a reason for every member of the society doing actions of the class X which is better than any reason in terms of independent interest for doing either X or Not-X'. Once this point is established, it will be obvious that the appropriate implication holds also for actual obligation, and the matter will not be brought up for discussion.

Given that the antecedent of the implication is logically equivalent to the contract ground (3, 3; 3, 4), the implication may be shown to hold by showing that the contract ground implies that there is a reason for doing actions of the class X which has the characteristic specified in the consequent, i.e., a reason better than any in terms of independent interest for doing either X or Not-X.

When we say that it is in everyone's interest to make a contract with everyone else to do actions of the class X, we are not speaking of an independent assessment of interests. It must be remembered, in this discussion, that X may be quite complex; that to speak of a class of actions is not strictly correct although it is convenient; we should strictly be speaking of complementary classes of actions and of numerous conditions embodied in the contracts. In saying that it is in everyone's interest to make a contract to do X, we are saying, *inter alia*, that it is in A's interest to make a contract with everyone else. But in saying that it is in his interest to make *precisely this* contract, i.e., a contract specifying precisely this (complex) X, we are not speaking of his independent interest. If his independent interest were in question, it may not be true that it is in his interest to make precisely this contract but some other more or less closely similar to it; some contract which benefits him more than this one irrespective of the benefits it confers upon others. But it may at the same time be true that it is in his interest to make precisely this contract with everyone else, because this is the best he can get in bargaining his interests against the interests of the others. And in saying this we cannot be speaking of his independent interest. In seeking to establish that it is in his interest to make precisely this contract with others, we could not use premisses which referred to his interest alone. We should need also premisses referring to the interests of other people, viz., that it is in their interest to make this contract with him. And when premisses referring to the interests of others are needed to establish that it is in a man's interest to do such and such, it is established that it is in his interest, assessed non-independently, to do such and such (1, 9). Thus in saying that it is in everyone's interest to make such and such a contract with everyone else, a non-independent assessment of interest is referred to.

Suppose now that there are classes of actions such that, if we consider any individual member of any society, we may say (*a*) that it may be against his interest, independently assessed, that he alone should do actions of these classes; but that (*b*) his and everyone else's greater interest is served by the presence rather than the absence of the requirement upon everyone to do actions of these classes, even though (*a*) is true, and even though, in speaking of his and everyone else's greater interest, interests are being assessed, not independently, but along with the interests of others. In speaking of a requirement to do certain classes of actions, we are speaking of the existence of a state of affairs in which people can be called upon to do actions of those classes.

If there are classes of actions of which (*a*) and (*b*) are true for every member of a society, we are compelled to admit that the requirement to do actions of these classes is a rational requirement. It is a requirement which is more conducive to everyone's interest than its absence, and we could not have a better ground than that for claiming practical rationality for it. But to say that the presence of this requirement is more conducive to everyone's interest than its absence is not to say that, for any individual we care to take, there are not other requirements more conducive still to his interest. If we think of an individual A_1, it may well be more conducive still to his interest that everyone except A_1 should be required to do actions of certain classes. But we do not have the corresponding argument, nor indeed any argument, for claiming rationality for this requirement. We have no reason for singling out A_1 from all the other individuals of the society. And to claim that this require-ment not only upon A_1, but upon everyone, is rational is absurd: to talk of a requirement, in a society of N members, upon everyone except $A_1, A_2 \ldots A_N$ is to talk gibberish, not to specify a require-ment for which rationality can be claimed. Clearly, many other requirements may be more conducive to A_1's interests than those so far considered, e.g., a requirement upon everyone to grant him his every whim. But it would be absurd to claim rationality for them. In the requirements rejected as irrational, the interests referred to are assessed independently: if any such requirement is in A_1's greatest interest, we establish that it is by considering the in-terest of A_1 apart from the interest of other individuals of the society.

If there are classes of action such that it is rational that every member of a society should be *required to do* actions of those classes, then we cannot deny that it is rational for individuals of the society to *do* such actions. For we are saying that a state of affairs in which everyone can be called upon to do actions of certain kinds is a rational state of affairs; and we cannot then deny that it is rational that action of those kinds be done; we cannot then deny that there is a reason for everyone's doing them. This is not to say that it is in *anyone's* independent interest that he alone should do them, for that would conflict with (*a*) which we are supposing to be true. It is to say that, despite (*a*), there is, by virtue of (*b*), a reason for everyone's doing such actions. But if (*a*) is true, then for any individual we care to consider, there may be a reason in terms of his independent interest for *not* doing them; and if, despite (*a*), there is a reason *for* his doing them, then it must be a reason which is better than a reason in terms of his independent interest. For we are saying that despite there being a reason in terms of his independent interest for not doing such actions, it is nonetheless rational for him to do them; and this is to say that there is a better reason for doing them than the reason in terms of his independent interest for not doing them. Moreover, this superior reason, as a reason for doing actions of the class in question, cannot be a reason in terms of his independent interest for, once we have said that it is against his independent interest to do actions of that class, we have ruled out the possibility of there being a reason in terms of his independent interest for doing them. The upshot is that if there are classes of action of which (*a*) and (*b*) are true, there is a reason for everyone doing actions of those classes which is better than any reason in terms of independent interest for not doing them. It is also better than any reason in terms of independent interest for doing them. The latter point, given the former, is obvious.

We must now ask whether there are classes of action of which (*a*) and (*b*) are true, and the answer is that there are: (*a*) and (*b*) are true of the classes of action specified in the contract ground. First, it may plainly not be in anyone's interest, independently assessed, to do actions of these classes. Therefore (*a*) is true. Second, it could not be in everyone's interest to make a contract to do actions of a certain class unless the requirement placed upon them by the contract was more conducive to everyone's interest than its absence. And as the interests referred to in the contract ground are, as we have seen, not independently assessed interests, (*b*) is also true. Thus, if the contract ground is true of a class of actions X, then (*a*) and (*b*) are true of X; and, as we have seen, if (*a*) and (*b*) are true of X, then there is a reason for everyone doing X which is better than any in terms of his independent interest for doing either X or Not-X. Consequently, from the contract ground asserted of a class of actions X, it follows that there is a reason for everyone doing X which is better than any in terms of his independent interest for doing either X or Not-X. This is the conclusion which we set out to prove. The second implication of the Reason-for-Acting/Obligation schema, as it applies to the basic made of the concept, is established.

It may be suggested that the conclusion does not follow without the additional premiss that other people, at least for the most part, do X. Someone may say, 'If the contract ground is true of X, but X is not for the most part done, it cannot be maintained that there is a reason for my doing X'. This is true of those cases, which are the majority, in which the contract ground takes the form: to do such and such provided most others most of the time also do such and such (3, 11). But the point is not inconsistent with anything I have said. For in such cases the X of which we have been speaking will be complex. It will be of the form: to do Y provided most people most of the time also do Y. And the claim is that from the contract ground asserted of this X it follows that there is a reason for everyone doing X, i.e., for doing Y provided most people most of the time also do Y.

I should point out, in concluding this section, that the argument to establish the connection between the contract ground and reasons for acting is independent of the earlier argument (3, 3) to establish that the contract ground implies a principle of abstract obligation. If this point should be missed, there is just a chance that I may be wrongly charged at a later stage (3, 15) with arguing in a circle.

14. THE MASTER CRIMINAL

I may be reminded that the contract ground is true of a society only if a penalty clause is included in the content of the contract (3, 10). It may seem to be a consequence that the contract ground implies that there is a reason for doing actions of the class specified only if a penalty is imposed for not doing them. It may then seem that the penalty is so connected with the reason that the Master Criminal, who has sufficient ingenuity and cunning to evade the penalties (3, 4), is an exception to the claims made in the previous section: that there is no reason for his doing actions of the classes in question.

The mistakes in this line of argument may be obvious, but there are several points of interest to be brought out by showing how it is mistaken. The fact that, in actual societies, penalty clauses have to be included is irrelevant to the point for which I argued in the previous section. Let us suppose that the content of a contract is $X+P$, e.g., not to steal provided most others most of the time do not steal (X) and to submit to an appropriate penalty if one does (P). Now the object of the previous section was to show that from the contract ground asserted of $X+P$ it follows that there is a reason for everyone doing X which is better than any in terms of independent interest; and that it follows also, although the point was not explicitly made, that if one does not do X, there is a reason for submitting to P which is better than any in terms of independent interest; and which therefore is not a reason in terms of independent interest. But the purpose of P is to provide a reason, which *is* in terms of independent interest for those who are not moved by other considerations. Thus the need for a penalty clause in actual societies is irrelevant to the point for which we argued in the previous section. We do not show that there is not a reason better than any in terms of independent interest by pointing out that, in actual societies, penalty clauses provide an additional reason which is in terms of independent interest.

Let me come at this from a different angle. I said earlier (3, 10) that the function of a penalty clause was to provide a motive for doing X, a point which now needs further analysis. If a penalty attaches to not doing X; if a man cannot evade the penalty upon not doing X; and if it is against his interest to suffer the penalty; then there is a reason in terms of his independent interest for doing X. This point can be established without employing premisses referring to the interests of other people. The belief that it is against his interest to suffer this penalty may provide him with a motive for doing X whereas the belief that X is obligatory may not. This is the point of the penalty clause: by providing a reason in terms of a man's independent interest for doing X it is more likely, in very many cases, that he will have a motive for doing X. But all this is irrelevant to the question of whether there is a reason for his doing X which is better than any in terms of his independent interest. And this was the point at issue in the last section. It is a contingent matter that penalty clauses are needed in actual societies; it is contingent upon the fact that a man's belief that he will suffer a penalty if he does not do X is more likely to provide him with a motive than some other beliefs. But it is easy to think of a society in which the facts about motivation are different; in which the belief that an action is obligatory, or the belief that it falls under the contract ground, always provides a motive for doing it. In such a society penalty clauses would not be needed, but it would be totally absurd to say that in such societies there was no reason for doing actions of the classes we are discussing. This is the absurdity to which we should be committed if we held that penalty clauses were a logically necessary condition of there being a reason for doing actions to which, in the usual run of societies, they are attached. For many classes of action, it is indeed a logically necessary condition of a man's having a reason for doing them that most of the people most of the time also do them; but that penalty clauses are required to ensure that they do is a contingent matter.

As the practical need for penalty clauses is irrelevant to the claim made in the previous section, it is also irrelevant that the Master Criminal has the ingenuity and cunning to evade the penalties. His peculiar talents have no bearing at all upon the question of whether there is a reason better than any in terms of independent interest for doing actions of certain classes; and they have no bearing upon the question whether there is such a reason for his doing them. The difference between the Master Criminal and his less talented fellows is that the penalty clause does not succeed in ensuring that there is a reason in terms of his independent interest for doing them. But the point is irrelevant to the claim that there is a reason *better* than any in terms of independent interest for his doing them. The fact is that there is such a reason for doing actions of certain classes *because* they are actions of those classes: because the classes are included in a true statement of the contract ground; and because of such classes (a) and (b) of the previous section are true. If we consider two societies which are identical save that penalties are needed to provide motives in one but not in the other, then if the contract ground is true of X in one of the societies, it will be true of $X + P$ in the other. It is the fact that X is included in the content of the contract, and that therefore (a) and (b) are true of X, which leads to the conclusion that there is a reason for doing X which is better than any in terms of independent interest for doing X or Not-X. And the fact that in actual societies P has to be added if the contract ground is to be true is neither here nor there.

It is however worth looking at the central argument of the previous section again with an eye specifically on the Master Criminal. We said that the requirement to do certain classes of action was a rational requirement and deduced from this that it was rational that everyone should do actions of those classes. This step may be challenged in the case of the Master Criminal. The propositions (*a*) and (*b*) of the previous section may be expressed in this way: in regard to certain classes of actions everyone's greater interest is served by the *presence rather than the absence* of the requirement upon everyone to do actions of these classes, even though it may not be in anyone's interest, assessed independently, that he alone should do actions of these classes, and even though, in speaking of people's greater interest, each person's interest is assessed, not independently, but along with the interest of others. Reflection will show that this claim is true of the Master Criminal: a state of affairs in which he is able to call upon others to do actions of these classes conduces more to his interest than a state of affairs in which he is not; and the fact that others are able to call upon him does not affect him either way just because he can evade the penalties which would make their calling upon him effective. I argued that the requirement to do actions of such classes was a rational requirement, and deduced that there was a reason better than any in terms of independent interest for everyone doing actions of these classes. The final step may be challenged on behalf of the Master Criminal; it may be said that there is a better reason for everyone else but not for him. If we ask why this is so, the answer will be that it is not is his *greater* interest to do those actions; his greater interest is served by everyone else doing them while he holds back. This is perfectly true, but it does not establish that there is not a reason for his doing them. There being a reason is not linked to greater interest in this simple way, except in pru- dential cases. It is perfectly true that the Master Criminal's greater interest is served by letting everyone else do actions of the kinds in question and not doing them himself. But, as was pointed out in the previous section, so is everyone else's. And it is precisely because this is so, and human motivation is what it is, that penalties are needed. True, if the penalties are suitably designed, they will ensure that it is in the greater interest of the ordinary run of people to act in the ways required than to act otherwise, and they will not have this result in the case of the Master Criminal. In his case, the device of penalties fails. But to suppose that the failure of such devices in this particular case has any bearing upon the rationality of certain kinds of action is ludicrous. The fact that penalties are needed to provide motives in actual societies has nothing to do with the claim that there is a reason of a certain kind for everyone doing actions of such and such classes. And the fact that the Master Criminal can evade the penalties has nothing to do with it either.

I shall now summarise the central points I have been making. Everyone's greater interest is served by the presence rather than the absence of a requirement to do actions of those classes specified by the contract ground. The requirement is rational; and the actions required are rational actions. In saying that they are rational, we are saying that there is a reason for everyone doing them which is better than any reason in terms of his independent interest; that this is so follows from the fact that the contract ground is true of such classes of actions. There are other requirements which may conduce more to an individual's interest than the one stated: one is the requirement upon everyone *except himself* to do actions of certain classes. But this requirement is not rational and cannot be made the basis for claims about reasons for acting. It is not true that it is in everyone's greater interest that everyone should do, rather than not do, actions of the classes specified in the contract ground. For any individual, it may be the case that his greater interest is served by everyone else doing such actions while he does not. It may be true of anyone, penalties apart; and whether it is true of anyone, taking penalties into account, is irrelevant to the issues discussed. But it cannot be rational to act in this way. It is rational only to act in accordance with requirements which are in the contractually harmonized interests of everyone. Requirements so determined are, as I have argued, rational requirements, and action in accordance with them is rational action: there is a reason for any man doing such actions which is better than any reason in terms of independent interest either for doing or for not doing them, even though his independent interest may be his greater interest. Where a man's greater interest is to do X rather than Not-X, and there is a requirement to do Not-X which is in the contractually harmonized interest of everyone, it is rational only for him to do Not-X.

I have spent a long time on these points because they are important. Suppose one of us can benefit himself by doing a wrong action in the sure knowledge that he will never be found out. We are inclined to think that although it is, *ex hypothesi*, immoral to do it, it is not irrational. My object has been to show that whatever we are inclined to say of such cases, we are committed to saying that it is irrational; that the concept of reason for acting is such that we are logically compelled to judge such action irrational. The Master Criminal cannot rationally exercise his talents, though he may count as a rational being if he does not exercise them. And if you or I have an opportunity to benefit from wrong action without risk of detection, we cannot rationally take our opportunity.

15. PROMISING AGAIN

We saw in chapter 2 that promises are made upon certain conditions (2, 6); and that if we are to be able to say correctly that promises have been made, simpliciter, these conditions must be so determined that promising upon these conditions is a rational exercise of the function (2, 8). We are now able to see that the contract ground determines the conditions so that they satisfy this requirement.

A contract is a mutual promise between two or more people; and we have been speaking in this chapter of contracts of which we can say that it is in everyone's interest to make them. In so speaking, we may be understood as saying that it is in everyone's interest to make such and such contracts upon certain conditions which are understood rather than explicitly stated. Alternatively, we may understand the contracts of which we have been speaking as containing a full specification of conditions. We have, in fact, adopted the second of these alternatives, and some of the conditions required have been brought out in previous sections (3, 9; 3, 11). Thus, in asserting the contract ground of a class of actions X, we are asserting that it is in everyone's interest to make a contract to do X provided . . ., the sentence being completed by a statement of conditions. I want now to draw a sharp distinction, in one respect, between the contracts (mutual promises) referred to in statements of the contract ground and promises made in daily life, and ask how the conditions are determined in the two cases. The answer in the first case is obvious: they are so chosen that it *is* in everyone's interest to make a contract in regard to the class of actions in question, *these* conditions being specified.

We now wish to know how to determine the conditions under which day-to-day promises must be made in order that exercises of the promising function shall be rational. The answer is given by applying the contract ground. We say:

> It is in everyone's interest to make a contract to count day-to-day utterances of 'I promise' as having made a promise if and only if, at the time appointed for fulfilment, the following conditions are satisfied: . . .

Two sets of conditions are involved in this statement of the contract ground: first, the conditions under which day-to-day utterances of 'I promise' are to count as having made a promise—the conditions for which a space is provided at the end of the statement; second, the conditions under which it is in everyone's interest to make such a contract in regard to day-to-day utterances of 'I promise'— conditions which would need to be stated explicitly in an actual application.

At first sight, it may seem that the two sets of conditions are the same, and that the proposed application of the contract ground is circular: it may seem that the contract ground could not be employed unless the set of conditions was antecedently known, and that it cannot therefore be employed to determine them. But the charge is unfounded. Even if the sets of conditions are the same, which is not, I think, entirely obvious, it is a mistake to suppose that, in order to apply the contract ground, we must antecedently know anything about conditions. The conditions required are such that the contract ground is true of a given class of such actions only if such and such conditions are specified; only if the conditions are such that it *is* in everyone's interest to make a contract to do such actions, *these* conditions being specified. The conditions required are not known antecedently to applications of the contract ground; they are determined, for this case and that, *in* applications of the contract ground. Consequently, even if the two sets of conditions are the same in the application considered, the charge of circularity is by no means warranted.

The next question is whether the set of conditions determined by the contract ground is such as to ensure that, if promises are understood to be made upon those conditions, the promising function is rationally exercised. The answer is that the set of conditions so determined guarantees just that. We saw in the previous section that the contract ground asserted of a class of actions is a reason for doing actions of that class which is better than any reason in terms of independent interest. If, as we may for convenience, we ignore the complication that any particular action of this class may also be a member of another class which there is a better reason still for not doing, we may say that the contract ground asserted of a class of actions X provides every reason for doing any particular action, x, of that class. Now the class of actions involved in the application of the contract ground discussed in this section is: counting day-to-day utterances of 'I promise' as having made a promise if such and such conditions are satisfied at the time appointed for doing the promised action, but not otherwise; e.g., acting towards the promiser in ways appropriate to promise breaking if and only if he does not do the action when all the conditions are satisfied. If the contract ground is true of action of this kind, then, as the argument of the previous section has shown, there is every reason for action of this kind. Or, as we may alternatively say, an exercise of the promising function which is controlled by conditions determined by the contract ground is a rational exercise of that function.[1]

This section completes the discussion of promising in chapter 2, and in particular gives body to two of the sections of that chapter (2, 6; 2, 8). We are now in a position to understand what is involved in speaking of a rational exercise of the promising function whereas our earlier understanding was inevitably skeletal. I think it is now obvious that in saying that the promising function must be exercised rationally if it is correctly to be judged that promises have been made, we are not committed to the position that an individual man cannot make a stupid promise[2]: the contract ground may or may not rescue a man from his own stupidity; in some cases it no doubt will, but in others, no doubt, it will not.

---

[1] It is a premiss of the argument of this section that the contract ground is a reason for acting. It is not a premiss that it implies an obligation principle. The argument to establish the former (3, 13) is independent of the argument to establish the latter (3, 3).

[2] See p. 69.

16. MORALITY, JUSTICE AND LAW

In this section, I shall make briefly and in my own way the same point as has been made recently by Professor John Rawls in his paper *Justice as Fairness*.[1] I shall argue that in developing a contract theory, a niche has already been carved for the notion of justice. In this respect, the theory is markedly superior to classical Utilitarianism which has always been embarrassed to find a place for the notion.

Justice may be ascribed to laws, actions and men. Laws will be considered first, and actions and men later. To say that a law is unjust is to say that it is unjust that people should be required to act as it enjoins. To say that a law forbidding coloured people from entering public houses is unjust is to say that it is unjust that coloured people should be required not to enter them. It is not to say that, if a black man defies the law, his action is unjust. Instead of saying that the law is unjust, we could say that the actions it requires are unfair to some people or that it fails to do justice between people's interests.[2] I have previously argued that if a class of actions is obligatory in a society it is in everyone's interest to make a contract to do actions of that class (3, 4), but no claim has been made that it is equally in everyone's interest. I shall now argue that it is not equally in everyone's interest for the very good reason that the requirements determined by the contract ground do justice between people's interests. Equality and justice are distinct concepts, and the claim that such-and-such is equally in everyone's interests is distinct from the claim that it does justice between everyone's interests. In the succeeding paragraphs we should be able to locate the tantalizing and elusive distinction between justice and equality.

I have to prove that the requirement to do X determined by the contract ground is a requirement which does justice between people's interests; a claim which has the consequence that a law which requires people to do X does justice between people's interests or is, more briefly, a just law. 'Justice' has a wider and a narrower use. In the narrower use a law or an action is said to be just only if

[1] *Philosophical Review* (1958).
[2] I have borrowed this expression from Professor R. M. Hare's *Freedom and Reason*, p. 129.

it is concerned with distribution of benefits, burdens or penalties, but there is no such restriction on the wider use. In the narrower use a law forbidding murder or blackmail or a law decreeing that those who steal sheep should be executed would not be said to be just or unjust. On the other hand, a law which decreed execution for an illegitimate sheep thief and deportation for one born in wedlock would be described as unjust, for it is concerned with distribution of punishment. In discussing the justice of laws, I shall be using 'justice' in the wider sense so that a law which decrees execution for a man who steals a sheep can be said to be unjust, and laws forbidding blackmail, murder and theft can be said to be just. This use may seem unnatural at the present time, but it is familiar enough in the history of the subject. For example, the wider use is involved in the term 'Natural Justice'. Moreover, we are committed to it in speaking of laws: it could not be denied that a law which forbade the murder of whites but not of blacks, or one which permitted the blackmail of peers but not of commoners, were both unjust. And we are thus committed to saying that laws relating to murder and blackmail which do not discriminate in these or other irrelevant ways are just laws. The wider use is forced upon us in speaking of laws. On the other hand, when the justice of actions is discussed in the next section, the narrower use will be adopted. The one use is appropriate for laws and the other for actions.

I shall now argue that a requirement to do X, as determined by the contract ground, is a requirement which does justice between people's interests. The discussion will be simplified by employing a fiction. I shall speak of people actually making contracts. This device is convenient; it is in no way a withdrawal from my insistence that claims about actual contract-making are quite alien to the theory. If it were in everyone's interest to make a certain contract; if everyone had a correct appreciation of his own interests; and if no one were thoroughly pig-headed or stupid in some other way; then everyone would make this contract. The second and third conditions are never likely to be satisfied, but we can suppose that they are and imaginatively consider the people of a society making contracts accordingly. These contracts would determine the classes of action which were abstractly obligatory in the society. As each class of action comes up for consideration, any entrenched legal, or quasi legal, institution which bears on the question has to be discounted, for such an institution may favour one group at the expense of another (3, 5; 3, 6). As each question of the form, 'Shall we make a contract in relation to X?', is discussed, each individual consults his own interests. He tries to consult only his own interests. But he is prevented from considering his interests to the exclusion of the interests of others by the fact that every other individual is also trying to consider only his own interests to the exclusion of others. The set of contracts arrived at under these conditions is one which caters for the interests of everyone so far as these interests are compatible with the interests of everyone else. The interests of everyone are contractually harmonized. It would be a mistake to think that the requirements of the obligation principles so determined are equally in the interest of everyone. For example, the rich man has more secured to him than the poor man; those who are ill-favoured in most respects have less secured to them than those who are well-favoured in most respects. In this sense, the requirements so determined are not equally in the interests of everyone. The fact is indisputable, but it is also indisputable that they do justice between the interests of everyone. It could not be otherwise if they are determined by everyone consulting his own interests so far as they are compatible with the interests of everyone else in circumstances in which no legal or quasi legal institution can give any individual a bargaining advantage over any other. We could not conceive of two men making a contract in the circumstances described which failed to do justice between their interests and we cannot conceive of a multitude doing so. If two men, each with a thorough understanding of his own interest and intent upon securing it, make a contract in a situation in which neither has a bargaining advantage over the other, it follows that that contract does justice between their interests. And what is true of two men making a contract is true of a whole society making a contract, each with the other. Contracts so made impose requirements to act which do justice between the interests of everyone concerned.

I have presented this in terms of a fiction, and I must emphasize that it is a fiction. Any suggestion that our remote ancestors actually made contracts with one another—quite apart from the lack of any historical evidence—meets with insuperable difficulties. The reality behind the fiction is that from the proposition that the requirement to do X is determined by the contract ground it follows that the requirement to do X does justice between the interests of everyone concerned. And from this it follows that a law which makes this requirement is a law which does justice between people's interests, or a just law. If 'just' is used in the narrower sense, the premiss would have to be added that the law was concerned with distribution.

The account may now be extended to ascriptions of justice to actions and men. I have argued that a law which requires of people those actions required by a basic obligation principle is a just law. The point could be expressed by saying that a law which confers a legal right where there is a moral right, as determined by the contract ground, is a just law, or that a law which accords people their moral rights is a just law. In considering the justice of laws, the term 'justice' was used in its wider sense; in considering the justice of actions, and therefore of men, it is used in its narrower sense. In saying that an action is unjust, a comment is being made upon the distribution effected in such an action, and only actions which effect a distribution of benefits, burdens or penalties can be said to be just or unjust. With this understanding, a just action is one which effects a distribution in accordance with the moral rights, as determined by the contract ground, of the recipients. And a just man is one who characteristically acts, in matters of distribution, so as to accord others their moral rights.

As an application of the concept of justice to actions we may consider the judgement that a certain law, although unjust, is administered justly. In saying that it is administered justly a comment is made upon the actions of the judges: the actions are said to be just even though the law is unjust. In imposing a penalty upon a man who has broken such a law, it cannot be said simply that a judge accords him his moral rights: one of his moral rights is being violated in being sentenced. But the action may still be just if, in the matter of the distribution of punishment, the judge accords him his moral right: if, for example, he does not treat him more harshly than another because he has taken a dislike to him, or because he is illegitimate or a Jew. In being punished under an unjust law, one of a man's moral rights is being violated, but it remains possible that another of his rights, his rights in the matter of the distribution of punishment, may be accorded to him. And if this is done, the action of the judge is a just action. In saying that an action is just, a comment is being made upon the distribution effected by it.

We thus see that contract theory, unlike classical Utilitarianism, is in no way embarrassed by the concept of justice. Judgements about the justice of laws, actions and men are related to the contract ground in the ways explained; and the relations are readily set out without any of the straining to be found in Utilitarian writers. Contract theory provides a natural place for the notion of justice.

17. NATURAL RIGHTS

I think we are in a position to make a take over bid for the term 'Natural Rights' and the corresponding terms 'Natural Justice' and 'Natural Law'. Natural rights have traditionally been thought of as the rights men have by virtue of being men; and that men have natural rights was, as I understand it, a presupposition of classical forms of social contract theory. As such there are no natural rights, for from the bare proposition that A is a man nothing follows about A's rights. The version of contract theory advocated here makes no such presupposition: it reveals the logical ground of propositions about rights. If, for any society, the contract ground is true of a certain class of actions, then the individuals of that society have the right to others doing actions of that class, provided it is a society in which some classes of actions are obligatory (3, 7). A distinction may be drawn between rights so determined and the rights which men may have as a result of actual promises received or actual contracts made. The term 'Natural Rights' suggests itself as a name for the former to distinguish them from the latter, and it will be adopted for that purpose. In the same way, we may speak of the corpus of obligation principles determined by the contract ground as embodying Natural Justice or as the system of Natural Law. The version of contract theory proposed reveals a perfectly proper use for three expressions whose propriety has often been doubted. Perhaps we may say that it explains what so many philosophers have been driving at when they have used them.

It is an inescapable consequence of the thesis presented in these pages that certain classes cannot have natural rights: animals, the human embryo, future generations, lunatics and children under the age of, say, ten. In the case of young children at least, my experience is that this consequence is found hard to accept. But it is a consequence of the theory; it is, I believe, true; and I think we should be willing to accept it. At first sight, it seems a harsh conclusion, but it is not nearly so harsh as it appears. It is a consequence of my thesis not because it makes no sense to talk of its being in the interests of young children, and individuals of the other classes, to make contracts, but because it is not in the interests of mature men and women to make contracts with them: either because they do not understand what is involved in making, and being bound by, a contract, or because they have no bargaining power, or both. It cannot be in my interest to make a contract with someone who does not understand what a contract is. In saying that young children, for example, do not have natural rights, we are saying that no child under the age of about ten years can have a right to mature men treating it in certain ways. We are not saying that no one has such a right: other mature men do. There is not the slightest doubt that the contract ground is true of many classes of action concerning the treatment of young children; and in consequence that mature members of societies have the right to other mature members treating children in certain ways and not treating them in other ways. But the children themselves cannot have any such right. When we do speak of children as having rights we must be understood as speaking of the rights which mature people have in regard to the treatment of them by other mature people.

We are inclined to take it, I think, that young children have rights because it is perfectly obvious that there are certain ways in which we ought to treat them and certain ways in which we ought not. But 'We ought to treat children in this way and not in that' is neutral between, 'We have an obligation to children to treat them in this way and not in that', and 'We have an obligation to mature members of our society to treat children in this way and not in that'. And it is neutral between, 'Children have the right to be treated in this way and not in that' and 'Mature members of societies have the right to children being treated in this way and not in that'. The fact therefore that we ought to treat children in some ways and not in others has no bearing on the issue in question.

In statements of the contract ground, the term 'everyone' refers to everyone who can be subject to obligation principles, and excludes, for example, animals and young children. The contract ground is undoubtedly true of many classes of action relating to the treatment of children. Quite apart from anything else, it is in everyone's interest that the rising generation should be equipped to take over the roles in society of the generation which precedes it. And it is in everyone's interest to make contracts to ensure that it is. It is natural to object at this point that the ways in which children ought to be treated depends upon the interests of the children and not upon the interests of the generations which precede them. The account offered, it may be said, makes it appear that children are tools to be fashioned for the convenience of their elders, a doctrine as vicious as a doctrine can be. But the truth is that there is no simple and straightforward dichotomy between the interests of children and the interests of mature people. The majority of mature people in any society are parents or grandparents who have affection for their children and grandchildren, and whose aim is to do the best for them in life. Thus, if it is in the child's interest to be treated in such and such a way, it is not always but very often *ipso facto* in the parents' interest that he should be treated in that way; and in saying that it is in everyone's interest to make contracts concerning the treatment of children, the interests of children are taken into account by virtue of the fact that the interests of parents are taken into account. Children do not have rights, but their interests are secured by the rights which their parents, and others, have to their being treated in such and such ways by other mature members of the society. It is not usually in the interest of parents to treat their children, or have others treat their children, as 'tools to be fashioned for the convenience of their elders'. The thesis that children cannot have rights is not so harsh as it might at first have appeared. It is, of course, a contingent matter that the interests of children are reflected in the interests of their parents; it is easy to imagine a society in which it is not so. In such a society it may indeed be in the interests of everyone to make contracts only to the extent of ensuring that the rising generation is equipped to take over the roles which its elders need it to take over for their own benefit. In this circumstance the morally correct treatment of children would no doubt be harsher than it is in our society. But the conclusion has to be accepted. In arguing that children cannot have rights, I am not arguing against an argument: there is no remotely respectable argument aiming to establish that they do. I am arguing only against what we are inclined to think. And there is no doubt that if we were members of the kind of society we are now considering, we should be inclined to think differently. We think as we do just because the interests of our children are our interests; and if, as in the society we are contemplating, it were not so, we should not be inclined to think as we do.

What we are inclined to think about the rights of young children is false, but I have tried to show that the consequences of its falsity are not so harsh as might at first sight appear. When our prejudices are overcome, the thesis advanced is seen to have the advantage of providing an intelligible answer to the question, 'When does that which begins life as a human embryo come to have rights? At the moment of conception? A few months later? At the moment of birth? Or when?' Anyone who wishes to opt for any of these alternatives must be armed with a reply to the further question 'Why?' And the history of our subject suggests that he is unlikely to be armed adequately. By contrast, we are able to give and defend an intelligible answer: children are not born with natural rights, nor are they bestowed upon them at the moment of conception; they grow into the possession of natural rights as they attain those states at which it becomes in the interest of mature people to make contracts with them. They come to have natural rights, that is, as they come to understand the notion of a contract and come to understand what it is to be under an obligation to other people.

18. NATIONS AND OTHER SOCIETIES

So far we have looked at the contract argument only as applied in a single society, and the nation has been our example. A nation has been thought of as the range of application of a particular set of laws. A society in general I shall take as the largest group of people to whom any given, substantially constant, set of rules apply. Rules may be provided by obligation principles, laws or authoritarian edicts, or by a combination; or they may be rules in the sense in which a tennis club has rules. The contract argument has application only in a society in which some of the rules are provided by obligation principles.

Taking the nation as unit, we distinguish between:

(a) distinct societies at this level
(b) sub-societies
(c) cross-societies
(d) greater societies

(a)—distinct societies at this level—are distinct nations and tribes i.e., distinct units; (b)—sub-societies—are societies all of whose members belong to the same unit, e.g., an English tennis club, Japanese criminals and the American Mothers' Union; (c)—cross societies—are societies whose members belong to different units, e.g., Freemasons, Roman Catholics, International Criminals and Orthodox Jews; (d)—greater societies—consist of the combination of two or more units. The only important instance is the society of humanity as a whole.

The contract argument can be applied to any of these types of society provided the individuals employ the concept of basic obligation in thinking about practical problems. Thus we can determine what classes of action are *abstractly* obligatory within any of these societies. In previous discussions, we have been concerned with the relations between abstract and actual obligation within a single society. We now have to see how to handle this relation for a conflict of abstract obligations which arises through a man's membership of two societies. Consider first a man who is a member of one of the units, i.e., a certain nation, and one of the sub-societies of that nation. Suppose he is an English criminal. As such he may have abstract obligations to other members of the same sub-society; for example, he may have an abstract obligation not to 'grass', not, that is, to disclose to the police the activities of other members of the sub-society. This is to say that as a member of the criminal society it may be in his interest to make a contract with everyone else against grassing; and it may be in everyone else's interest to make the same contract with him. But as a member of the unit, i.e., the English people, it may also be in his interest to make a contract with everyone else to help the police in their criminal enquiries. It may be in his interest because, as with the Master Criminal, it would be an effective way of ensuring that others (non-criminals) assist in the maintenance of law and order, and he benefits from this no less than everyone else—provided he is clever enough to avoid getting caught himself.

It may be in his interest to make both these contracts. He thus has conflicting abstract obligations, one as a member of the criminal sub-society, and one as a member of the unit. When such a conflict occurs it can be resolved only by applying the contract argument to the unit, i.e., to that society which includes, but is not included in, the other. The interests of everyone who stands to be affected by the class of actions in question can be taken into account only by applying the argument to the including society. True moral judgement is not to be achieved by ignoring the interest of anyone, and not, *ipso facto*, by ignoring the interests of those members of the unit who are not members of the sub-society. The point holds equally, of course, when the sub-society is a cricket club or the Mothers' Union. It is not asserted that the obligation in the including society always takes precedence. For example, it may well be in everyone's interest to make a contract whereby important obligations owed to each other by the members of sub-societies take precedence over comparatively unimportant obligations owed to each other as members of the unit. But whether or not this is so, or in which cases it is so, is determined by an application of the contract ground to the unit.

As a sub-society stands to the unit, so the unit stands to the greater society of humanity as a whole. What we have called a sub-society is a sub-society of a nation, and, in the same way, a nation is a sub-society of humanity as a whole. Thus the same principle for deter-mining superiorities among obligations applies: the contract argu-ment must be applied to the including, not to the included, society. If we are to speak of our obligations as members of the society of humanity as a whole, the theory requires us to say that there are some classes of actions regarding which it is in the interest of every man on the surface of the earth to make a contract with every other. The objection may be made that some of us know nothing about the interests of people in remote corners of the earth and therefore nothing about what contracts it is in their interest to make. Conse-quently, the objection goes, if we found ourselves in a moral situation with one of them we would, according to the theory, not know what we ought to do. But in fact we often would know.

The answer to this is that if we do know what we ought to do, by that token, we know something of the interests of the man our action affects—unless we hold the incredible view that what we ought to do is independent of the interests of those affected. The fact is that most of us know a good deal about general characteristics of human interests. There is also a good deal we do not know about individual interests. But there are also a good many moral situations which we could not handle without more knowledge. Most of us know enough to begin discussing the question: Is it in the interest of every human being to make a contract to wage war against a regime like Hitler's? We also know enough to take the discussion quite a long way. But most of us would not know enough, nor have enough imagination, nor enough human sympathy, to give a decent statement of the escape clauses which would alone do justice to individual German men and women in hellish situations. It does not follow that there is something wrong with the principles set out; only that we are not morally omniscient and would be partly wrong in the moral judgements we would make.

If a man has conflicting obligations as a result of his membership of a nation and a cross-society, it can be resolved only by asking what his obligation is as a member of humanity as a whole, for that is the only society to which the contract ground can be applied to resolve it. Suppose a man is a member of the nation N and the cross-society C, and that he has an obligation to every member of N which conflicts with an obligation to every member of C. To apply the contract ground to resolve it we have to find a society such that it is true of everyone. It is no good taking the society C for that excludes some members of N, and it is no good taking the society N for that excludes some members of C; nor is it any good taking the overlap of C and N, for that excludes some members of both C and N. The only society left to which the contract argument can be applied is humanity as a whole.

My treatment of possible conflicts due to a man's membership of more than one society has been brief because it is a problem which more or less takes care of itself. The really hard work lies in establishing the validity of the contract argument as applied to a single society. Once that is done, the rest falls fairly naturally and simply into place. I hope I have said enough to make it seem that this is so. If I were to attempt more by way of illustration, I should be handicapped by my conviction that moral differences between societies are nothing like so common as is generally thought. A casual glance seems to show that the requirements of obligation principles differ enormously from society to society. No doubt there are differences, but they are not enormous. The belief that they are results partly from confounding obligations with customs, and partly from the contemporary shyness of ascribing truth and falsity to moral judgements. A custom, e.g., raising one's hat to a lady, spiking peas individually or burying the dead with ham, is something which it is in people's interests to respect because, and only because, it is done, i.e., customary. I do not know whether this 'definition' will fit all uses of the word 'custom'; but using it in this way marks a distinction which is worth marking. There is no doubt at all that customs differ enormously from one society to another. But if X is customary, it is not obligatory by virtue of being X; it is obligatory because it is customary, and because ignoring customs causes offence. It is quite plausible to say that it is in the interest of every member of a society to make a contract to respect the customs of that society, because neglecting to do so causes offence. But it is totally implausible to say that it is in everyone's interest to make a contract to burp after a meal to show appreciation. It might as well be said of taking off one's shoes or swinging on the chandelier. Thus the enormous difference of customs from one society to another does not reflect a difference in obligation principles: it is the same principle throughout, viz., to respect the customs of the society to which one belongs. The obligation is no doubt a weak one, but this is not a point which need be pursued.

On the second point, for reasons by now evident, I cannot share the contemporary shyness of ascribing truth or falsity to moral judgements. Consequently, when we find two societies with different moral beliefs, we are not forced to conclude that there is a difference in obligation principles. The alternative remains that the beliefs of one or both are straightforwardly false. And I think it is a safe bet that this alternative will quite often turn out to be the correct one. In this chapter it has been my aim to discover the proper methods of determining which are true and which false when the proposition is one of basic obligation.

CHAPTER 4

THE GROUND OF ULTRA OBLIGATIONS

A distinction between two moral modes of the concept of obligation was introduced at the beginning of chapter 2. In this chapter, the second of these modes, ultra obligation, will be further elucidated. This done, the ground of propositions in terms of this notion will be set out. To establish the ground of basic obligations has been a long and difficult task, but I can promise that the problem is much simpler for ultra obligations.

It was argued earlier (2, 2) that a basic obligation implied and was implied by a right. The first step in elucidating the notion of ultra obligation is to bring out its connection, or lack of connection, with that concept.

1. ULTRA OBLIGATION AND RIGHTS

When Sir Philip Sidney lay dying on the field of Zutphen, fatally wounded and parched with thirst, he was brought by another soldier a mug of water. Instead of drinking it himself with thought for nothing but his own plight, he gave it to another man who lay beside him in a similar condition. This, most people would agree, is a morally good action of outstanding merit. But moral goodness is not in question at the moment. The question concerns the concept of a right, and the right of the other soldier to receive the water from Sidney. It is plain, I think, that he had no such right. Sidney's action is one of great beneficence which confers upon him a benefit greater than any he is entitled to by right. I argued earlier (3, 12) that people have the right to limited beneficence, and that others have a basic obligation to accord them this degree of beneficence. But the limit is exceeded in this case: Sidney had no basic obligation to give the water to the other man, and the other man did not have the right to receive it.[1]

Suppose that, instead of giving the water to the other man, Sidney had drunk it himself, as most of us would have done. Imagine now

---

[1] This case is discussed with a different purpose by G. E. Moore and Professor H. J. Paton in *The Philosophy of G. E. Moore*, pp. 126 and 618 ff.

that a third soldier, fit and hearty despite the battle, had told Sidney that he ought to have given it to the other man. His stricture is not justified. Yet, as already argued (2, 8), when a basic obligation is violated, others are justified in trying to get the agent to act differently in a similar situation in future. The second soldier did not have the right to the water, and no stricture upon Sidney would have been justified if he had drunk it himself. He had no basic obligation to give the water to the other.

Despite this it is almost certain that Sidney believed *he* ought to act as he did. If we were in a position to question him and ask, 'Did you think you had an obligation to give the water to the other man?' it is almost certain that he would have answered that he did. And even if it is not true, it does not matter; for we can imagine someone in an identical situation who would have answered in this way. In supposing that Sidney would have agreed that he ought to give the water to the other, we are not supposing that he would also have agreed that a man of *different character*, in the identical situation, ought to have done the same thing. A man can intelligibly hold that in a certain situation *he* ought to do such-and-such and at the same time refuse to extend this judgement to another man of different stamp. The situation is as follows:

(*a*) It is not the case that Sidney had an obligation to give the water to the other man

(*b*) It is the case that Sidney believed he had an obligation to give the water to the other man

There are now two alternatives. Either we can say that Sidney was mistaken and that he did not have an obligation to act as he did; or, alternatively, that two distinct modes of the concept of obligation are involved here and that (*a*) and (*b*) should read:

(*a'*) It is not the case that Sidney had a basic obligation to give the water to the other man

(*b'*) It is the case that Sidney believed he had an ultra obligation to give the water to the other man

With the latter understanding of the position it remains an open question whether he was right or mistaken. It remains an open question whether any man of his character in that situation has an ultra obligation to act as he did. It is not for a moment suggested that whether a man has an ultra obligation is a matter of what he believes.

So far as the argument has gone, either of these alternatives is as good as the other. Subsequent argument is designed to show that the second must be accepted. I shall try to show that ought judgements of the same kind as Sidney's, which are only *less* exacting in their requirements, play an important part in the lives of large numbers of people. They are not the prerogative of men of morally outstanding character, but also have their place in the moral lives of more ordinary folk. To reject so large a body of moral judgement as false is absurd. The philosophical task is to chart it correctly in the total pattern of moral thought. Before discussing the place of ultra obligations in the lives of more ordinary men, it will be well worth looking at the words of another man who, by general consent, was of distinguished moral character.

Dr Albert Schweitzer records in his autobiography that after becoming a missionary doctor he was often approached by others who wanted, or thought they wanted, to make a similar venture. He has, he says, only rarely been able to give immediate encouragement. Often those who asked for his opinion were moved merely by a restless spirit, failing to find satisfaction in their present lives. Often it was quite secondary considerations which provided their motive. He gives the following judgement on the kind of man who alone should follow his example:[1]

Only a person who can find a value in every sort of activity and devote himself to each one with full consciousness of duty, has the inward right to take as his object some extraordinary activity instead of that which falls naturally to his lot. Only a person who feels his preference to be a matter of course, not something out of the ordinary, and who has no thought of heroism, but just recognizes a duty with sober enthusiasm, is capable of becoming a spiritual adventurer

The word 'duty' occurs twice in this brief passage. The purpose in quoting it is to stress that in using this word Schweitzer is talking about an ultra obligation, not a basic obligation. We can see this in two distinct ways. I shall suppose that Schweitzer knows exactly what he is talking about and that his words are of precisely the kind to be considered by any man who is thinking of adopting such a life. What we have to notice is how very *personal* the requirements are which have to be satisfied before he would recommend it. Anyone thinking of the kind of life in question is being told in effect to ask

---

[1] Albert Schweitzer, *My Life and Thought*, p. 110.

himself: Is your *character* right for it? Can *you* find a value in every sort of activity and devote yourself to it with full consciousness of a demand upon *you*? Is your character such that this life is a matter of course for *you*?

These words reveal a great deal about the ground of judgements of ultra obligation which is to be discussed later. The present purpose is to point out that such considerations are ludicrously irrelevant to the questions of what a man's basic obligations are. They are precisely right for helping a man to decide what is ultra obligatory upon him. They are totally and comically irrelevant to the question of what is basically obligatory upon him. If a teacher is explaining to his class why they ought not to adopt a life of crime he does not tell them seriously to face the question whether their character is right for it; he does not say, 'If your character is of such-and-such a kind, adopt a life of crime, but not otherwise'. Or if he does, he had better cease to be a teacher for he does not understand the first thing about morality. Similarly, if we wish to explain to a man why he ought to do his job properly or keep his promises or refrain from telling lies, it is not to the point to suggest that he takes a good look at his own character to see whether he is up to it. The grounds of judgements of ultra obligation are quite different from the grounds of judgements of basic obligation.

The second way to see that the kind of judgement which Schweitzer is making is one of ultra obligation is to ask, of his own case, whether anyone had the *right* to his becoming a missionary doctor in Equatorial Africa. The obvious candidates for such a right are the natives themselves, and it is easy at least to show that nobody thought they had it. If a man has decided to act in such a way as to accord some group of people their rights we would not expect morally reputable people to try to persuade him to act otherwise. But after Schweitzer had decided to go to Africa, practically everyone tried to persuade him to change his mind; his friends, his relatives and all his colleagues at the University of Strasbourg. I think it is obvious in any case that, although a group of people can have a right to a man's doing properly the job he has chosen, no group can have the right to his doing any particular job. Unless he had promised them to do it, the concept of rights is out of place here. It might as well be suggested that a particular group can have the right to a man's occupying his leisure in a particular way.

The first step, and a large step, has now been taken towards drawing the distinction between basic and ultra obligation: whereas a basic obligation implies a right and vice versa, it is characteristic of an ultra obligation that it does not; and the ground of ultra obligations is different from the ground of basic obligations in ways which have begun to appear.

2. CHRISTIANITY, ULTRA OBLIGATION AND RIGHTS

It is widely held that we have an obligation to help others who are in trouble, and philosophers have supplied the name: the obligation of beneficence. I have already argued briefly (3, 12) that we have a *basic* obligation of limited beneficence. This is one of the few substantial moral questions to be discussed in these pages, and it must be looked at in a little more detail at this point. It may be doubted whether any degree of beneficence is required by a basic obligation; whether in general—in the absence of any special relation such as that of benefactor or parent—we have the right to help from other people. The question is settled by applying the contract ground. Is it in everyone's interest to make a contract to help others when they need help? The answer plainly depends upon the degree of help needed; upon the differential between the benefit to be conferred and the inconvenience to the agent in conferring it. It also depends upon the fact that some people need more help more often than others; a contract to help others who are in trouble, without any restriction, would impose a disadvantage upon the relatively trouble free; and it cannot be in everyone's interest to make such a contract. A further relevant consideration is that some people prefer to be independent, and that in many cases it is in their interest to be so; they are that sort of person. The existence of a class of people who, in general, rationally prefer to fend for themselves and live independent lives has the result that the contract ground is true only of help required in special circumstances: the kind of circumstances in which even the most independent person would welcome help. Such considerations make it plain that there are strict limitations upon the help from others to which people are entitled by right, and that the basic obligation of beneficence is an obligation of strictly limited beneficence. On the other hand, there can be no doubt that we have a basic obligation to help others in some circumstances, and the case considered earlier provides an example.

If I come across a man in a diabetic coma and can save his life by lifting a telephone, dialling 999 and asking for insulin, I have a basic obligation to do so. This is the sort of help which anyone, even the most trouble free, might need: anyone might find himself in a position in which his life can be saved by another at practically no trouble to the other. It is the sort of help which would be welcomed by even the most independent minded person; it is not in anyone's interest, however independent he may be, to reject this modicum of help to avoid a premature death. And it is the sort of help in which the benefit conferred greatly outweighs the inconvenience to the agent. The contract ground is true of help required in such a situation, and we have a basic obligation to give such help in such a situation.

This discussion of the requirements of a particular obligation principle could be continued for pages, but it would not be illuminating to prolong it. Sufficient has been said to establish that we have a basic obligation of limited beneficence and that its requirements are not very exacting. Many actions which we witness daily, and many more which we can imagine, go far beyond its requirements: they give more help to others than they are entitled to by right; or they give help to others in circumstances in which they have no right to help at all. Examples of such actions are Sir Philip Sidney's handing the water to the other soldier and Dr Schweitzer's going to Equatorial Africa as a missionary doctor. It is because they do more than is required by the basic obligation of beneficence that I have used the expression 'ultra obligation'.

Common ideas on what degree of beneficence is obligatory are an amalgam of what is basically obligatory upon all men and what is ultra obligatory on men of certain character. The basic obligation of beneficence is not very exacting. It is the ultra obligations of different people of different character which are, in their different ways and their different degrees, more exacting. We have as social creatures a set of basic obligations, each to the other. The set includes an obligation to a limited degree of beneficence. Superimposed upon this, practically everyone has ultra obligations, though they are not usually so exacting as those of Sidney and Schweitzer. Having an ultra obligation to act in certain ways is a matter of having a certain character. This has already begun to appear and it will appear more fully later. Knowing that one has an ultra obligation to act in certain ways is a matter of knowing one's own character. It is probably true to say that the most important influence in Western civilization both for forming character and for revealing people's characters to themselves is the teaching of Christ. This is not to say that it is the only influence, nor that it has been the most important influence in the lives of many men who have been more or less distinguished. It is only to say that if we look at Western civilization over the last two thousand years we are hard put to it to name any other influence whose overall effect has been greater. This suggests that we should look at the teaching of Christ in relation to what has been said here about ultra obligation, basic obligation and rights.

We shall think of the Mosaic Law—excluding its ceremonial parts—as playing in Palestine in the time of Christ the same role as the set of basic obligations in present society; the role of a set of basic obligations upon which the ultra obligations of different people are superimposed. It is indeed the case that most of the actions enjoined by the Decalogue are actions which are accepted as being basically obligatory in present society; certainly this is true of the fifth to tenth Commandments, and, with a not implausible interpretation, the same can be said of the third. But I do not wish to push the parallel too far. The most I wish to claim is that there is an illuminating comparison to be made between, on the one hand, the Mosaic Law and the teaching of Christ and, on the other, the set of basic obligations and the recognition by many people of ultra obligations.

Christ's ethical teaching consists in nearly all cases of a comment upon the Law. It was never his intention to replace the Law but to supplement it:

For verily I say unto you, Till heaven and earth pass, one jot nor one tittle shall in no wise pass from the law, till all be fulfilled. Whosoever therefore shall break one of these least commandments . . . he shall be called least in the kingdom of heaven: but whosoever shall do and teach them, the same shall be called great in the kingdom of heaven.[1]

But obedience to the Law is *not enough*. Christ demands of his disciples far more than this:

For verily I say unto you, that except your righteousness shall exceed the righteousness of the scribes and Pharisees, ye shall in no case enter into the kingdom of heaven.[2]

[1] Matt. 5 vv. 18–19. [1] Matt. 5 v. 20.

Obey the Law, certainly, Christ says; there can never be any justification for failing to do that. But inheritance of the kingdom of heaven requires far more of you than this. Then with the formula, 'Ye have heard that it was said by them of old time . . . But I say unto you . . .', he explains how each Commandment is to be reinterpreted so that it makes far greater demands upon the moral capacity of his followers than have ever been made before.

But not only does Christ require his disciples to obey the Law, interpreted with an altogether new stringency; he requires them again and again to forgo their own rights under the law. Thus, as recorded by Luke,[1] when a young man asks him to intercede on his behalf so that his brother may allow him his share of the inheritance, Christ says in effect: Never mind about your share of the inheritance; never mind about your rights; the growth of your soul is much more important than the growth of your material wealth. And again, never mind your right to recompense. When a man strikes you on one cheek, turn the other one to him also. If a man sues you, under the Law, for your coat, give him your cloak as well; never mind your rights to your own property. Christ demands of his disciples that they should pay strict respect to the rights of others, but display no corresponding enthusiasm in claiming their own.

Two thousand years of history have thrown up few men who have adopted Christ's teaching through and through. But numerous people have adopted what we may call an all-embracing mode of life under his influence. We have considered Albert Schweitzer and Sir Philip Sidney as examples, and there are many more—many a priest, teacher, missionary and monk. Many again take on charitable activities under the influence of his teaching. But even more people, without becoming priests or teachers or missionaries and without becoming charity workers, allow his teaching to inform the orthodox modes of life they have chosen. Many a clerk and civil engineer, many a bricklayer and barrister live lives informed more or less by it. Few men attain the heights Christ had mapped out for us; but in more or less watered down form, in part or in whole, his teaching guides the lives of large numbers of men. It is this fact which makes it so difficult to notice the distinction between basic and ultra obligation. If men divided sharply into those who obeyed the Mosaic Law merely and those who followed the teaching of Christ to the letter,

[1] Luke 12 vv. 13-15

there would be no difficulty in seeing the difference. It would not be difficult to see that the man who says, 'This man has sued me for my coat; I ought to give him my cloak as well', is making a different kind of judgement from another who says, 'This man is not satisfied with the job I did for him, and I did make a botch of it; I ought not to charge him'. In the first case the man had no right to the cloak; but in the second he had the right not to be charged. Here the distinction is clear, but we do not often come across men such as the first speaker in our daily lives. We read of Sidney and Schweitzer, but we seldom come across people of their stamp. Instead our daily intercourse is with men who follow, either consciously or unconsciously, some less exacting version of Christ's teaching. Thus many of the moral ought judgements which we encounter in our daily lives and many which we find ourselves making are in terms of ultra obligation while others are in terms of basic obligation. And for the most part, we have no clear ideas on which are which. It is only by considering men of outstanding moral worth that we are able clearly to perceive the distinction.

In saying all this, I do not want to suggest that the teaching of Christ is the only influence which leads men to go beyond their basic obligations to others. It is patently untrue of parts of the world untouched by his influence and it is also untrue of those parts in which his teaching is made known to everyone. Nor need the influence be specifically religious—unless the word is understood in a wildly extended sense. As we shall see, any man, whether a great religious leader or a great artist or just a parent or a friend—any man who can reveal to another some truth which he did not know about his character—may also reveal to the other that a certain mode of life, or a certain colouring of a life already adopted, is ultra obligatory upon him. Christ's teaching was taken as an example, and as the most prominent and well known example, of this phenomenon.

The conclusion must be that two distinct modes of the concept of obligation are involved in moral thought, but that the distinction between them can be clearly perceived only by considering extreme examples. The two modes are named basic and ultra obligation. We have seen that they differ in their logical relations to rights: if A has a basic obligation to B to do an action x, then B has the right to A's doing x and vice versa; but if A has an ultra obligation to B to do x, B does not have a right to A's doing x; A's ultra obligation to B

is to do *more* for *B* than he has the right to. If I have a basic obligation to tell you the truth in a given set of circumstances, then you have the right to my telling you the truth in those circumstances, and vice versa. But Sidney's ultra obligation to give the other soldier the water does not imply that the other had a right to the water. Sidney's ultra obligation is to do more for him than he has the right to. It has also begun to appear that the ground of basic and ultra obligations is different. In the succeeding sections, I shall be leading up to the discussion of the ground of ultra obligations.

3. FULFILMENT

Different men find happiness or fulfilment in quite different modes of life. Tom, let us say, is married and has two sons. He works behind the counter in a grocer's shop, takes his wife to the cinema once a week and goes to the pub with his friends on another. He enjoys playing with the children and taking them to the sea in a small family saloon on a summer week-end. Each June they go to Margate for an annual holiday. Tom may be perfectly happy in this life. It may not be possible to suggest any change which would make him happier. Jeremy is a different sort of man. He is a bachelor advertising executive who runs a vintage Bentley. Children are of no interest to him, and a sequence of affairs is more to his taste than a settled married life. He spends many months each year abroad on his firm's business, and uses a large expense account with discrimination in the capitals of Europe. He has two holidays each year, one for winter sports and another beginning on August 12th. Jeremy too may be perfectly happy in this life; it may not be possible to suggest any change which would make him happier. We could say that, in their respective lives, Tom and Jeremy fulfil themselves. The word is perhaps slightly pretentious, but it is not so badly out of place as 'happiness' in talking of the lives of some other men. If we look at the lives of many great artists, and to a lesser extent of many great thinkers, we could not say that they were aiming at being happy. Happiness is too tame a notion to do justice to the purpose of their lives. An artist like Van Gogh, a thinker like Nietzsche and a teacher like Christ are in the grip of a demonic urge which it would be inept to describe as seeking happiness. The least we can do is talk of their striving to fulfil themselves. The word is only slightly pretentious when used of the lives of Tom and Jeremy; it is more appropriate than 'happiness' in speaking of many men who engage our attention long after their deaths. For these reasons it will be adopted here. The most important question a man has to ask himself is: In what mode of life—in what combination of activities and states—will I find my fulfilment? For enormous numbers of people the answer follows a fairly standard pattern: Marry a pretty girl who can cook; have some children; do a job—it is not critically important what job—as well as the next man; earn as much as I can; own my own house and car; engage in recreations and entertainments to taste; love my neighbour with some fraction of my enthusiasm for myself. There will be some men for whom one activity will predominate in importance over any other. The fulfilment of a man may lie principally in being a poet, a perfect husband or a philosopher; in devoting his life to helping others or caring for sick animals; or in giving his children and the children of his relatives the opportunities that he did not have. Usually, there will be secondary activities in any life of fulfilment, but we can imagine men for whom any of these aims is the heart of that life.

Whether a man is right or wrong in adopting any mode of life depends upon the sort of man he is. It depends upon the character of the man. Collingwood records in his Autobiography that as a small boy he chanced upon a copy of Kant's *Grundlegung zur Metaphysik der Sitten* on his father's shelves:

I felt that the contents of this book, although I could not understand them, were somehow my business: a matter personal to myself, or rather to some future self of my own. It was not like the common boyish intention to 'be an engine driver when I grow up' for there was no desire in it; I did not, in any natural sense of the word, 'want' to master the Kantian ethics when I should be old enough; but I felt as if a veil had been lifted and my destiny revealed.[1]

It may be one's destiny to be a philosopher like Collingwood, or a poet or a musician; or to live like Tom or Jeremy; or, like Albert Schweitzer, to devote oneself to the service of other people. A man's destiny—the mode of life in which he will find fulfilment—may be revealed to him by a friend, a religious teacher, a parent, an artist or simply by a chance encounter with a small book on his father's shelves. Alternatively, it may need no revealing. In any case it is determined by the character of the man.

[1] R. G. Collingwood, *An Autobiography* (Oxford), p. 4.

4. REASON FOR ADOPTING A MODE OF LIFE

Whether a man's fulfilment lies in being a poet or in the service of other people, the ground for saying that he ought to adopt one mode of life or the other is that he will thereby fulfil himself. If this is not so he ought not to adopt it. It was on this point that Schweitzer was so insistent that would-be missionaries should satisfy themselves. He demanded of each individual that he should look deep into his character and ensure that the life is a matter of course for *him*. Such advice is not usually available for a man who is deciding whether or not to be a poet, but it is plain enough that it is appropriate in the same way. So far the ground of the judgements that one man ought to be a poet and that another ought to devote his life to other people is the same. But there is also a difference of importance. In being a poet a man may give pleasure to many people. Many poets have. But in saying that his fulfilment lies in being a poet, we are not saying that it *consists in* devoting himself to other people: it consists in being a poet. On the other hand, in saying that a man's fulfilment lies in the service of others, we are saying just this, viz., that it lies in the service of others. The ground of the judgement that a mode of life ought to be adopted is always that it leads to fulfilment; but different lives fulfil different people, and sometimes a man's fulfilment consists in devoting himself to other people. *The difference between a prudential judgement and a judgement of ultra obligation begins at this point*. When a man's fulfilment consists in the devotion of his own capacities to the interests of others, the judgement that he ought to adopt this life is one of ultra obligation. Otherwise it is prudential. The same point holds when some part of a man's fulfilment consists in devoting some part of his life to others, and living for the rest as Tom or Jeremy do. For example, a man may judge, either by himself or with help from others, that he ought to spend one afternoon a week assisting with orphaned children, or that he ought regularly to give a large proportion of an ample income to charity. Provided a certain stipulation about motives, which is to be discussed in a moment, is satisfied, such judgements are of ultra obligation, while all other judgements he makes about the kind of life he ought to live may be prudential.

Ultra obligations require beneficent action, and they require a greater degree of beneficence than basic obligations. To say that a man ought to devote his life, or part of his life, to others is to make a judgement of ultra obligation: ultra obligation because devoting one's life to others is not merely respecting one's basic obligation of beneficence. Devoting one's life to others is doing more for others than the basic obligation requires. It is doing more for others than they are entitled to by right.

An important point has now to be made about the relative merits of the reasons for the adoption of different modes of life by different people. In making it I shall assume that the kinds of life in question do not characteristically involve the violation of basic obligations. The qualification is important: without it the point to be made does not stand. Isolated conflicts can, of course, occur: a particular action which falls under a class which is prudentially or ultra obligatory may also fall under a class which is forbidden by a basic obligation. The supposition is that the classes of action involved in the lives in question are not forbidden by basic obligations. With this understanding suppose there are two men, A and B, such that

$R(a)$ A's fulfilment lies in being a poet

and $R(b)$ B's fulfilment lies in devoting himself to others

$R(a)$ is a better reason for A's becoming a poet than for A's adopting any other life; and $R(b)$ is a better reason for B's devoting himself to others than for B's adopting any other life. The propositions establish respectively that A ought to become a poet and that B ought to devote his life to others. The important point to be made is that $R(b)$ is in no sense a better reason for B's devoting his life to others than $R(a)$ is for A's devoting himself to poetry; nor, of course, vice versa. As reasons for A's choosing one life and B's choosing a different one, they are one as good as the other. The point can be made alternatively by saying that there is no mode of the concept of obligation in which we could correctly say that A ought to emulate B or that B ought to emulate A. All modes of the concept have the implication of better reason than . . .; so that if we could say that A ought to emulate B we should have to admit that there was a reason for A's devoting his life to others which is better than his reason for becoming a poet. The argument of this section has been designed to show that it is not so: the only good reason for adopting a mode of life is that one's character decrees it; and this is independent of the question of whether the mode of life consists in the service of others or anything else. Locke remarked in the *Essay*[1] upon the futile quest for the *summum bonum*. If the quest is, as Locke took it, for a mode of life of which we can correctly say that everyone ought to adopt it, then the quest is indeed futile. There is no such mode of life. And even if there were, the reason for everyone's adopting it would not be that it is such and such a mode of life but that everyone's fulfilment lies in adopting it. On the other hand, using '*summum bonum*' differently, we may say that the *summum bonum* is that state in which each man fulfils himself so far as he can while also according to every other man his rights; while also doing those actions enjoined by, and refraining from those actions forbidden by, the contract ground.

We have been considering two men: the fulfilment of the first lies in being a poet; of the second in devoting himself to other people. In saying that no reason can be given for either emulating the other, I am not denying that one life is morally better than the other. Of course the man who devotes his life to other people lives a morally better life than the poet. It is just this comment we are making in saying he is a good *man*. We should not say that the poet was a good man—not unless he was apart from being a poet. We say, recent fashions apart, that Schweitzer was a good man. But although T. S. Eliot was a good poet, we do not say he was a good man—not unless he was quite apart from being a poet. A life devoted to the service of other people *is* a morally better life than a poet's life, qua poet's. But it now transpires that the fact that one life is morally better than another is *not a reason for adopting it*. If it were, we should be able to give to a man whose fulfilment lies in writing poetry a reason for devoting himself to good works. Of course, if one life characteristically involves violating the rights of others, and another life does not, the second is morally better than the first, and there is a reason for adopting the second rather than the first. But the reason is not that it is morally better. The reason is that the first life characteristically involves doing actions which the contract ground provides good reason for not doing.

If anyone should feel that this discussion makes the notion of moral good seem less important than he would have thought, I can only say that I believe his feeling is justified. The points made will be confirmed and developed in chapter 5.

---

[1] *Essay Concerning Human Understanding*, Bk. II, ch. 21, sec. 55.

5. ULTRA OBLIGATION AND ALTRUISTIC MOTIVES

To adopt a certain mode of life is to do characteristically, though not necessarily without occasional omissions, actions of a certain class or classes. Suppose a man helps regularly at an orphanage on Saturday afternoons, although he is not required to by a basic obligation. Suppose further than he does so only for the sake of the good opinion of his neighbours. In general, we suppose that a man characteristically does more than a basic obligation requires for the sake of the applause. His motive is, as we should say, not above suspicion. Now the enjoyment of applause may certainly be an element in his fulfilment, or, to use a more natural expression in this context, his happiness. Thus it can be established that he ought to do this class of actions on the ground that they bring applause, and that enjoyment of applause is an element in his happiness. And as it appears that the class of actions goes beyond the requirement of basic obligations, it may seem that we have sufficient to establish that the judgement that he ought to act in this way is one of ultra obligation. But a closer look at the situation will show that it is not so. The reason given for the ought judgement is that the class of actions enjoined brings applause and that the receipt of applause is an element in his fulfilment. All that is thus established is that he ought to do actions of this class if applause is likely to be forthcoming; if there are witnesses. But, except in special cases in which an action as such gives offence, there can be no basic obligation to act in certain ways only when witnesses are present. The argument therefore, contrary to initial appearance, does not establish that the man ought to act beyond the requirements of basic obligation, and one of the necessary conditions for a judgement of ultra obligation is not satisfied. It is, after all, prudential. It is not unlike a man claiming that he has an ultra obligation to do extra services to help attractive women. Unless there is a basic obligation to help attractive women in ways in which one is not required to help plain ones, no one can have an ultra obligation to do so.

But suppose witnesses always were present, that actions more beneficent than those required by basic obligation always called forth applause, and that the receipt of such applause was an element in a man's fulfilment. The reason 'Such actions always occasion applause' is, in this circumstance, a reason for doing, without exception, actions which are more beneficent than those required by basic obligation. We also have enough to establish that the man ought to do such actions. But we should be mistaken if we thought this judgement to be one of ultra obligation. The concept of ultra obligation was introduced by speaking of a man's fulfilment consisting in devoting himself to others; by contrasting him, for example, with a poet, whose fulfilment consists in writing poetry. In saying that a man's fulfilment, or part of his fulfilment, lies in devoting his life, or part of his life, to others, we are not saying simply that it lies in doing actions of certain classes. It might lie in doing such actions for the sake of the applause, for witnesses may always be present. To say that his fulfilment lies in devoting himself to others is not to make a comment only upon the kinds of action he ought to do; it is to make a comment also upon the motives from which he ought to do them. Doing such actions from selfish motives is not devoting oneself to others; it is devoting oneself to oneself. To devote oneself to others is to do such actions from altruistic motives.

For some men over large sectors of their lives, and for many men over smaller sectors of their lives, a reason can be given for judging that they ought, from altruistic motives, to do actions which do for others more than they are entitled to by right. The reason is that their fulfilment, or some part of their fulfilment, consists in acting in such ways from altruistic motives. It is important to stress at this point that we are speaking of a *reason* for the judgement that a man ought to do actions of certain classes from certain *motives*. In *The Right and the Good*, Sir David Ross persists in a mistake which has done more than its fair share towards fouling moral philosophy. He writes:

. . . the attempt to base rightness on conduciveness to the advantage or pleasure of the agent . . . comes to grief over the fact, which stares us in the face . . . that as soon as a man does an action *because* he thinks he will promote his own interests thereby, he is acting not from a sense of its rightness but from self interest.[1]

Action which I call ultra obligatory is a sub-class of action which Ross would call right; and I shall assume that he would say of the fulfilment of the agent the same as he says of his advantage or pleasure. His argument rests upon a horrible confusion between the

[1] p. 16.

reason for an ought judgement and a motive for action. In the first half of the paragraph, he is speaking of a reason; in the second of a motive. And he argues that because acting from a certain kind of motive, self interest, is not acting morally, therefore the thesis that reasons for ought judgements are in terms of self interest comes to grief. But, as is obvious once the muddle is pointed out, no such conclusion follows. Let us see how the matter stands in relation to what has been said about ultra obligation. The proper reason for a judgement of ultra obligation is certainly in terms of the agent's interest[1]: it is to the effect that he will find fulfilment in a certain mode of life. But the judgement for which it is a reason is the judgement that he ought to do actions of certain kinds *from altruistic motives;* that he ought to do actions of certain kinds, his motive being that he believes they will benefit others and his desire to benefit others (1, 3). If it is true that a man has an ultra obligation to do actions of the class X from altruistic motives, and if he characteristically does actions of that class from such motives, then he is acting in accordance with reason. He is acting rationally. He is acting rationally because he is fulfilling himself, and there is every reason for a man's so acting—provided, of course, that in doing so, he does not violate the rights of others. But if he characteristically does actions of that class from selfish motives, he is not fulfilling himself. If, for example, his motive is the belief that he will fulfil himself in such action and the desire to fulfil himself, then in acting from that motive he is *not* fulfilling himself: if his fulfilment lies in acting from altruistic motives he does not fulfil himself in acting from selfish motives. And in failing to fulfil himself he is acting irrationally, for there is every reason for his acting differently. Thus a man upon whom a certain class of actions is ultra obligatory acts rationally only if he does actions of that class from altruistic motives. But this conclusion is perfectly compatible with the reason for the ought judgement being in terms of his own interest: that in action of the kind enjoined, he will find his fulfilment. It is seen to be compatible as soon as the distinction is kept clear between a motive and a reason.

[1] But, as we shall see later (4, 7), not in terms of his interest assessed *independently* of the interest of others.

6. THE GROUND OF ULTRA OBLIGATIONS

The ground of propositions of ultra obligation can be set down immediately, X representing a class of actions:

Doing X from altruistic motives is an element in A's fulfilment
and
Doing X is doing more for others than they are entitled to by right
conjointly imply
A has an abstract ultra obligation to do X from altruistic motives

The ultra obligation in the conclusion of the argument is abstract. Any individual action which falls under the class X may also fall under a class which is forbidden by a basic obligation. The situation when such conflicts occur will be discussed in a short while.

The objection may be lodged that any argument such as this is totally remote from any actual moral discussion which occurs in day to day life. The answer must be that it is not remote from the kind of discussion in which Schweitzer engaged with potential missionaries, and it is not remote from countless other cases of the same kind. The truth of the first premiss is precisely the question at issue in such discussions. The second premiss is indeed not explicit but, as the distinction between basic and ultra obligations is not drawn, it is not surprising. The argument is indeed remote from the majority of moral discussions because very few of them are concerned with the classes of action which are ultra obligatory upon people. Discussions which centre round the notion of ultra obligation are usually between people who know each other fairly well, and know the kind of actions which are ultra obligatory upon each other. The questions at issue are questions of fact and consistency. The conclusion of the argument stated so far is a premiss of the greater number of discussions. The point at issue is whether some particular action x is a member of the class X. Given that it is, there is no further dispute about the next stage in the schema, viz.,

A has an abstract ultra obligation to do X from altruistic motives, and A can do x
implies
A has an abstract ultra obligation to do x from altruistic motives

The discussion may be concerned exclusively with the question of whether x is a member of the class X. That the fundamental argument set out is remote from the majority of practical discussions need cause us no concern.

I have so far related ultra obligations only to the basic obligation of limited beneficence, saying that an ultra obligation is an obligation to do more for others than they are entitled to by right under that basic obligation. The account now needs extension. Reflection on the contract ground will show, I think, that the beneficence which husbands owe to wives and vice versa under a *basic* obligation is greater than that decreed by the basic obligation of limited beneficence. The same applies to the beneficence owed by parents to children, friends to friends and so on. But these obligations, although they require more than the basic obligation of limited beneficence, are not ultra obligations; they are basic because derived from the contract ground. Thus an ultra obligation is not adequately explained as an obligation to do more for others, from altruistic motives, than they are entitled to by right under the basic obligation of limited beneficence. It is properly explained as an obligation to do more for people of a certain class than they are entitled to by right under the basic obligation of beneficence which the agent owes to people of that class. For example, a man owes more beneficence to his wife than to Tom, Dick and Harry: he owes more as a matter of basic obligation. Thus, since a man can have basic obligations to his wife or to his friends which he does not have to people at large, so can he have ultra obligations to his wife and friends which he does not have to people at large. By contrast, he cannot have an ultra obligation to blondes: he has no basic obligation to blondes as a class of people.

I must deal finally in this section with the possibility of a conflict between a basic and an ultra obligation. Suppose a certain class of actions is ultra obligatory upon a man, but a particular action which falls under this class falls also under a class which an abstract basic obligation forbids. Suppose, for example, that in fulfilling his ultra obligation he would do a great benefit to A but doing so would involve violating a basic obligation as a result of which a quite minor injury is suffered by B. This is a case in which there is a conflict not between two abstract basic obligations, but between an abstract basic and an abstract ultra obligation, but it is plain that the same procedure for determining what is actually obligatory applies as when the conflict is between two abstract basic obligations (3, 12). The contract ground is applied in just the same way, but in this case it is not a question of a particular action x falling under two classes X_1 and X_2 which are such that both X_1 and Not-X_2 satisfy the contract ground. The position is that Not-X_2 satisfies it and X_1 satisfies the ground of abstract ultra obligations. The resulting actual obligation is *basic*, not *ultra*, because the action which is actually obligatory satisfies the contract ground as applied to a conflict of obligations. If the abstract ultra obligation is superior, the resulting obligation would enjoin a class of complementary actions: it would enjoin the ultra obligatory action upon all those who had such an ultra obligation; and it would require of everyone that they did not claim as an actual right the abstract right which would have been actual if it were not for the conflict.

7. ULTRA OBLIGATION AND REASON FOR ACTING

It has been a central purpose of this work to establish a theory about the relation between the concepts of obligation and reason for acting and thus show how propositions about obligations are relevant to action. These relations are stated in the final implication of the Reason-for-Acting/Obligation schema which, in general form, is:

P
implies
A ought (   ) to do x
implies
There is a reason for A's doing x which is better than . . .

The appropriate P has been brought to light for prudential obligation (1, 8); for basic obligations arising out of promises (Ch. 2); for basic obligations which do not arise out of promises (Ch. 3) and for ultra obligations (this chapter). The final implication has been established for the former three cases (1, 8; 2, 10; and 3, 13–14 respectively) and it remains to show that it holds for abstract ultra obligation. As remarked earlier, once it is shown to hold for the abstract modes, it is obvious that the appropriate implication holds for the actual modes. The final implication for abstract ultra obligation is:

A has an abstract ultra obligation to do x from altruistic motives
implies

There is a reason for A's doing x from altruistic motives which is better than any in terms of his overall *independent* interest for doing either x or not-x

It is fairly easy to show that this implication holds. If A has an abstract ultra obligation to do x from altruistic motives, it is because part of his fulfilment lies in doing from such motives, actions of the class X. Doing actions of this class from such motives is an element in his fulfilment while failing to do them is not. There is thus a reason for his doing them. But although the reason is in terms of his fulfilment, it is not in terms of his interest assessed independently of the interests of others. He cannot have an ultra obligation unless part of his fulfilment lies in devoting himself to other people, and we cannot determine the classes of actions, or the particular actions, which are ultra obligatory upon him without employing premises about the interests of other people. In consequence, the reason for his doing such actions is not in terms of his independent interest (1, 9). His fulfilment consists in acting in the interests of others; it consists in doing, from altruistic motives, more for others than is their right. The poet considered earlier is a different case. His fulfilment consists in being a poet; it does not consist in doing, from any motive whatever, more for others than is their right. And if his fulfilment lies in being a poet, there is a reason for his acting in certain ways which *is* in terms of his independent interest.

If a certain class of actions is ultra obligatory upon a man, his fulfilment, or part of it, lies in doing actions of that class and not in promoting his independent interest by not doing them: in relation to such actions his interest in serving others is greater than his interest in serving himself without regard to others. Thus there is a reason for his doing such actions which is better than any in terms of his independent interest, and the final implication of the schema, as it applies to ultra obligation, holds.

I have now argued that the Reason-for-Acting/Obligation schema proposed in chapter 1 holds for all modes of the concept of obligation. The argument has not been set out for the actual modes, but it is evident that the schema applies here once it is shown that it holds for the abstract modes. The schema provides what might be called an analysis of the concept of obligation: it reveals the common thread which holds the distinct modes of the concept together and reveals also distinctions between them. Further distinctions would be brought out by looking at the relations between the various modes and other concepts in the same field: by the kind of investigation carried out in chapter 2 for basic obligation, rights, blame, moral good and trustworthiness.

To have shown that the schema holds for all modes of the concept is to have shown, *inter alia*, that the proposition that A ought ( ) to do x implies that there is a reason for A's doing x which is better than . . . Obligation judgements are related to action, or are practical, by virtue of this implication. To explain the practicality of moral judgement, no prescriptive theory is needed, nor any theory which falls under the title of 'Ethics without Propositions'.

The investigation of obligation is now complete and I turn to the notion of moral good.

CHAPTER 5

GOOD

I shall argue that the ground of propositions in terms of moral good always refers to the fulfilment of basic obligations or ultra obligations. If I succeed, I shall have vindicated Kant's saying that:

the concept of good and evil must not be determined before the moral law (of which it seems it must be the foundation), but only after it and by means of it.[1]

It seems, as Kant says, that judgements of moral good are logically prior to judgements of what ought to be done; it has seemed so to countless Utilitarian philosophers. The converse is the truth: the structure of morals can be made intelligible only if the grounds of judgements of obligation are set out first, so that the discharge of obligations can be referred to in the grounds of judgements of moral good. The thesis for which I argue is deontological in the sense that it takes the concept of obligation to be, in this way, fundamental among moral concepts. But it is teleological in the sense that the concepts of fulfilment, for ultra obligation, and of its being in every-one's interest to make contracts, for basic obligation, are teleological concepts. I should like to think of it as a complex teleological theory which attempts to remedy the defects of simple teleological theories by taking obligation as the fundamental moral concept.

I. MORALLY BETTER THAN

It is, it seems to me, a very easy matter to obtain a grasp of judge-ments of moral good once we have available the work already done on judgements of obligation. I shall approach the problem not directly but by discussing judgements in terms of *morally better than*. Motives, actions, men, intentions, qualities of character and states of mind can all be assessed as being one morally better than another. I shall illustrate my position by discussing motives, actions and men.

[1] *Critique of Practical Reason*, ed. Abbott, 1907, p. 154.

Motives

Some kinds of motive, in most kinds of situation, are *more likely to lead to right action* than others. This is the fact which we mark in saying that this kind of motive, in this kind of situation, is a morally better motive than another. And the ground of the judgement that it is a morally better motive is that it is more likely, in the kind of situation in question, to lead to action which is obligatory upon the agent, i.e., right action. The point is illustrated by considering some typical cases, confining ourselves in the first instance to motives for doing actions which are basically obligatory. The motive for doing such an action may be the belief that it is right plus the desire to do right; or it may be the belief that one will otherwise run into trouble plus the desire to avoid trouble. It will be agreed that the former is a morally better motive, and it is plain that it is more likely to lead to right action. It leads to right action, as the latter does not, when there is no danger of running into trouble; when, that is, an agent who acts, as a matter of course, from this kind of motive can avoid the penalties of doing wrong. For similar reasons, a benevolent motive, e.g., the belief that an action is in the interest of another person plus the desire to act in his interest, is a morally better motive than the desire to avoid trouble or the fear of disapproval: the former leads to right action when there is no danger of trouble nor of disapproval. There are, however, kinds of situation in which a benevolent motive must be judged less good than the belief that an action is right and the desire to do right. In judging examination results, the belief that an action will help someone you like plus the desire to help those you like is the less likely to lead to right action: it is quite likely to lead to awarding a candidate a higher class than he deserves. In such a situation the 'sense of duty' is a morally better motive than benevolence.

Ultra obligations are obligations to do actions of certain classes from altruistic motives. If the action requirement, as distinct from the motive requirement, of an ultra obligation is done for the sake of the applause, the obligation is not fulfilled at all. Thus, in the case of ultra obligations, an altruistic motive is morally better than any other kind of motive: it is more likely to lead to obligatory action than any other kind of motive because it is the only kind of motive which can lead to obligatory action.

This is all I have to say about the assessment of one kind of motive as morally better than another. To summarize: some kinds of motive are more likely to lead to the fulfilment of basic or ultra obligations than other kinds. It is this fact that we mark in saying that a motive of such a kind is morally better than a motive of another kind. And the ground of the proposition that a motive of the kind M_1 is morally better than a motive of the kind M_2 is that M_1 is more likely than M_2 to lead to obligatory action in the kind of situation in question. The ground for judging one quality of character or state of mind as morally better than another is very similar.

Actions

One action may fulfil a basic obligation which another does not; one may fulfil an ultra obligation which another fails to fulfil; one may fulfil an ultra obligation while another fulfils only a basic obligation; one may fulfil an ultra obligation which requires more in the service of others than a second. Such are the facts to be marked by saying that the first mentioned action of each pair is a morally better action than the second. And each of these propositions is a ground for saying that the first mentioned action is a morally better action than the second. Both the propositions that action A_1 fulfils an obligation which A_2 fails to fulfil, and that A_1 fulfils a more demanding obligation than A_2 are grounds for the proposition that A_1 is a morally better action than A_2. By a more demanding obligation is meant an obligation requiring the agent to do more in the interests of other people than a less demanding obligation; as, for example, an ultra obligation requires more to be done in the interests of other people than a basic obligation.

It is not clear to me whether, in everyday life, we judge one action as morally better than another without taking into account the motive from which it was done. We do not normally use 'morally good' in connection with action without consideration of the motive, but, as will be explained, more is involved in judging an action to be morally *good*. The point is, however, of little importance: the previous paragraphs have made it clear what our grounds would be for judging some motives as morally better than others and for judging some actions as morally better than others if the judgements were made independently of each other.

Men

When we speak of one man as morally better than another we are
making a judgement about more or less lasting periods of the lives of
both. We can say, for example, that one man was better than another
when they were both young but not in later life; or we can say that
one was better than another taking their whole lives in view. But we
could not say that one was better than another on his 21st birthday—
though we could say that he did better actions on that day. Some
men characteristically do morally better actions than others, and do
them from an appropriate motive. This is the fact which we mark
by saying that some men are morally better men than others. The
ground of the proposition that A is a morally better man that B is
that he characteristically does morally better actions from an appropriate motive.

I have now set out the grounds of propositions that X is morally
better than Y, where X and Y may be motives, actions or men.
The account is easily extended to intentions, qualities of character
and states of mind. Thus in stating the ground of any proposition
that one thing is morally better than another reference is made to the
fulfilment of obligations. But the ground of propositions of basic and
ultra obligation makes no reference to anything being morally better
than anything else, nor to anything being morally good. Kant's
insight, expressed in the quotation at the beginning of this chapter,
is right. Moral good is a coping stone of morality, not a foundation
stone.

2. MORALLY GOOD

So far I have spoken only of the judgement that X is morally better
than Y. It is now time to consider the judgement that X is morally
good, and in doing so I shall confine myself to actions and men. Our
actual use of these terms does not mark any clear cut distinctions,
and there is a certain haziness of usage which can be brought against
what I shall say. My defence is that I am recording a marked tendency, and it is a tendency which I think is worth marking more
forcefully.

There are very many cases in which we should have to concede
that A was a morally better man than B, but in which we should not
judge that A was a morally good man. For example, suppose that A

and *B* were criminals of equal iniquity, but that one was kind to his family while the other was not. In such a case we should have to concede that the second was morally better than the first, but we should not say that he was a morally good man. Again, if of two thugs bent on robbery one held back, from an appropriate motive, while the other assaulted the night watchman, we should have to concede that he was a morally better man than the other though we should not judge that he was a morally good man. We should also have to concede that his action was morally better, though we should not judge that it was morally good. The reason for this is that 'Morally Good' is a medal struck for those who give distinguished service. We could arrange men, in a rough and ready way, upon a scale such that we should have to concede that any man at a higher point on it was morally better than a man at a lower point. But we should not thereby be committed to judging that he was morally good. 'Morally Good' is a medal awarded only to those at the higher points on the scale. In saying, in the most characteristic use of the expression, that a man is morally good, we are saying that he is morally better than, and usually a good deal better than, the average moral agent. We are saying that he stands out above the average in respect of the moral quality of the actions he characteristically does. And the more he stands out, the more willing we are, and the more willing we should be, to say that he is a morally good man. Many of our judgements of moral good are more specific: we speak of good fathers and good employers. Such judgements, in contrast to judgements about good bakers and good business men, are moral judgements. And the point made by them is the same: the characteristic actions of a good father and a good employer, so far as they affect their children and employees respectively, stand out, in respect of moral quality, in comparison with the characteristic actions of the average parent and the average employer.

3. MORAL GOOD AND ULTRA AND BASIC OBLIGATION

In a society in which most people most of the time respect their basic obligations, a man worthy of the title 'Morally Good' must be one who has and respects ultra obligations. If it were not so, far from being morally distinguished and standing out above the standard moral agent, he is an instance of the standard moral agent. If he has and respects ultra obligations to other people in general he is said to be a good man. If his ultra obligations are to specific classes of people, such as children or employees, he is said to be a good father or a good employer (as distinct from a good business man or a good baker). Moral goodness is attributed to people who characteristically do more, either for people in general or for specific classes of people, than they are entitled to by right.

It is now plain, and it is most important, that the proposition that A is a morally good man does not imply that anyone has a basic obligation to emulate him. To hold that it did would be to hold that a man could have a basic obligation characteristically to do more for others than they are entitled to by right, which is self-contradictory. Similarly, the proposition that x is a morally good action does not imply that anyone has a basic obligation to do it, for a morally good action accords someone more than his right, and it is self-contradictory to speak of a basic obligation to accord another more than his right. Again, the proposition that A is a morally better man than anyone else does not imply that anyone has a basic obligation to emulate him, and the proposition that x is the morally best action open to me does not imply that I have a basic obligation to do it.

It may seem that in a society in which people are, as we might say, lax about respecting their basic obligations, moral goodness may be attributed to a man who merely respects his basic obligations. In such a situation, it may seem that others have a basic obligation to emulate him. But if it were so, it would not be because he is morally good. It would be because he does respect his basic obligations. The position is similar in a situation in which, as we might say, most basic obligations are for the most part respected but there is one which is not. It may seem that others would have a basic obligation to emulate a man who respects this cinderella. But if it were so it would be because this man respected this obligation, and not because he was good. And in any case it is not so. As argued earlier (3, 11), the content of a basic obligation is to do X provided others for the most part also do X. If they do not there is no basic obligation. Thus the only ought propositions which could be established about the actions of a man in the situations considered is a proposition of ultra obligation.[1]

It is now established that the propositions that A is a morally good

[1] See p. 119.

man and that x is a morally good action do not imply that anyone has a basic obligation to emulate A or to do x. I shall later distinguish from moral good the notion of a man's good, and show that similar points apply. The proposition that E is an element in a man's good does not imply that anyone has a basic obligation to produce it. And the proposition that the action x produces most good (the good of all men affected by the action being considered) does not imply that anyone has a basic obligation to do x. The consequence is that, as predicted earlier (2, 9), attempts to ground a moral system in the concepts of good result in a system innocent of the concept of a right. It is for this reason that justice provides so much difficulty for Utilitarianism.

I shall now look at the situation in terms of the residual use of 'ought' (1, 11). If A is a morally good man does it follow that anyone ought (rationally) to emulate him, i.e., that there is good reason for anyone doing so? And if an action is morally good, does it follow that there is good reason for anyone doing it? It does not follow in either case. What does follow is that *if* B is *aiming* at being a morally good man of the same kind as A, then there is good reason for his emulating A. There is, this is to say, good reason for emulation only for a man who has moral intent of a particular kind. A similar point can be made about a morally good action. Consequently, any would-be Utilitarian who hopes to found a system on the notion of moral good will produce one which contains reasons for acting only for those who are already intent upon a moral life of one kind or another. And such a system, I submit, even if it could accommodate the notions of rights and justice, is not good enough. Either there is point in acting morally or there is not. If there is no point, morality might as well be forgotten. But if there is point, we should be able to give reasons for so acting to any man whatever his intent may be. Whether we should thereby provide him with a motive is another matter. But it *is* another matter.

4. A MAN'S GOOD

In this section I shall propose a definition of 'a man's good', and I shall argue that when we speak of a man's good we employ a concept which is quite distinct from that involved in judgements of moral good. In the section following, I shall climb a few rungs down the ladder, and argue that the definition is defective in such a way as to show that the concepts are not totally distinct but have, like the concepts of prudential, basic and ultra obligation, a common element. For the present, however, it is the differences between the two concepts, and not the common element, to which we attend. These differences compel us to say that while 'moral good' is, of course, a moral term, 'a man's good' is not.

I shall argue that a man's good may be defined as follows:

Df_1 A thing or an activity is an element in a man's good if and only if it is in his interest to possess it or do it.

If we ask what kinds of thing can be elements in a man's good, we are asking what kinds of things it can be in his interest to have. The (probably incomplete) answer is: The possession of (i) material things; (ii) states of body such as health, good eyesight and stamina; (iii) states of character; (iv) talents and skills; (v) opportunities to engage in activities he enjoys; and (vi) human relationships. There is room for considerable diversity in the good of different men, particularly in the possession of material things: a wine cellar for one; a collection of mummified butterflies for another. But the diversity may go further: some poets and musicians have been able to do their best work when they were sickly. For such men, health may not be an element in their good. Cases of this kind could be multiplied *ad infinitum*, in imagination if not in fact.

Consider a fairly typical man from a particular profession, a dentist, say. Some of the elements in his good under the various headings are: (i) a surgery, house and car; (ii) general good health, strength and stamina; (iii) kindness, sympathy and patience; (iv) the talents and skills which a dentist needs; (v) the opportunities to have a nap after lunch and to rest at week-ends; (vi) a wife and a family, and friends with whom to enjoy his leisure. There will be many more elements in his good, and they will vary to some extent from one dentist to another. But the list is fairly representative. It would be the most natural thing in the world to say, 'Having (or being) ... is for his own good', where the sentence is completed by any of the items listed. It is only less natural to say of any of them that it is an element in his good.

The entries under one of the headings stand out as assessable as morally good as well as elements in a man's good. These are qualities of character, of which the examples given are kindness, sympathy and patience. But the question whether these are morally good qualities is quite distinct from the question whether they are elements in the man's good and is answered upon an entirely different ground. The ground for judging that a quality of character is morally good is very like the ground for making the same judgement of a motive: it is that that quality of character is more likely than others to lead to obligatory actions being done, not by any individual, but in a society in which obligations are for the most part respected. But the ground of the judgement that these qualities are elements in the dentist's good is simply that if he does not possess them he will probably lose most of his patients. He may indeed not lose them; he may be the only dentist within a ten mile radius in an area where the public transport is deplorable. If so, it need not be in his interest to have the qualities of kindness, sympathy and patience; he will no doubt keep most of his patients whether he has them or not. If he is a hard hearted man who is unaffected by the discomfort of his patients and unaffected by social disapproval, we cannot say that it is in his interest to possess these qualities and we cannot say that they are elements in his good. But it is plain enough that these considerations have no bearing upon the question of whether kindness, patience and sympathy are morally good qualities of character.

There may be a tendency to think that the other items listed cannot be elements in a man's *good* if they are put to morally wrong purposes. The source of this idea is the belief that when 'good' is applied in the human sphere, it must be a moral term; not when we speak of a good cricketer or a good cook, but when we speak of a good man or a man's good. When we talk of good knives or good wines, 'good' is not a moral term; but, it seems to be thought, it must be a moral term when it applies to men. So far as I can see, there is no warrant for this assumption: it seems to arise from a tendency to confuse the notion of a man's good with that of a good man, i.e., a morally good man. And this is just the confusion we are trying to avoid.

Consider again the elements other than qualities of character which can be constituents of a man's good: the possession of (i) material things; (ii) states of body; (iv) talents and skills; (v) opportunities and (vi) human relationships. Any of them can be put to morally wrong purposes. A material possession such as a surgery or a house can be converted to dope peddling; strength can be used to do murder; a talent for accounting can be turned to fiddling the books; the opportunity to play golf on Sunday may be used for adultery, and friendship with the managing director to stab a rival executive in the back. How are these facts to be allowed to reflect on the claim that each of these possessions can be an element in a man's good? Should we say that such things are to count as elements in a man's good only if they are put to harmless uses? Or should we say that they are elements in his good come what may? If we adopt the latter course, the definition we have given of a man's good stands; but if we adopt the former it will have to be modified. We should have to say that X was an element in a man's good if and only if

Df_2 (1) it was in his interest to have X, and
     (2) X was not put to morally wrong purposes

Suppose two different men both own a jemmy. One is a collector, the other a burglar. The collector's interest is served by having it lying harmlessly in a show case; the burglar's by putting it to its normal use. Are we to say that the possession of the jemmy is an element in the good of the collector but not of the burglar on this ground? Or are we to say that it is an element in the good of both?

The question can be answered by leaving on one side the kind of people we are most naturally inclined to consider—decent law abiding folk—and turning our attention instead to a family of criminals. The Plugs, we will suppose, have been in criminal practice for generations just as a neighbouring family has been in the grocery business. The head of the family, Fingers, is an accomplished pick-pocket, with a substantial income. The elder children have received the best training available and are launched on successful careers; one has even entered the white collar branch of the profession as a confidence man. The time has now come to consider the education of young Steve. Fingers has decided, having a keen eye for the boy's talents, that he should be apprenticed to a safe-breaker; not any safe-breaker but the best available, whose headquarters are many miles away. But Mrs Plug, like many mothers before her, cannot endure the thought of her youngest being sent away to school. She pleads with Fingers, but he stands firm. 'We must think of the boy's future', he insists. 'It's for his own good that he should be sent away'. Eventually, like other doting mothers, Mrs Plug capitulates, and young Steve is sent away to school for *his own good*.

The discussion between the parents Plug is unfamiliar to us, but it is strikingly parallel to a type of discussion often heard. Parents decide upon a course of action for their son because it is for his own good. In this case they have decided that a certain course of training is for Steve's good. We can now return to our alternative proposed definitions of a man's good, the first of which represents 'a man's good' as a non-moral, the second as a moral, term. If we adopt the second definition we shall be committed to saying without more ado that the Plugs' judgement that a certain course of training was for Steve's good is simply false, for his training is to be put to morally wrong purposes. The position is plainly absurd: the question can be decided upon no *a priori* ground; it is decided by asking what *is* in Steve's interest, and the answer depends upon his talents, inclinations, the chances of keeping out of prison, and so on. Someone may object, 'But it cannot possibly be for a boy's good to bring him up as a criminal!' An opinion is thus expressed about a matter of fact which is supported, for example, by describing the dire effects of spending years in prison when he is caught, and perhaps stressing the diminished chances of heaven which result. The judgement is supported by talking about the boy's *interests*. It provides no objection to the definition offered. Indeed it supports it. The correct definition is the first; and its being correct shows that the notion of a man's good is not a moral notion at all.

5. GOOD AND ITS MODES

In discussing the grounds of propositions in terms of 'morally better than' and 'morally good' we saw, *inter alia*, that some kinds of motive are more likely to lead to right action than others and that we mark the fact by saying that they are morally better motives (5, 1–2). A mutual implication holds between 'Motives of the kind M_1 are more likely to lead to right action than motives of the kind M_2' and 'Motives of the kind M_1 are morally better than motives of the kind M_2'. The equivalence may be expressed by writing, 'M_1 is a morally better motive than M_2' implies and is implied by 'M_1 is likely, *in a higher degree than* M_2, to lead to obligatory action'. Similarly, on the basis of the earlier discussion, we may define 'morally better action' by saying that 'X_1 is a morally better action than X_2' implies and is implied by 'X_1 fulfils an obligation which is demanding in a higher degree than the obligation fulfilled by X_2' (provided, for cases in which one action is better than another because it fulfils an obligation which the second does not, we are prepared to say that the second, in failing to fulfil any obligation, fulfils a less demanding obligation).[1] And we may define 'morally better man' by saying that 'A_1 is morally better than A_2' implies and is implied by 'A_1 characteristically fulfils obligations which are demanding in a higher degree than the obligations fulfilled by A_2'. When we transfer from 'morally better than' to 'morally good' the definitions are adjusted by replacing the reference to the second motive (M_2), action (X_2) and man (A_2) by a reference to some standard; the standard in the case of the morally good man, for example, is, as explained previously, the average moral agent. In each of these definitions, the phrase 'in a higher degree than' occurs.

The phrase 'in a higher degree than' also occurs in the definition of 'a man's good'; the defect of that definition referred to previously (5, 4) is that the point is not made explicit by it. It becomes explicit in pointing out that 'Having or doing X is an element in A's good' is not equivalent to 'It is in A's interest to have or do X' but to 'Having or doing X is in A's interest in a higher degree than some alternative or alternatives' (the alternatives in question being made plain by the context). The point is easily missed by using 'interest' to mean greatest interest.

Let us use the word 'characteristic' sufficiently widely to allow us to say that it is a characteristic of a motive that it is likely to lead to right action; that it is a characteristic of a man that he characteristically acts so as to fulfil obligations; and that it is a characteristic of a man that it is in his interest to do certain actions and possess certain things. We may now say that, when 'good' is used in one of the ways so far discussed, any proposition in terms of good is logically equivalent to the proposition that some characteristic is possessed in a relatively high degree. Saying, for example, that M is a good motive, is equivalent to saying that M has in a relatively high degree the characteristic of being likely to lead to right action; and saying that such and such is an element in A's good is equivalent

---

[1] See p. 179 for the meaning of 'demanding'.

to saying that A has the characteristic, in a relatively high degree, of its being in his interest to possess such and such.

The notion of the morally good and of a man's good thus turn out not to be totally distinct concepts: propositions in terms of both are logically equivalent to the proposition that some characteristic, using 'characteristic' in the wide sense indicated, is possessed in a relatively high degree. But there are still differences between the concepts: different characteristics are referred to when we employ them. In fact, we have been concerned with four different characteristics, depending upon whether we are speaking of a good motive, a good action, a good man or a man's good. But the first three have it in common that they are moral characteristics while the fourth is not; a fact which is marked by our distinguishing between the notion of moral good and the non-moral notion of a man's good. By saying that the first three are moral characteristics, I mean that a moral term, 'right action' or an equivalent, is used in specifying them; and in saying that the fourth is not a moral characteristic, I mean that no moral term is used in specifying it.

We now see that we may speak of *Good and its Modes* as we previously spoke of *Obligation and its Modes*. It is interesting, though perhaps not very important, to ask whether the common element we have found when 'good' is used to speak of the morally good and of a man's good is to be found also in other uses of the term. It has often been said that in some of its uses 'good' means efficient, and that when we speak of a good saw, or a good pen, we use 'good' in a sense quite different from the moral sense. It is an alternative to suggest that the common element to be found in other uses is to be found in this one too: that the proposition that S is a good saw is logically equivalent to the proposition that some characteristic is possessed in a high degree; the characteristic of contributing to an aim which some group of people have in using it. Thus, we might suggest that 'X is a better saw, (pen, ashtray, teapot) than Y' is equivalent to 'X contributes in a higher degree than Y to the aim which some group of people, carpenters (writers, smokers, housewives), have in using it'.

Again, it has been suggested that 'good' sometimes (or even always) means pleasant: when we speak, for example, of a good cigar or a good wine. And again it is an alternative to suggest that when, in some contexts, we say 'X is a better apple (cigar, wine) than Y' the proposition expressed is equivalent to: X contributes in a higher degree than Y to the pleasure of some group of people who eat them (smoke them, drink them). The common element is found again; the difference between this use and others lies in the characteristic which is said to be possessed in a relatively high degree. 'Characteristic' has been used in a wide sense. If we use it in a narrower sense, we may say that all sorts of characteristics, e.g., sweetness and size (for apples), length and fragrance (for cigars) and mellowness and body (for wines) are relevant in deciding whether one apple (cigar, wine) is better than another; whether, that is, it contributes in a higher degree to the pleasure of some group of people than the other.

I do not know whether a thorough-going and illuminating job can be made of working out the equivalences suggested in the last two paragraphs. I have done no more than suggest the lines along which they might go. Such uses of 'good' are philosophically important only if they help us to understand the concepts of moral good and a man's good. If any light has been thrown upon these concepts in these pages it has been done by first studying the notion of obligation and then showing how the terms 'morally good' and 'morally better than' are used to make comments upon the fulfilment of obligations; and by contrasting a man's good, in this respect, with moral good. Other uses of 'good' have not helped us, and we may perhaps leave them in the philosophical penumbra where they rightly belong.

6. UTILITARIANISM AND CONTRACT THEORY

By Utilitarianism I mean the type of theory which holds that the proposition

Of all the actions open to an agent A, x produces the most good

implies that A ought to do x. I shall argue that this implication does not hold whatever mode of the concept of obligation is involved in the consequent. The notion of everyone's interest as contractually harmonized with the interest of everyone else is the logical ground of morality; the notion of the greatest good cannot be. The argument of this section is designed to show that it cannot.

The contract ground, taken alone, implies a general principle of abstract obligation. To arrive at an actual obligation in an individual case, more is required; a matter which has already been considered at length. Utilitarianism, in the form considered here, deals directly with the individual case. Rule Utilitarianism, which does not, will be considered later. It is not clear which mode of the notion of good is intended by Utilitarians to be involved in their first principle. But I have already argued (5, 3) that no proposition that such-and-such is morally good can have the implication which the Utilitarian requires, and I shall take it that it is the notion of a man's good which is involved. I think, in fact, that this interpretation comes closest to the main stream of Utilitarian thought, e.g., Bentham, Mill, Sidgwick and Rashdall. But I also think that some of the superficial plausibility of the Utilitarian position arises from not being clear which mode of the notion is involved; from not being clear, indeed, that there are two modes which could be involved.

The Utilitarian first principle must be applicable to a case in which only the actions x and not-x are open to an agent and are such that

(*P*) By doing x, A can do slightly more good for B than he can do for himself by doing not-x

The Utilitarian is committed to saying that P implies that A ought to do x. G. E. Moore would object to this formulation because he holds that the conception of A's good as distinguished from B's is nonsensical. Sidgwick argues that the implication does hold. The arguments of both these philosophers—and they are the most acute and careful of the Utilitarians—will be examined later and found wanting. For the present, I shall argue independently that the implication does not hold.

Suppose that the implicandum asserts that A has a *basic* obligation. It is quite obvious that P does not imply that B has the *right* to A's doing x: to think it does is to fail completely to understand the concept of a right. And if it does not imply that B has the right to A's doing x, it does not imply that A has a basic obligation to do x. There is no need, however, to rely on this argument, for another is available which shows at the same time that P does not imply that A has an ultra obligation to do x. If it implied either, it would imply also that

There is a reason for A's doing x which is better than any in terms of his overall independent interest for doing not-x

The reason referred to could only be *P*, and the implication holds only if *P* is a better reason than the proposition

(*Q*) Doing not-*x* is in *A*'s overall independent interest

Sidgwick holds that it is. But it should be decisive to point out that if *A* denied that *P* was a better reason than *Q* and acted accordingly, he would emerge with no blemish whatever upon his rationality. There would be no ground for saying that he had been unreasonable. All he has done is to look after himself in a situation in which he could do somewhat more good for someone else by acting differently, and no one could say that this was an *unreasonable* way to conduct himself. *P* does not imply that *A* has either a basic or an ultra obligation to do *x*.

If *A* has an ultra obligation to do the most good and *P* is true, *then* it follows that *A* has an ultra obligation to do *x*; and it also follows that there is a reason for *his* doing *x* better than any in terms of his independent interest for doing not-*x*. But equally obviously it does not follow without the premiss that *A* has an ultra obligation to do the most good. And this premiss, while it may be true as asserted of some people, will be false as asserted of others. Similarly, *P* does imply that *if A* is aiming at doing the most good, and *x* produces the most good, then there is good reason for *A*'s doing *x*. If he is aiming at doing the most good and *P* is true, then it follows that he ought (rationally) to do *x*. But again it does not follow if *A* is not aiming at doing the most good.

The Utilitarian's first principle is impotent. Taken by itself it does not imply that *A* has a basic obligation to do *x*, nor that he has an ultra obligation to do *x*, nor, as Moore held, that he has a reason as good as he could have for doing *x*. It implies nothing of moral interest.

There are, it seems to me, two causes for philosophers having thought otherwise. (1) They have not been clear that a man's good is not a moral notion. If it is thought that *P* is a moral judgement and the alleged consequent is thought of in terms of *moral* obligation, the connection may appear to hold. For 'moral obligation' easily slips into meaning the obligation which a moral man has, i.e., the obligation of a man who is aiming at being moral. And the argument easily slips into the form: if a man is aiming at being moral, and *x* is the most moral thing he can do (as *P*, thought of as a moral judgement, seems to assert), then he ought to do x. This argument is a thinly disguised version of the one we have just seen to be valid, viz., *if* a man is aiming at doing the most good, and P is true, then it follows that he ought to do x. But when it is cleared of these confusions, it transparently does nothing towards establishing that A has a basic or an ultra obligation to do x. (2) The proposition that my doing x is for my own greatest good implies that I ought (prudentially) to do x. It is tempting to see the moral case as analogous, and to think that the proposition that my doing x is for *the* greatest good, irrespective of persons, implies that I ought (morally) to do x. To this temptation, Sidgwick yielded.

I shall now examine arguments put forward by Moore and Sidgwick which, if valid, would demolish my conclusion.

Moore

Moore holds that:

> ... if it is *good absolutely* that I should have (anything), then everyone has as much reason for aiming at *my* having it as I have myself.[1]

This principle may be expressed in the form:

> ... if it is *absolutely best* that I should have (anything), then everyone has reason as good as he could have for aiming at *my* having it as I have myself

If this is true, the argument I used to show that the Utilitarian first principle, taken alone, does not imply that there is good reason for anyone doing anything is refuted; for Moore is saying that the proposition that if I am in a position in which I can produce something for another man, his having which is better than anything I could produce for myself, then I have reason as good as I could have for producing that for him. I have now to show that Moore's argument does not establish his conclusion. After saying that he will reveal a 'confusion involved in the conception of "my own good" as distinguished from "the good of others"', he argues as follows:

What, then, is meant by 'my own good'? In what sense can a thing be good *for me*? It is obvious, if we reflect, that the only thing which can belong to me, which can be *mine*, is something which is good, and not the fact that it is good. When, therefore, I talk of anything I get as 'my

---

[1] *Principia Ethica*, p. 99.

own good', I must mean either that the thing I get is good, or that my possessing it is good. In both cases it is only the thing or the possession of it which is *mine*, and not *the goodness* of that thing or possession. There is no longer any meaning in attaching the 'my' to our predicate, and saying: the possession of this *by me* is *my* good. Even if we interpret this by 'My possession of this is what *I* think good', the same still holds: for *what* I think is that my possession of it is good *simply ;* and, if I think rightly, then the truth is that my possession of it *is* good simply—not, in any sense, *my* good; and, if I think wrongly, it is not good at all. In short, when I talk of a thing as 'my own good' all that I can mean is that something which will be exclusively mine, as my own pleasure is mine . . . is also *good absolutely ;* or rather that my possession of it is *good absolutely.* The *good* of it can in no possible sense be 'private' or belong to me; any more than a thing can *exist* privately or *for* one person only. The only reason I can have for aiming at 'my own good', is that it is *good absolutely* that what I so call should belong to me— *good absolutely* that I should *have* something, which, if I have it, others cannot have. But if it is *good absolutely* that I should have it, then everyone has as much reason for aiming at *my* having it, as I have myself.[1]

This argument may be at first sight unintelligible. When Moore asks, 'In what sense can a thing be good for me ?' posing apparently a difficulty, we may want to reply, 'Well, isn't it perfectly obvious in what sense a thing can be good for me? It is good for me in the sense that it is in my interest to have it'. When a father tells his son that such-and-such is not *good for him*, is it not obvious that he is saying that it is not in his interest to have it? And when I say that being a philosopher is an element in my good, is it not obvious that I am saying, rightly or wrongly, that it is in my interest to be a philosopher?

I think this answer is not only obvious but also correct. But Moore's argument becomes lucidly intelligible the instant we remember that he thinks 'good' is the name of a quality which is, in important respects, like the quality named by 'yellow'; in fact in all respects except that one is natural and the other non-natural. Moore's position is internally consistent as we would expect. And once we remember that he thinks 'good' names a quality like that named by 'yellow', his apparently unintelligible remarks become perfectly intelligible. For example, '. . . it is only the thing or the possession of it which is *mine*, and not the goodness of that thing

---

[1] *Principia Ethica*, p. 98.

or possession'. Compare: it is only the thing or the possession of it which is *mine*, and not the yellowness of that thing or possession.

Whether Moore's argument is valid, and whether his principle is true, depends therefore upon the question whether good is a quality like yellow in the relevant respects. And it needs little reflection to see that it is not. The fact is that we can intelligibly talk of my good, my own good, your good, his good, an element in my good but not in yours, and so on. But it makes nonsense to talk of my yellow, my own yellow, your yellow, his yellow, an element in my yellow but not in yours and so on. Thus the comparison between good and yellow breaks down at precisely that point at which it must hold if it is to establish Moore's conclusion. He decides, long before he comes to the present argument, that good is a quality, which he explicitly compares with yellow. He then employs his conclusion to show that there is a confusion in talking of my good as distinguished from the good of others, just as there is a confusion in talking about my yellow as distinguished from the yellow of others. But the argument does not establish any such conclusion. All it shows is that there are ways in which good is not like yellow; in fact, that he was wrong in the first place to assimilate the two. Moore is not entitled to hold, on the strength of the argument he has produced, that '. . . if it is good absolutely that I should have anything, then everyone has as much reason for aiming at my having it as I have myself'. There is no conception of good absolutely as distinct from my good, your good, his good and so.

Sidgwick

Sidgwick does not reject the distinction between my good and the good of others. He argues in the following way for a principle which would, taken with the principle that '. . . as a rational being I am bound to aim at good generally', establish that we have an obligation to produce the greatest amount of good, irrespective of whose good it is. He writes as follows:

So far we have only been considering the 'Good on the Whole' of a single individual: but just as this notion is constructed by comparison and integration of. . .different 'goods'. . .so we have formed the notion of Universal Good by comparison and integration of the goods of all individual human—or sentient—existences. And here again, just as in the former case, by considering the relation of the integrant parts to the whole and to each other, I obtain the self-evident principle that the good of any one individual is of no more importance, from the point of view (if I may say so) of the Universe, than the good of any other; unless, that is, there are special grounds for believing that more good is likely to be realised in the one case than in the other . . .[1]

Sidgwick cannot have meant his expression 'the point of view of the Universe' to be taken seriously. He knew as well as anyone that this was a nonsensical expression, and his rider 'if I may say so' shows that he did. It was probably included as an aid to understanding and with no intention that it should be thought of as an element in a cogent proof. Leaving it out, the passage runs, 'I obtain the self-evident principle that the good of any one individual is of no more importance than the good of any other'. Now the first thing I want to show is that when a certain defect is removed from the formulation of this principle, it becomes apparent that it is not a self-evident principle at all but a contingent proposition which is false when asserted of many individuals. The defect concerns the way in which Sidgwick talks about importance: a thing cannot be simply of importance; it must be of importance *to someone*, or of importance for a purpose someone has. To say that such-and-such is important, and to deny that it is of importance to anyone is to talk nonsense. Sidgwick's principle is therefore improperly expressed; after 'importance' we must add 'to him', 'to me', 'to everyone' or some such expression. With this emendation, the principle is: '. . . the good of any one individual is of no more importance to him . . . than the good of any other'. It is plain that, far from being a self-evident principle, this proposition is contingent, and false when asserted of very many people. It seems that Sidgwick has been misled into thinking he has said something self-evident and significant at this point by using the word 'importance' *in vacuo*.

It is worth trying to alter Sidgwick's principle so that it does make an important claim. It may be done by writing, '. . . the good of any one individual *ought* not to be of any more importance to him than the good of any other'. As 'ought not to be of importance' is a curious expression, I write the principle in the form, 'No man ought to prefer his own good to that of another *merely because it is his own*'. I think this may well be what Sidgwick meant. But now we have another problem, for he says it is self-evident, but also offers

---

[1] *Methods of Ethics*, 1907, p. 382.

a proof of it. In view of the argument I have already given that it is false, I cannot accept that it is self-evident. But we must look at Sidgwick's proof to see if it reveals something wrong with the contrary proof given here. His argument goes like this: Consider an *individual* man and his good. He may be able to act in such a way as to obtain a good for himself *now*, or in another incompatible way so as to obtain a good for himself *at a later date*. Sidgwick says that he ought not to prefer either of these goods to the other *merely because one is Now and the other is Hereafter*. No one will dispute it: it is the principle of prudence. It is a necessary truth that a man ought (prudentially) to aim at his own greatest overall good. But Sidgwick seems to think that he can argue by analogy to the principle that no one ought to prefer one good to another *merely because one is his own and the other another's*. In other words he assumes that

prudential ought: good now: good hereafter

is analogous to

moral ought: good for self: good for others

He assumes that if a principle in terms of the former three concepts is true, then the corresponding principle in terms of the latter three is true. It must remain a mystery how a thinker of the stature of Sidgwick came to make such an assumption. There is no reason whatever for believing it to be true.

7. RULE UTILITARIANISM

It may seem surprising that I have concentrated attention upon Act Utilitarianism at the expense of Rule Utilitarianism; the second of these theories, or the second version of the theory, appears to find more favour among contemporary philosophers who look for a proposition in terms of the greatest good as the ground of morality. And it may seem both naïve and unjust to concentrate criticism upon a version of Utilitarian theory which many philosophers have abandoned in favour of a superior version. Rule Utilitarianism suffers, it seems to me, from the lack of systematic exposition. But so far as I understand it,[1] it is a theory which either falls by the arguments already used against Act Utilitarianism; or it turns out

---

[1] I rely largely on the account given in John Hosper's *Human Conduct* (Harcourt Brace and World).

to be an underdeveloped version of the theory for which I have argued in these pages.

A Rule Utilitarian holds that the proposition that the universal adoption of certain rules produces the greatest good is the ground for judging that everyone ought to adopt them; ought, that is, to act as they enjoin. I shall assume that in making this claim, a Rule Utilitarian is employing the notion of a man's good and not the notion of moral good. Now at first sight at least, it seems that the arguments of the previous section can be turned against this claim just as they can be turned against Act Utilitarianism. Suppose there is a rule R such that:

> By adopting R along with everyone else, A can do the greatest good for others; but he can do the greatest good for himself by not adopting R.[1]

If it is claimed that this proposition implies that A ought to adopt R, then, whatever mode of the concept of obligation is involved, it seems plain that the arguments of the previous section show that it is not so. But I think a Rule Utilitarian would reply that the rules of which he is speaking are such that the proposition just considered could not be true of them; that they are rules such that their universal adoption does the greatest good for *everyone*. And that the ground for judging that everyone ought to adopt them is that they have this characteristic. I shall now argue that, if he takes this line, his ground turns, upon investigation, into the contract ground and Rule Utilitarianism into the theory I have developed in the preceding chapters.

If the claim is that there are rules such that everyone's acting in the way enjoined by them produces the greatest good for everyone, it is a false claim. For any rule we consider, a Master Criminal (3, 14) may be imagined who is an exception: his acting in that way does not produce the greatest good for him. The difficulty may, however, be avoided by claiming not that the *adoption* of the rule, i.e., acting as it enjoins, produces the greatest good for everyone but that the *requirement* made by the rule does (3, 13); that a state of affairs in which everyone can be called upon to act as it enjoins produces the greatest good for everyone. To this claim, as we have seen, the Master Criminal is no exception. With this emendation, let us suppose that a certain rule makes a requirement R, and examine

[1] Cf. p. 191.

the claim that R produces the greatest good for everyone; for A, B, C ... The trouble now is that there may be no R such that it produces the *greatest* good for A and B and C ... For if we formulate a requirement which produces the greatest good for A, B may be such a man that not just that requirement, but some modification of it, produces the greatest good for him. And C may be such that the greatest good for him is produced by some other modification (3, 13). The point which emerges is that the Rule Utilitarian should not be talking about the production of the greatest good. He should be talking about the production of the greatest good for everyone so far as that is compatible with the production of the greatest good for everyone else. And now, of course, we are not speaking of the greatest good for anyone.

The Utilitarian ground has now become:

> The requirements made by certain rules (which may be very complex) produce the greatest good for everyone so far as that is compatible with the greatest good of everyone else;

and we must compare it with the contract ground. We are able to say that it is in everyone's interest to make a contract to do a (complex) X partly because a contract to do X places upon us a requirement to do X. That is the point of a contract. Of course, the requirement not to murder, commit arson, steal, rape and so on is not placed upon us by a contract. We have made no contracts about such classes of action. It is placed upon us by the obligation principle which is implied by the contract ground. But the class of actions required by the obligation principle just is the class of actions of which the contract ground is true. And the precise form of the requirement is determined by the fact that the contract ground is true of just that requirement, and not of some other more or less similar to it (3, 13).

The contract ground determines certain requirements. The Rule Utilitarian has, so it appears, a different formula for determining requirements. But what does he mean by 'the greatest good for everyone so far as that is compatible with the greatest good for everyone else'? And how are we to set about specifying the requirements which satisfy this formula? It is no good turning to the literature to find an answer. Uncritical use of the expressions 'the greatest good', 'the best effects' and their like has concealed from Utilitarians the fact that their putative ground must take the form we have now given to it if it is to be true of any rule. And consequently no answer to the questions we are now asking is forthcoming. All we can do is to suggest an answer, or rather, canvass an answer which suggests itself: that the requirements are determined by asking of any which is proposed whether, under the conditions specified earlier (3, 5–6), it is in everyone's interest to make a contract with everyone else which places that requirement upon them all. I think that if I had been a Rule Utilitarian, and were presented with the work we now have behind us, I should feel compelled to accept this interpretation. It seems to me that the notion of contract is *demanded* as soon as we find ourselves committed to talking of requirements determined by the greatest good of everyone so far as it is compatible with the greatest good of everyone else; it is demanded if we are to *begin* to understand what we are supposed to do to find out what such requirements might be. They are requirements determined by asking: what contracts would everyone make with everyone else if no entrenched legal institutions affected the question, if everyone knew all the relevant facts and was intent upon securing his (independent) interest so far as he could, i.e., what contracts is it in everyone's interest to make with everyone else, entrenched legal institutions which bear upon the question being discounted? If 'Requirement *R*' is an answer to this question, and it is then said that *R* is not a requirement which 'produces the greatest good for everyone so far as that is compatible with the greatest good of everyone else' then I have no idea what could be meant by saying that some requirements do have this characteristic. I can make no sense of the Rule Utilitarian's ground unless it is understood as an alternative formulation of the contract ground.

Should a Rule Utilitarian accept the interpretation offered, then his theory has turned into the theory for which I have argued. His acceptance would have the added advantage of providing him with an argument, which he shows no inclination to supply himself, to establish that our now common ground does imply a judgement of obligation (3, 3). Should he reject the interpretation, then the onus is upon him both to make his ground intelligible and to provide arguments for the claim that it implies ought judgements. It is not really a tolerable presumption of many Utilitarians that the onus is upon others to prove them wrong and not upon them to prove themselves right.

EPILOGUE

Hume said:

Be a philosopher; but amidst all your philosophy, be still a man.

I shall now stop being a philosopher and make some comments, as a man interested in practical morality, upon the thesis for which I have argued. The aim of moral philosophy, as it seems to me, is to enhance our understanding of moral judgement and of the demand made upon us by morality. In trying to fulfil this aim, I have argued for a philosophical position which is not neutral between different moral positions: if anyone has been convinced by what I have written, he might find that he has, as a result, to modify his moral views on some points. The fact that the theory is of this kind may lead to the assumption that it is put forward primarily as a decision procedure for moral questions. And it may then be criticized, like other moral philosophies before it, on the ground that it is far too difficult and complex to wield in the solution of such problems. I have once or twice in the preceding pages referred to the danger of overestimating its value as a decision procedure, and I think I should now make it clear where I stand on this question.

Morality, I have argued, divides into two segments which are keyed in distinct modes of the concept of obligation. Questions of ultra obligation are, in the end, questions about men's characters. They are most likely to be settled for any man by a novelist, a playwright, or by a friend who just talks and listens: by anyone who has insight into character and into the different kinds of character to be found among men; not by anyone who could be called a scientist. Questions of basic obligation are of a different nature. They arise because people need to live together in societies, and they arise so far as people's interests conflict. There is, so far as I can see, no reason to suppose that such questions should be simple to answer. Indeed, if I am anywhere near right in what I have written, they are of great complexity. There is a common prejudice, descended perhaps from the greatest of all moral philosophers, that it must be a simple matter to solve moral problems. If it is not, simple folk, it has seemed, cannot be good men. But after our discussion of moral good, if not before, the mistake in such reasoning is obvious: it is like saying that a candidate in a physics examination, who is incapable of doing work of the originality he describes, cannot be a good candidate; or that a man cannot be a good engineer if he is incapable of working out for himself the principles which he employs so competently. Goodness does not require originality of thought; and a simple man can be a good man while the thought required to solve moral problems is far from simple.

When questions of basic obligation are understood to be of a different character from questions of ultra obligation; when we have grasped their complexity; and when we have realized their fundamental importance to us all, it becomes a disturbing thought that there is no class of people whose *job* it is to think about them. I do not mean to suggest, that in the absence of such a profession, our common moral beliefs are substantially wrong; I called them at an earlier point (3, 8) a body of coarse grained truth. They are substantially right because all of us, or almost all of us, know perfectly well in practice that in moral discussion we are concerned with men's interests. But our ignorance of the exact way in which we are concerned with them results in marginal injustice to many and serious injustice to some. The exact way in which basic morality is concerned with human interests is revealed, I believe, by the mutual implication between obligation principles and the contract ground. If I am right, and if it is a complex matter to find the exact form of the principles so determined—to work out principles which contractually harmonize the interests of *everyone*—then the conclusion is only too obvious: it is work for professionals. We do not need bishops, journalists, scoutmasters and Members of Parliament, all professionals in their way, making amateur pronouncements on moral questions; and all too often merely repeating what they learned in their childhood from their own kind. We need moral scientists.

A science is a systematic body of knowledge, whether quantitative or not. I think it likely that questions of basic morality, but not of ultra morality, can be investigated scientifically, and the results organized as a body of knowledge. I see no reason why they should not be, and it seems desirable that they should be. But a science requires techniques for its development, and it needs open minded investigators to develop them. It needs scientists. The thesis for which I have argued does, of course, provide an outline decision procedure for moral questions, but it would be easy to overestimate its value in amateur hands. The outcome of our amateur application would indeed be broadly correct; but our moral opinions are broadly correct in any case and they were formed before we had ever heard of the contract ground. My thesis may or may not be a contribution to moral philosophy, but it is of little value as a decision procedure until its application is entrusted to professionals: men who have developed techniques for its application and whose job it is to apply it. So applied, we might hope that, in time, we should be able to say that moral opinion at large was something better than broadly correct.

At this point I peter out, for there is nothing more that I can say. It is not obvious, from what I have written, how moral scientists should go about their work. Or, if it is obvious, it is obvious only in outline. I do not know what means they would find it best to adopt to determine people's interests, except that they would be empirical means. I do not know how they would tackle the problem of discounting entrenched legal and quasi legal institutions and assessing people's interests in their absence. And I do not know, except in the most general way, how they would best set about determining moral requirements so that they are in the contractually harmonized interests of everyone; how they would go about devising penalties which satisfy the conditions which must be satisfied (3, 10); determining complementary classes; accommodating interests which run counter to the general interest; and qualifying obligation principles against relevant changes in the interests of those to whom they apply (3, 9). These problems and many others would be solved, if at all, in the field: in attempting to make a science, whether quantitative or not, of basic morality. They are not philosophical but technical questions; and a philosophical work is no place to discuss them even if its author knew how to begin. If he could think that, in trying to advance moral philosophy, he had written the prolegomena to the science of morals, he should and would be satisfied. But upon that and other questions time must be left to judge.

INDEX

(References obtainable from the table of contents are not given in the index)

actions
  classes of, 42, 45, 87–9, 91, 97–9, 172–3
  compensatory classes of, 110, 112, 113
  complementary classes of, 114–15, 120–
    3, 174, 203
  individual, 42, 45, 121–6, 173–4
  justice of, 143, 146–7
  morally better, 179, 188
  morally good, 180–3, 188, 190
aims, 18, 22, 34
  and morality, 4, 23–4, 183, 192–3
annoyance, avoidable, 121, 126–8, 130
appraisal, moral, 2, 177–81
as if, 88, 89
Austin, J. L., 46, 48, 49
authority, an, 90, 107

bargaining power, 113–14, 132, 145,
    148
beneficence, limited, 125, 159–60, 173
benefits, distribution of, 144, 146
Bentham, 13, 90–1, 191
blame, 50, 63, 106
Broad, C. D., 8
burdens, distribution of, 144, 146

care
  degree of, 128–30
  reasonable, 126, 128–30
Cartesian bedrock, 108
catalyst, 120
cause, 8
character, 36, 156–8, 160–1, 163, 165–7,
    201
  qualities of, 177, 179, 180, 184–5
  and reason for acting, 166–8
characteristic, moral, 189
'characteristic'
  narrow use of, 190
  wide use of, 188–90
children, 114–15
  rights of, 148–50
Christ, 161–3, 164
Church, Roman Catholic, 118
Collingwood, R. G., 165

contract, 42, 46, 88, 89, 140
  form of, 118–19, 135
  implicit, 88, 89
  renewal of, 111–14
  revision of, 112–14
contract argument
  completion of, 104–5
  limit to application of, 108
  objections to, 98–9, 109–10
  rule for breaking, 103
contract ground, 43, 94, 95–154, 159–60,
    168, 173–4, 190–1, 198–200, 202–3
  truth value of, 95, 103–5, 109, 115–16
Criminal, Master, 101, 151, 198
criminals
  and reasons for acting, 85
  and rights, 85
customs, 154

Decalogue, 161
decision procedure, 90, 105, 201, 203
demand, moral, 2, 29
dentist, 184–5
deontology, 7, 46, 177
deserts, and rights, 38–9
desire, 9–17, 90
  and morality, 23–4
destitute, the, 109–11
disapproval, social, 185
disposition, 11–12
drills, pneumatic, 126–8
duty, 157
  sense of, 178

egoism, 7, 114
Eliot, T. S., 168
employers, 181–2
endowments, natural, 109
ennui, 11–12
equality, 92, 93, 109, 143, 145
Ethics without propositions, 176
evaluative concept, 129
Ewing, A. C., 24
expectations, 51,
explanation, moral, 2–4, 73–4, 129–31

favoured class, 90
force, 83, 90, 104–5
fraud, 54
free-for-all, 92
frut, telling the, 72–3
fulfilment, 169

game
  promising-, 66–7
  truth-telling, 65–6
God, 118, 120
good
  and efficiency, 189
  intrinsic, 5, 6
  a man's, 5, 6, 58–61, 188–9, 190, 193, 198
  moral, 7, 106, 155, 168, 180, 198, 202
  moral, and promises, 51, 63
  moral, and reason for acting, 168, 183
  my/other's, 191, 193–7
  and pleasure, 189–90
good faith, 58–9, 61–2, 74
good reason
  and greater good, 86
  and rights, 39, 75
'good reason'
  idle uses of, 23
  superficial uses of, 33–5
good will, 23, 114
Government, 91
  Contract of, 118
grassing, 151

Hamlyn, D. W., 46
happiness, 164–5, 169
Hardy, G. H., 34, 39
help, measure of, 124–5, 159–60
holy wills, 106
horse and cart, 76
humanity as a whole, 151–3
Hume, 49–51, 63, 70, 201

ill-favoured, the, 109, 145
immoral action, irrationality of, 139–40
imperative of skill, 35
implication, 2, 26
importance, 196
impossibility, physical, 42
in a higher degree than, 187–90
in some sense, 92–100
inference, kinds of, 128–9
injustice, 202
insult, 63–5
institutions, legal and quasi legal, 144–5, 203

intentions, 177, 180
interests
  and desires, 12
  children's, 149
  contractually harmonized, 117, 123–6, 139, 145, 190, 202–3
  and good, 183–7
  independent, 31, 43, 92, 101–2, 132–5, 136–40, 171 n., 174–6
  non-independent, 30, 43, 101–2, 132–5, 136–40, 174–6
  and obligation principles, 90–3
  of offenders, 117
  overall, 21, 27–8
  present and future, 21–7
  and reason for acting, 15–19
  selective, 90, 91

Jeremy, 164–6
justice, 117–18
  natural, 144, 147
'justice', wide and narrow uses, 143–4, 146
Juvenile court, 47, 80

Kant, 6–7, 29, 35, 106, 165, 177, 180
killing, 130
kindnesses, returning, 63–5

law(s), 87, 102–4, 105, 118, 127
  justice of, 143–7
  Mosaic, 161–3
  natural, 90, 147
  positive, 87, 90
  unjust, 103, 105
legal system, 118
  quasi, 105
Locke, 168

means-ends, 22, 34–5
Melden, A. I., 9–10
men
  justice of, 143, 146–7
  morally better, 180, 188
  morally good, 180–3, 188, 190, 202
Mill, J. S., 77, 191
Moore, G. E., 2, 37, 77, 191, 192, 193
moral agent, average, 181, 188
moral argument, day to day, 1–4, 131, 172–3
moral judgements, truth value of, 154
moral problems, technical, 126
moral truth, unknown, 120
moralist, 117

morality
  being outside, 104
  coping stone of, 180
  ethical part of, 36
  foundation stone of, 180
  legalistic part of, 36
  practical, 201
  structure of, 177
morally better than, 168, 178–9, 187–9
motive, 7, 8, 9, 12, 20, 22, 27, 36, 47, 114,
    116–17, 136–7, 138–9, 166, 169–71
  altruistic, 36, 170–1, 175
  benevolent, 178
  explanation, 14
  moral assessment of, 20, 178–9, 187–8
  morally better, 178–9, 187–8
  morally good, 188, 190
  and reasons for acting, 15, 20, 114,
    170–1
  selfish, 170
murder, 3–4, 73

nations, 87, 118, 150–4
nature, human, 116
nature, state of, 88, 108–9
negligence, 126, 128–30
neutrality, abstract, 97–8, 103
Nietzsche, 164
Nowell-Smith, P. H., 9–10

objections, material, 100
obligations
  abstract and actual, 24, 25, 35, 43–4, 52,
    89, 121–2, 173–4
  basic, 6, 23, 32, 35, 36, 75, 155–6,
    159–61, 169, 177–81, 191–2, 201–3
  conflict of, 44–5, 97–9, 121–2, 151–4,
    167, 173–4
  demanding, 179, 188
  fulfilment of, 177–83, 187–90
  legal, 102–3
  moral, 24, 25, 35, 43, 102
  objective, 24, 25, 28, 35
  prima facie, 7, 25, 31, 45
  prudential, 24, 25, 26–8, 35, 193, 196–7
  subjective, 24, 25, 28, 35
  superiority among, 122
  ultra, 6, 7, 23, 32, 35, 36, 42, 44, 87, 115,
    119, 122, 125–6, 177–81, 191–2,
    201–2
obligation principles, 87–93, 199, 202
  application of, 123–6
  form of, 119
  general, 87, 98, 123, 131
  sparse set of, 104

specific, 87, 120–1, 131
offenders
  rights of, 116–17
  right to punish, 116–17
old, the, 112–14
ought (rationally), 33, 75–6, 108, 183,
    192
'ought', senses of, 24–5

parents, 120, 149, 181–2, 186–7
  rights of, 114–15
Paton, H. J., 155 n.
penalties, 92–3, 116–20, 135–40, 203
  distribution of, 144, 146
  justice of, 117, 146
Pickard-Cambridge, W. A., 57, 61, 74
pickpockets, 115
Plug, Fingers, 186–7
poet, 166–8
Pope, the, 118
posteriority, logical, 103, 105, 177
Prescriptive theories, 29, 176
Price, Richard, 24, 25
Prichard, H. A., 5–6, 7
principles, moral, 90, 92
privileges, rights and, 40
pro-attitude, 9
promises
  and blame, 50, 51, 63, 72, 88
  criminal, 55
  day to day, 140–2
  insincere, 49, 84
  and moral good, 50, 51, 63, 72
  and reason for acting, 50, 51, 63, 68, 72,
    88
  rejection of, 54–5, 65
  and rights, 50, 57, 61–3, 76–7, 88
  stupid, 69, 142
  and threats, 53, 57
  and trustworthiness, 50, 51, 63, 72, 88
promising, 42, 87–8
  and actual obligation, 52
  controlling conditions, 53–6, 71–2, 74
  and holy wills, 106
  offer and acceptance, 54–5, 56, 65, 74
  primary function, 47, 51, 72, 81–3
  secondary function, 47, 57, 80–3
  simpliciter, 53, 56, 63
  utility of, 75–8
promising function, rational exercise of,
    56, 67–8, 74, 79, 83, 140–2
punishment, present instruments of, 117

Rashdall, Hastings, 37, 77, 191
Rawls, John, 46, 143

reasons for acting, 7–8
  and abstract and actual obligation, 32–3,
    43–5
  assessment of, 19–24
  and character, 166–8
  and criminals, 85
  and motives, 15, 20, 114, 170–1
  and Prescriptivism, 29, 176
  and promising, 50, 51, 63, 68, 72, 85–6, 88
  prudential, 22, 27
  and rights, 39, 75–6
  there being/A's having, 12, 17, 20, 21–4,
    25
  and Utilitarianism, 75–8, 191–2
reason for a judgement, 1–4, 7, 8, 18–19,
    32–3
reason for a judgement, the, 1–6
recidivist, 117
requirements, 90–3, 132–4, 139, 143, 198
  justice of, 143–7
  rationality of, 133, 139
retaliation, 118–19
rights
  abstract and actual, 57
  abstract, and criminals, 85
  and basic obligation, 36, 107, 155, 159,
    191–2
  and benevolent authorities, 107
  of children, 148–50
  and deserts, 38–9
  different kinds of, 37–8
  and good reason, 39, 75
  growing into, 150
  and a man's good, 191
  moral and legal, 37, 146
  and moral good, 182–3
  natural, 114, 147
  of offenders, 116–17
  and privileges, 40
  and promising, 50, 57, 61–3, 76–7, 88
  and ultra obligation, 37
'right to', 38
'right to expect', 38
rising generation, 114–15, 149
Ross, Sir David, 7, 24, 31, 45, 57, 170,
rules, 198
  tyrant's, 105
Rule Utilitarianism, 74, 78–9, 191
Ryle, Gilbert, 13

schema, Reason-for-Acting/Obligation,

    26, 28, 32, 36, 42, 43, 44, 79, 87, 131,
    174–6
Schweitzer, Albert, 157–8, 160–6, 172
scientist, 201
  moral, 202–3
Searle, J. R., 46
self-interest, 171
service
  distinguished, 181
  of others, 166–8, 170–1
Sidgwick, Henry, 50–1, 55, 84, 191, 193
Sidney, Sir Philip, 155–7, 160–4
Singer, M. G., 37
social contract
  classical theorists, 118, 147
  societies, 87–154
    cross, 151, 153
    edict ruled, 90–3, 106–8
    greater, 151, 152
    of holy wills, 106–8
    moral differences between, 93–4, 153–4
    sub, 151–2
    tyrant ruled, 104–5
  states of affairs, unjust, 105
  states of mind, 177, 179, 180
  structure, conceptual, 106
  suffering, unnecessary, 126
  summum bonum, 168

tailoring, 73, 129
taxes, 102, 115
teleology, 7, 46, 177
Tom, 164–6
Tom, Dick and Harry, 119, 123, 173
Toulmin, S. E., 8
tribes, 151
trustworthiness, 50, 88, 106
truth
  coarse grained, 111, 202
  telling the, 65, 72–3

unit, 87, 151
Utilitarianism, 2, 5, 37, 51, 78, 84–6, 90–1,
    143, 147, 177, 183

Van Gogh, 164

yellow, 194–5
young, the, 112–14

Zutphen, 155